Gay and Lesbian Plays Today

Gay and Lesbian Plays Today

SELECTED AND INTRODUCED BY TERRY HELBING

■

BELLE REPRIEVE
Bette Bourne, Peggy Shaw, Paul Shaw, and Lois Weaver

EYE OF THE GULL
Jane Chambers as revised by Vita Dennis

ONE TIT, A DYKE, & GIN!
Pennell Somsen

A QUIET END
Robin Swados

TELL
Victor Bumbalo

INTIMACIES/MORE INTIMACIES
Michael Kearns

ANNUNCIATION
Carl Morse

▼

HEINEMANN ⊠ PORTSMOUTH, NH

Heinemann Educational Books, Inc.
361 Hanover Street   Portsmouth, NH 03801—3959
Offices and agents throughout the world

Library of Congress Cataloging in Publication Data

Gay and lesbian plays today/selected and introduced by Terry
    Helbing.
        p.   cm.
    Contents: Introduction/Terry Helbing — Belle reprieve/Bette
Bourne . . . [et al.] — Eye of the gull/Jane Chambers as revised by
Vita Dennis — One tit, a dyke, & gin!/Pennell Somsen — A quiet
end/Robin Swados — Tell/Victor Bumbalo — Intimacies and more
intimacies/Michael Kearns — Annunciation/Carl Morse.
    ISBN 0—435—08618—9
    1. Gay men — Drama. 2. Lesbians — Drama. 3. Gays' writings,
American. 4. Lesbians' writings, American. 5. American drama — 20th
century. I. Helbing, Terry, 1951—   .
PS627.H67G38 1992
812'.54080355 — dc20   92—21957
                                                            CIP

Printed in the United States of America
93 94 95 96 97 5 4 3 2 1

Contents

■

▼

▼

Acknowledgements

■

Thank you to the following people — no doubt, an incomplete list — who, in various capacities, made it possible for me to do this book: Rachel Green, Nancy Johnson, John Hammond, Paul Bellman, Felice Picano, Doris and "Cak" O'Neill, Nicholas Deutsch, and the authors included here, for writing such excellent work, so that it was a pleasure to select them.

Introduction

■

In the almost quarter century since the Stonewall Riots in New York's Greenwich Village, the landmark event that now serves as the impetus of the modern gay/lesbian rights movement, that movement has made amazing progress in a relatively short time — despite the fact that achievement of full rights and equality, in which the subculture simply becomes part of what New York City Mayor David Dinkins calls "the gorgeous mosaic," has not yet happened. The gay community still faces tough problems — gay bashing, the health crisis, and discrimination (from the right wing and others), to name three — but it is marshaling its forces and people to achieve the end goal of full equality.

Although we have lost so many of our best and brightest to the plague, gay/lesbian culture continues to grow and thrive. Shortly after I cofounded the Gay Theatre Alliance in the mid-1970s, I began to maintain a list of active lesbian/gay theatre companies, which then comprised no more than a dozen or so addresses; that list is now handled by our successor, The Purple Circuit, and their recent updated list contains over fifty companies!

Covering shows for my weekly column, "The Fourth Wall," for *New York Native*, I am continually impressed by the diversity of issues and the varied approaches to them to be found in the community: AIDS, of course, but also gay parenting, the eternal quest for true love and affection, "the whole nine yards" if you will. What is even more impressive in New York City is that gay-themed plays are not limited to being produced by gay theatre companies. Plays open on, off, and off off Broadway, produced independently or by resident companies, and they sink or swim solely on their artistic merits and quality or lack of them. Of course sexuality has its theatrical place, but examples of what my Meridian Gay Theatre cofounder, Terry Miller, used to call "dick-wiggling theatre" come down the pike far less often now than they did ten or fifteen years ago.

The seven plays I have chosen for this volume reflect the aforementioned quality and diversity for which we can feel so justifiably proud. The plays are discussed here in the order in which they appear.

Split Britches and Bloolips — the groups responsible for *Belle Reprieve* — both take their names from bits of history (the former is a habilimentary convenience, the latter a sexual innuendo). They have been presenting their unique takes on gay/lesbian/feminist theatre for years. The women are perhaps best known for their eponymous *Split Britches*, the men (who are British) for works like *Lust in Space*. When members of the two groups collaborated for the first time to create *Belle Reprieve*, they gave literal (and delightful) embodiment to the subtitle of Charles Ludlam's *Conquest of the Universe, or When Queens Collide*. Their "fractured fairy tale" version of the themes and character types of Williams's *A Streetcar Named Desire* is a delicious joining of the groups' talents for satire, music, and crossdressing. A work that comes across so well because of the performing style of the authors may seem a curious choice as the lead play in this volume, but their cosexual pleasure in creating the work still comes across, even though the printed page can never match the vibrancy of their live performance. Naturally, "But ya are, Blanche, ya are" appears as a line of dialogue here, but they most definitely disprove their own line "We haven't arrived yet" — as writer/performers, they have, folks, they have. Lyrics from their encore, "I Love My Art," sum it up for both sides of the footlights: "It's so entrancing/ the song and dancing . . . /I love the glamour, I love the drama/ I love, I love, I love my art."

The late Jane Chambers arrived on the playwriting scene in the mid-1970s, at a time when there was an unfortunate dearth of productions by quality women playwrights. Performers like Susan Sullivan (of *Falcon Crest* and Tylenol commercials fame) and Jean Smart (formerly of *Designing Women*) enhanced their reputations in *A Late Snow* and *Last Summer at Bluefish Cove*, the latter now frequently taught at colleges and universities in modern drama and contemporary women playwrights courses. While women like Maria Irene Fornes (who goes back even further than Chambers), Megan Terry, Marsha Norman, Tina Howe, and Caryl Churchill have forged ahead to write excellent plays that do get produced with healthy frequency, a woman of Chambers's talent (she died of a brain tumor in 1983) is sorely missed, not because of her gender, but because of the excellence of her work. Her *Eye of the Gull*, recently produced for the first time in a version somewhat revised by Vita Dennis, was written prior to her better-known works, but the essences of her women characters appear here. As she does in her other works, Chambers effectively uses humor and a nice mix of characters to bring her dramatic points across.

Pennell Somsen sent me *One Tit, A Dyke, & Gin!* (her first play) in response to a request for scripts that I made in my weekly column. In it, she successfully combines laughter and consciousness raising, as a heterosexual woman who has had a mastectomy is accidentally locked in her doctor's office, then found by a gay female security guard. They strike up a friendship as they cope with the situation, demonstrating that human connection and caring interaction are essential — and eminently possible — regardless of sexual preference. This first effort bodes very well for performer Somsen's newfound profession.

As the second decade of the plague drags on, many gay male playwrights naturally choose characters and situations that address the ramifications and the far-reaching effects of AIDS. The most dramaturgically traditional of such plays included here is Robin Swados's *A Quiet End*, which has already had numerous productions in various cities and countries. The themes of human interaction, friendship, and simply caring are highly evident here, as three men who have lost their jobs and apartments share a rundown apartment that has been converted into an AIDS hospice. By play's end, two of the men have died and the third has moved back with his Midwestern nuclear family, but this work demonstrates the crucial importance of your "chosen" family, particularly if you are lesbian or gay and even if the family is chosen for you. Take these lines of dialogue: "I enjoyed my *life*, I really did," but "I get ruffled inside. I'm not an outside person like you. ... What the hell do you think would happen if all of a sudden I got better? You think everything would just fall into place?" A sympathetic character voices his "wanting to make what's left of your life meaningful. Filling it with some warmth." They emphasize, in their way, that, as Chambers said in the special introduction to the hardcover edition of *Last Summer at Bluefish Cove*, written a couple of years before her death, "life is not a crap shoot; it is what we who love each other do together, and that is, in itself, sufficient meaning." The approach to the disease is decidedly traditional here, with little or no discussion of holistic approaches or organizations like HEAL, but there is no lack of warmth in Swados's impressive effort.

Safer-sex eroticism takes two unusual forms in Victor Bumbalo's *Tell*, a companion piece to his *Show*. Here a man hospitalized with an unnamed (but obvious) disease is able to reawaken his sexual feelings thanks to a description a visitor provides of his own sexual experience, and to satisfy these feelings via the hand of a lonely nurse who, while being a caring professional to her patient, fulfills her own need to connect and satisfies some of her own sexual inclinations. The play touchingly demonstrates that sexual feelings don't disappear with age or after a diagnosis of illness, and that they can find some kind of release in unorthodox but risk-free ways.

Michael Kearns's solo performance pieces, *intimacies* and *more intimacies*, which he has performed at various locations around the country, emphasize that AIDS is no longer a gay disease; no doubt Magic Johnson would concur. By including disparate people — a Hispanic flamenco dancer, a Catholic priest, a street hooker, a Southern religious fanatic — in his portraits of twelve diagnosed people, he powerfully reminds us of the truth of the activist slogans "a virus knows no morals" and "AIDS does not discriminate." His characters "smell like life," as he says, in their varying reactions to the medical crisis they face in common.

Carl Morse is known primarily as a poet — he's even edited poetry anthologies — but with *Annunciation* he successfully demonstrates that he is capable of crossing over from one genre to another. The play was seen in New York in 1991 as part of an evening of short gay plays, and this charming, sweet effort stays true to his poetic style. He affirms that gay people come in all shapes and sizes and, by raising the consciousness of his very pregnant protagonist, reminds those who might need to hear it that there is no shame in — nor did they fail by — having a gay child; in fact, it can be rather a pleasure. It is also gratifying to come across a gay play in which a topic other than AIDS is the primary focus. (This by no means negates the validity of that subject matter, a validity that has become all too relevant and prevalent over the last decade.)

It is my fervent hope that these seven scripts will give you important slices — although by no means the whole pie — of contemporary gay/lesbian life as expressed in the theatrical idiom. Ideally, the lessons, humor, and love present in these authors' works are such that you cannot but choose to carry them with you as you live — and enjoy — your life to its fullest.

Terry Helbing
January 1992
New York City

Belle Reprieve

■

A COLLABORATION

BY

BETTE BOURNE

PEGGY SHAW

PAUL SHAW

&

LOIS WEAVER

▼

Belle Reprieve

Belle Reprieve was first presented at The Drill Hall Arts Centre, London, on January 8, 1991. It was directed by Lois Weaver; the sets were designed by Nancy Bardawil and Matthew Owen; the costumes were designed by Susan Young; music was composed and directed by Laka Daisical and Phil Booth; and the lighting was by Liz Poulter. Production was in association with The Club at La MaMa E.T.C., New York City, and opened at La MaMa on February 14, 1991. Lighting for the New York production was by Howard Thies. The cast in order of appearance was as follows:

MITCH . . . . Paul Shaw

STELLA . . . . Lois Weaver

STANLEY . . . . Peggy Shaw

BLANCHE . . . . Bette Bourne

CHARACTERS

MITCH . . . . a fairy disguised as a man

STELLA . . . . a woman disguised as a woman

STANLEY . . . . a butch lesbian

BLANCHE . . . . a man in a dress

PLACE

An empty stage. The backdrop is a scrim painted to resemble the interior of a 1940s New Orleans apartment. There are three high-tension wires strung across the stage. Throughout the play, various painted cloth curtains are pulled across these wires to denote a change in scenery or mood.

TIME

Four o'clock in the morning.

ACT I

MITCH is wheeling three large boxes onstage with a handtruck. One is designed to resemble a steamer trunk. The second is square, large enough to hold an actor, and shaped to resemble a card table, which it becomes in later scenes. The third is tall, rectangular, and large enough to hold another actor. It is turned on its back to represent a bathtub in the second act.

MITCH. Inside this box it's four o'clock in the morning. I know that sounds incredible but it's true. I know because it's *my* four o'clock in the morning. Every time it comes around, I put it in this box. I've been doing it for years now. At four o'clock in the morning, the thread that holds us to the earth is at its most slender, and all the creatures that never see sunlight come out to make mincemeat of well-laid plans. So you can imagine what it's like in there. If you listen closely you can hear them shuffling about, like the sound of rain or chittering birds. It reminds me of a soundtrack, the beginning of a movie . . . (*Stella appears drinking a coke behind the scrim*) a clean slate. Darkness all around. Small sounds that give a taste of an atmosphere, a head turning, a body lit from behind, shadows in a dark, tiled hallway, a blues piano. (*Pianist strikes a match and begins to play the blues*)

STELLA. (*Moving to center from behind scrim, still drinking the coke*) Is there something you want? What can I do for you? Do you know who I am, what I feel, how I think? You want my body. My soul, my food, my bed, my skin, my hands? You want to touch me, hold me, lick me, smell me, eat me, have me? You think you need a little more time to decide? Well, you've got a little over an hour to have your fill. Meanwhile

5
▼

... (*Mitch enters with last box, swatting bugs*) I'm surprised there aren't more bugs out this time of year. All the ones that are out seem to be buzzing around my head.

MITCH. No, there's plenty for both of us. Don't feel singled out.

STELLA. I think it's 'cuz I eat so much sugar that they're attracted to me. Sugar in my blood. And my veins are close to the surface.

MITCH. You know that they excrete something to digest your blood, that's why they leave that bump on your skin.

STELLA. I always worry that they carry things with them, transferring them from person to person.

MITCH. That's an old wives' tale. This country has no tradition of disease being spread by mosquitoes. You're mistaken.

STELLA. Well, every year I make one big mistake. I wonder what it will be this year?

MITCH. This mistake, is it at a particular time, or can't you tell when it's coming?

STELLA. I can usually feel it coming ...

BLANCHE. (*From inside box*) I've always depended on the strangeness of strangers.

STELLA. Or at least after the fact I thought I knew it was coming.

MITCH. Isn't there something you can do to stop it happening?

STELLA. Such as ...

MITCH. Change the script!

STELLA. Change the script. Ha ha. You want me to do *what* in these shoes? The script is not the problem. I've changed the script.

MITCH. It's a start.

STELLA. Look, I'm supposed to wander around in a state of narcotized sensuality. That's my part. (*Blanche and Stanley speak simultaneously from inside the two largest boxes*)

BLANCHE. You didn't see, Miss Stella, see what I saw, the long parade to the graveyard. The mortgage on the house, death is expensive, Miss Stella, death is expensive.

STANLEY. Is that so? You don't say, hey Stella wasn't we happy before she showed up. Didn't we see those colored lights you and me. Didn't we see those colored lights.

STELLA. And anyway, it's too late. It's already started.

STANLEY. Hey Stella! (*Coming out of stage right box*)

▼

STELLA. Don't holler at me like that, Stanley.

STANLEY. Hey Stella, Stella baby! Catch!

STELLA. What!

STANLEY. Meat.

BLANCHE. (*Emerging from stage left box*) Are we here? Is this the place? Are my necessaries disembarked? How sweet it is to arrive at a new place for the first time. The future stretching out in front of us like a clean, white carpet. There's the stir and rustle of endless possibility in the air.

STANLEY. You don't say.

STELLA. Honey, we're in exactly the same place we started out from.

BLANCHE. Started out? What do you mean started out? You mean we haven't arrived?

STELLA. No, we haven't arrived, but don't worry about that now. You just take it easy.

STANLEY. Something smells fishy around here and it's not me.

STELLA. (*To Stanley*) Now you be kind to my sister. Tell her how nice she looks.

BLANCHE. I can't stand being in between. I just can't bear it.

STELLA. (*To Stanley*) You should try to understand her a little better, she's just different.

STANLEY. Different? You can say that again.

BLANCHE. I have never regretted my decision to be unique.

STANLEY. I'm gonna put an end to this charade here and now.

BLANCHE. (*As Stanley moves to center stage with trunk and becomes a customs agent*) That my plans of late have gone somewhat awry is the price one has to pay if life is to be superb.

STANLEY. (*To Blanche*) Ticket please.

BLANCHE. (*To Mitch*) Young man, don't I know you?

MITCH. We were engaged to be married.

STANLEY. Ticket please!

BLANCHE. Did I break your heart?

MITCH. No, you broke my leg.

BLANCHE. I must be stonger than I thought.

STANLEY. Ticket please!

BLANCHE. Oh, well, all right, I have it here somewhere. (*Rummages through her bag*) Which ticket do you mean, the one that got me here or the one that will take me away?

STANLEY. Both.

BLANCHE. Oh, well I don't seem to have either at the moment. Although we must have gotten here somehow, we can't have walked, we have a heavy load. However, I present myself as overwhelming evidence that I am actually here.

STANLEY. While we're at it, I'm gonna need your passport.

BLANCHE. Passport? I wasn't aware that we were crossing any borders. What borders?

STANLEY. Passport.

BLANCHE. (*Rummaging around*) Passport, passport . . . (*Mitch steps forward with her passport and hands it to Stanley*)

STANLEY. (*Still staring at Mitch*) Name?

BLANCHE. Blanche DuBois.

STANLEY. That's not what it says here.

BLANCHE. I assure you that is who I am. My namesake is a role played by that incandescent star, Vivien Leigh, and although the resemblance is not immediately striking I have been told we have the same shoulders.

STANLEY. (*Looking at passport photo*) Then who's this here?

BLANCHE. The information in that document is a convention which allows me to pass in the world without let or hindrance. If you'll just notice the message inside the front cover, the Queen of England herself not only requests this but requires it.

STANLEY. You don't look anything like this photograph.

BLANCHE. I believe nature is there to be improved upon.

STANLEY. You're lying.

BLANCHE. Well, that's one way of looking at it.

STANLEY. Is there another?!

BLANCHE. You wouldn't treat me like this if I wasn't at the end of my rope!

STANLEY. (*Slamming fist on trunk*) But ya are Blanche, ya are. (*Cat screams from Mitch and Stella*)

BLANCHE. What was that?

STANLEY. Cats. I'm afraid I'm going to have to perform an intimate search.

BLANCHE. My body?

STANLEY. Your luggage.

BLANCHE. Stella, how do I look?

STELLA. Fresh as a daisy.

STANLEY. One that's been picked a few days.

MITCH. Look, can't we just scrub 'round the search and get on with the scenes of brutal humiliation and sexual passion?

STANLEY. I'm afraid we have to find a motive in this case, and I believe it's in this trunk. (*To Mitch*) Why don't you mind your own business?

BLANCHE. How dare you speak to my ex-fiancé like that!

STANLEY. Your ex-fiancé?! This man is your ex-fiancé?

BLANCHE. That's right.

MITCH. I told her I loved her and she pushed me down the stairwell, but I forgave her as any decent man would.

STANLEY. That's not what it says in the script. In the script it says you treated her like shit because you're a stuck-up mommy's boy.

MITCH. That's a lie!

BLANCHE. I think I'm going to faint.

STELLA. Is all this really necessary?

STANLEY. Look, have you any idea how many people we have come in here saying they're Blanche DuBois, clutching tiny handbags and fainting in the foyer? I'm afraid I'll have to subject this case to the closest possible scrutiny before I allow any of you to pass any further.

BLANCHE. I see, you want me to come clean by showing my dirty laundry to the world.

STANLEY. You got it.

BLANCHE. I think I'll go into the dressing room and burst into tears.

STELLA. We're in this up to our asses now. There's no going back.

BLANCHE. Hold me Stella, I think I feel a flashback coming on. (*Lights flash, music plays, a curtain painted like a grotesque piece of torn lace is pulled on stage behind the action, the actors shuffling backward around trunk*) And so it was that I set out to prove to the world that I was indeed myself. A difficult enough task, you might say, for anyone.

STELLA. She threw herself at the feet of an unforgiving world to prove her identity.

MITCH. The answer was somewhere in that trunk.

STANLEY. (*Thumping fist on trunk as music and lights stop flashing*)
This is gonna cost you, lady. What did you think, you were
gonna get a free ride or something? (*About to open trunk*) What
do we have here?

BLANCHE. Please open the doors one at a time! If you open them
all at once pink things and fur things, dainty things, delicate
and wistful things might pop out.

STANLEY. I'll open them one at a time. First things first. (*Music
starts. Stanley pulls out a jacket and tosses it to Stella, then pulls out
a scarf and throws it to Mitch*)

BLANCHE. I won't take it personally the way you're treating
everything I own in the world.

STANLEY. Let's see, what are little girls made of? (*Singing*) I put
my right hand in, I pull my right hand out (*Pulls it out empty
and laughs*), I put my right hand in (*Pulls out dress on hanger and
puts it around his neck*) and I shake it all about.

BLANCHE. I can't approve of any of this, just as you can't approve
of my entire life.

STANLEY. I do the hokey-pokey and I turn myself around. That's
what it's all about. So this is what little girls are made of.
Tiaras, diamond tiaras. (*Puts tiara on his head*) And what's this?
(*Pulling out gold bracelet and putting it on*) A solid gold Cadillac.
This must be worth a fortune. And what have we got here? A
box of valuables. (*Tossing the contents onto the floor*) Love
letters, scrap books, newspaper clippings.

BLANCHE. Everybody has something they don't want others to
touch because of their intimate nature.

STANLEY. (*Singing, as Mitch picks up newspaper clippings*) I put my
right foot in, I take my right foot out, I put my right foot in
and I shake it all about . . . (*Stanley pulls out high-heeled shoe*)

MITCH. (*As Stanley continues singing*) There was a time when
everyone was trying to get a piece of her. These are the pieces
left over, "Tipped for the Top," "What an Angel." Now the
angel's in the kitchen, washing the dishes and picking her
teeth.

BLANCHE. (*As Mitch hands her newspaper clippings*) I don't see how
any of this relates to my own life except in the way people
perceive my fall.

10
▼

STANLEY. I put my left hand in ... (*Shaking the box violently from inside*)

BLANCHE. (*Ripping up the newspaper clippings*) Tearing ... I hear tearing ... be careful ... the wings, you're tearing them!

STANLEY. They're just animals, lady, what's the matter with you?

BLANCHE. But they've been faithful their whole lives. There are things we don't know here.

STANLEY. Things are different now. (*Still struggling inside box*) I pull the white-feathered excited body of one swan off the white-feathered excited body of another swan. (*He pulls out handful of feathers*)

BLANCHE. What right have you to interfere with nature?

STANLEY. (*Pulling feathers apart to reveal that they are a boa, which he drapes across his shoulders*) And shake it all about.

BLANCHE. Birds of a feather.

STANLEY. I put my left hand in ... (*Pulling hand quickly out*) Oww, Stella, Stella!

STELLA. What?

STANLEY. I burned my hand.

STELLA. Oh, Stanley, it's just candle wax.

STANLEY. I know but it hurts.

STELLA. Some people think it's sexy.

STANLEY. (*Pulling hand away from her*) I can see where it might be sexy if I knew it was coming. I put my left hand in, I pull my left hand out ... oh, a little cheerleading doll ... (*Breaks off the arm*) the arm is busted ... the rubber band must be broken inside.

BLANCHE. My mother gave me that.

STANLEY. (*Dancing doll on top of trunk*) And I shake it all about ...

BLANCHE. And before that, it was her mother's.

STANLEY. (*Slamming doll down*) Look, lady, I'm just trying to do my job here.

BLANCHE. Yes, of course.

STANLEY. And my job is to make sure you're not smuggling something personal in this here trunk. (*Reaching into trunk*) Let's see, what's this? And what is this? (*Pulling out purse*)

BLANCHE. This contains all of my hopes and dreams ... this is my hope chest.

STANLEY. Hopes and dreams? Forget it. (*Sticking hand into purse*) I put my whole body in, I take my whole body out. (*Pulling out scarf*) I grab myself a frilly thing and shake it all about. I pin it on my shoulders and I sashay up and down, that's what it's all about. Yes? I put my right hand in, I take my right hand out ... (*Pulls out hand covered in blood. Blanche and Stella exit. Mitch enters in fading light to roll away trunk, music and lights slowly fade out. In blackout*) I am suddenly aware that the atmosphere has changed. It's dark. The night has a thousand eyes and they're all looking at me. They're burning into me, burning into my chest. If I don't sleep now, I never will ... don't panic ... the night seems to last forever ... don't panic ... I'm scared, I'm wrong, the night is making me feel ... (*Lights return suddenly on a curtain with a painting of an oversized clawed foot of a bathtub and a straight razor lying on a tiled floor. Stella is onstage with Stanley. She is wearing a cheerleading outfit and carries a cheerleading doll*) Vivien Leigh, huh? O.K., that's your story and I'm stuck with it for now. But let's see if you can keep up the deception day after day, week after week in front of me. Let that be a challenge to our relationship. But meanwhile, relax, make yourself at home, have a drink. Tell me about yourself, stuff I haven't heard before, recent stuff like how've you been lately. I got all the time in the world and I'm all ears.

STELLA. Stanley, you come out here and let Blanche finish dressing. (*Stanley exits*) I let her keep her hopes and dreams, just like I let her keep her cheerleading memories. I pretended they were mine as well, came to know them as I know my own face in the mirror. A face that was not a twin of my older sister.

BLANCHE. (*Entering stage left in a bathrobe*) I think I handled that really well. It's a tricky business, deception in the face of legal documents. Thank heavens for bathrooms, they always make me feel so new.

STELLA. Blanche, honey, are you all right in there? There was no answer, but I could hear her splashing and the sound of her radio.

BLANCHE. I can always refresh my spirits in the bathroom.

STELLA. Blanche, I brought you your lemon coke.

BLANCHE. All right sweetie. Be right out.

STELLA. I'll wait out here.

BLANCHE. I don't want you to have to wait on me.

STELLA. I like waiting on you Blanche, it feels more like home.

BLANCHE. I must admit, I do like to be waited on.

STELLA. Well, I'm waiting.

BLANCHE. One day I'll probably just dissolve in the bath. They'll come looking for me, but there'll be nothing left. "Drag Queen Dissolves in Bathtub," that'll be the headline. "All that was left was a full head of hair clogging up the plughole. She was exceptional even in death. . . ." I wonder where I'll end up. In the sea, I suppose.

STELLA. I'm waiting, Blanche.

BLANCHE. Just a few last finishing touches.

STELLA. Waiting. Waiting in the wings. Waiting for her to get off the phone.

BLANCHE. You wouldn't want me to go out looking a mess, now would you?

STELLA. Waiting for her to come home from Woolworth's with the new Tangee lipstick. And when I wasn't waiting I was following. I used to follow her into the bathroom. I loved the way she touched her cheek with the back of her hand. How she let her hand come to rest just slightly between her breasts as she took one last look in the mirror. I used to study the way she adjusted her hips and twisted her thighs in that funny way when she was changing her shoes. Then she would fling open the bathroom door and sail down the staircase into the front room to receive her gentlemen callers.

BLANCHE. (*Colliding into Stella, who drops the doll*) My doll, it's broken!

STELLA. (*Laughingly*) No it isn't.

BLANCHE. I did. I broke it.

STELLA. No, honey. You didn't.

BLANCHE. Yes I did. I broke it.

STELLA. (*Shaking Blanche*) No, Blanche, it was already broken.

BLANCHE. I don't know why I'm like this today.

STELLA. .(*Embracing her*) Blanche, you know what this reminds me of? My homecoming corsage, remember? Before the homecoming parade, when the band and all the floats were gathering in front of the war memorial. It was your senior year, you were the captain of the cheerleaders, and I was the mascot. And they gave us these big orange and maroon chrysanthemums with ribbon streamers; mine was just as big as yours.

BLANCHE. And I pinned it on your shoulder and you were so proud of its size and excited by the smell of it.

STELLA. I felt every bit as tall and glamorous as the real cheerleaders, the majorettes, the homecoming court, even Miss Mississippi herself. I stood in that November air imagining all the things a grownup woman could be ... and then, that great big ole fooball player came walking across the red dirt and smacked right into me.

BLANCHE. And your poor corsage, it started to bleed, it started to lose its petals one by one.

STELLA. And I started to cry. I threw a god–awful fit.

BLANCHE. You certainly did.

STELLA. My whole life was disappearing with those dripping petals. How was I going to present myself in the same parade with Miss Mississippi, her in her strapless gown and me with a handful of petals. But you put your big strong arms around me and set me right up there on the float with ...

BLANCHE. The beauty queen herself. And there you were, all puffy–eyed and corsageless ...

STELLA. Right next to the great white virgin, with her round bare shoulders and her rhinestone tiara.

BLANCHE. (*As music starts*) And I took your picture and it was in the papers. (*Blanche takes off bathrobe to reveal cheerleading outfit and they sing*)

Under the Covers

When life is unfair, and the world makes you sick
I know somewhere that's bliss on a stick.
(*Stella*) Somewhere to go when things are unsteady
(*Blanche*) Somewhere to go with Coco and Teddy.

Under the covers, the pillows and laces
We both can share, those soft cotton places

(*Stella*) Lying together like spoons in a drawer
(*Blanche*)Then turning over to have an explore ...

Under the covers, those smooth satin covers
We share our dreams
(*Stella*) Like goose downy lovers
(*Blanche*) Tucked in together like girls in the dorm
Under the covers everything's cozy and warm ...

(*They pull hidden pom-poms from each other's sleeves and cheer*)
AMO, AMAS, AMAT
WE LOVE OUR TEAM A LOT
WE'RE GONNA FIGHT FIGHT FIGHT
WE'RE GONNA WIN WIN WIN
WE'RE GONNA BE ... (*Blanche*) FABULOUS.

(*Tap dance break*)

Under the covers, it's you and it's me now
Our pleasure grows, because we are two now
Lean on a pillow and look in my eyes
Spreading our knowledge and sharing our thighs
Under the covers, our fingers exploring
Those hidden dreams, we've found there is something
(*Stella pulls a hand covered in menstrual blood out from under her
    skirt*)
Mother has maybe forgotten to tell
Tho' if she found out
We'd found out
She'd give us hell.

STANLEY. (*Yelling from backstage*) Stella!
BLANCHE & STELLA. She'd give us hell.
STANLEY. Stella!
BLANCHE & STELLA. She'd give us ... (*Song dissolves into laughter*)
STANLEY. When are you hens gonna end that conversation?
STELLA. Oh, you can't hear us.
STANLEY. Well, you can hear me, and I say hush up!
STELLA. This is my house too, Stanley, and I'll talk as much as ...
BLANCHE. (*Interrupting her*) Please don't start another row, I

couldn't bear it . . . (*She exits*)

STELLA. I tried to follow her, but I got stuck. Stuck in the bathroom, where I saw myself in the medicine chest mirror. I stopped there and I stared. For three days I stared. I wasn't her little sister. And in the mirror I saw the road split, and I took mine . . .

STANLEY. (*Grabbing Stella*) Stella. (*They hug, Stella exits, Stanley goes to bathroom and starts shaving. Lights dim*)

MITCH. (*Entering stage right. He carries a painting of a card table, which he places over the front of the square box*) Now and then I reached out to touch his wrists. They glittered with a dozen golden bracelets that matched the large earrings he wore. He was like a shimmering waterfall of gold, his whole front covered with golden pendants that looked like coins. Beneath, he wore a purple semitransparent shift that matched the dark makeup around his large bedroom eyes. There was something both fierce and warm in his face. He was glowing with a pagan intensity that matched the intense feelings brimming up in my heart, which in turn matched the brimming purple wine that was being poured, seemingly without end, into our glittering golden goblets that matched the shafts of golden scorching sunlight that poured through the high windows down onto the banqueting table, where they were scattered in a dozen colors as they hit the gold in the glass. Finally, he rose from his throne, which was covered in a mantle of blue macaw feathers that cost ten dollars per square inch and matched the cerulean blue of the deep-piled carpet reputedly made by the tiny fingers of ten-year-old eunuchs within the forbidden city in Peking. Then he began to dance . . .

STANLEY. (*Grabbing Mitch by the shoulders*) You know, a bum like me can grow up in a great country like this and be her lover, which is a hell of a better job than being president of the United States.

MITCH. You're a lucky man.

STANLEY. You know, when I think about her, it's like food, I want to eat her, just put her whole leg in my mouth, or her face, or her hands . . .

MITCH. That's a mouthful!

STANLEY. I feel so hungry when I think of her, I could eat my car, I could eat dirt, I could eat a brick wall. I have to, I have no choice. I have to touch things, and my hands bring them to my mouth.

MITCH. Your big hands!

STANLEY. Feelings grow inside me, and sometimes they fly out of me so fast and then smack, I'm out of control. When it comes to big hands, I have no competition. (*Stanley takes a swig of beer*)

MITCH. When it comes to big hands, she knows she's got your big hands all over her. (*He takes a swig*)

STANLEY. (*Challenging him to arm wrestle*) My big pioneer hands all over her rocky mountains.

MITCH. (*Taking the challenge*) All over her livestock and vegetation.

STANLEY. Her buffaloes and prairies.

MITCH. Her thick forests and golden sunsets.

STANLEY. All over her stars!

MITCH. She's in your hands!

STANLEY. She's in my hands and ... yeeaaa ... (*Stanley pins Mitch's arm down*)

MITCH. That's right! Bite me! Bite me! Suck on me ... oops.

STANLEY. (*Pulling away from Mitch*) What are you talking about?

MITCH. Mosquitoes! Biting me, biting me ...

STANLEY. (*They both slap at bugs*) Suck on me, suck on my body!

MITCH. What do you think I'm here for, your entertainment? A Coney Island for you?

STANLEY. A joyride on my ankle! A suck on my wrist! I'll eliminate you! (*Mimes machine gun and makes gun noise*)

MITCH. Remove you from my space! Pow!

STANLEY. Away from my body, you aggravating hungry bugger.

MITCH. Bugger off! Away with you!

STANLEY. You're spoiled ... Splat!

MITCH. You're educated ... Squash!

STANLEY. You remind me of my fate.

MITCH. You remind me of my immortality! Leave me my blood.

STANLEY. Blood!

MITCH. Bloody sheet.

STANLEY. Bloody night.

MITCH. Blood on your hand!

STANLEY. It's my hand, I'm dealing the cards.

MITCH. (*Running after Stanley around box*) Deal me!

STANLEY. If you want another card I'll hit you with it.

MITCH. Hit me!

STANLEY. When it comes to big hands I got no competition.

MITCH. Take me!

STANLEY. Your shuffle.

MITCH. Cut me in!

STANLEY. Throw your checkbook out the window!

MITCH. Empty my pockets!

STANLEY. I'm a royal flush, I win every time. (*Challenging him to arm wrestle*)

MITCH. (*Taking the challenge*) I'm the last sailboat across the horizon before the sun sets.

STANLEY. Nobody can audition for my part.

MITCH. I flop and smash and throw things.

STANLEY. I turn and punch the air!

MITCH. I sweat.

STANLEY. I smell.

MITCH. I smell!

STANLEY. I smell of car oil, I smell of your blood.

MITCH. I smell of . . . cologne!

STANLEY. I'm hungry, ha, hungry! I'm gonna eat rough memories.

MITCH. I'm gonna eat tough dreams.

STANLEY. Digest hard words. Hard, hard words.

MITCH. I'm gonna spit them out!

STANLEY. It's gonna cost you my hunger!

MITCH. I'm gonna pay!

STANLEY. (*Grabbing Mitch*) I'm gonna eat my car. I'm gonna eat dirt!

MITCH. I'm gonna eat a tree! Eat your whole leg!

STANLEY. I'm gonna eat the sun and then I'll sweat!

STANLEY & MITCH. (*In a frenzy*) Bite me! Bite me! Suck on me!

BLANCHE. (*Opening the bathroom curtain and entering*) Suck my wrist.

STANLEY. (*Singing*)

I'm a Man

When I was a little boy, at the age of five
I had something in my pocket, kept a lot of folks alive
Now I'm a man, made twenty-one
I'll tell you baby, we can have a lot of fun
'Cos I'm a man
Spelled M ... A ... N ... Man
Oohh ... oowww ... oowww

All you pretty women, standing in a line
I can make love to you, in an hour's time
'Cos I'm a man
Spelled M ... A ... N ... Man

(*Dance break*)

The line I shoot will never miss
When I make love to you baby, it comes to this
I'm a man
Spelled M ... A ... N ... Man
Oowww ... oowww ... owww ... I'm a man, yes I am, I'm a
   man ...

(*Gradually noticing Blanche has a finger up her nose*) Hold it, hold it.
   (*To Blanche*) Is there something I can help you with?
BLANCHE. Please could you give me a tissue. I think I've got
   something stuck up my nose.
STANLEY. Would you like me to have a look?
BLANCHE. Please don't trouble. I think a tissue would probably
   do it.
STANLEY. (*Handing her a tissue*) Here.
BLANCHE. Probably a boogey, I expect.
STANLEY. An acquaintance of mine lost his sense of smell from
   having a booger stuck up his nose ... better?
BLANCHE. Not really, no.
MITCH. Can I help?
BLANCHE. Oh no, please, it's only something stuck up my nose.
MITCH. Try sticking your little finger in as far as it'll go.

STANLEY. Then blow your nose.

MITCH. Please let me look, I happen to be a doctor.

BLANCHE. It's very kind of you.

MITCH. Turn around to the light please. Now look up. Now look
down. Now look up again ... I can see it ... keep still ...
(*He twists the tissue and pokes it up her nose*) There!

BLANCHE. Oh dear, what a relief, it was agonizing.

MITCH. (*Holding up the tissue*) It looks like a piece of Christmas
Pudding.

BLANCHE. Thank you very much indeed.

MITCH. Not at all.

BLANCHE. How lucky for me you happened to be here.

MITCH. Anybody could have done it.

BLANCHE. Never mind, you did and I'm most grateful.

MITCH. There's my train ... Goodbye. (*He exits*)

BLANCHE. And that's how it all began, just through me getting a
booger stuck up my nose. (*She turns to face Stanley, then walks
away upstage left as lights dim and music starts. Mitch enters and
motions for Blanche to dance with him, as Stanley shuffles a deck of
cards*)

STANLEY. Hey Mitch, you in this game or what?

MITCH. Deal me out. I'm talking to Miss DuBois. (*They begin to
dance as Stella wanders on*)

STELLA. Look, we made enchantment.

STANLEY. Who turned that on? Turn it off.

STELLA. Ah-h-h-h let them have their music.

STANLEY. I said turn it off!

STELLA. What are you doing?

STANLEY. That's the last time anybody plays music during my
game. Now get OUT! OUT! (*Mitch and Blanche exit*) Everybody
get out! (*To pianist*) OUT! (*Music stops, Stella is laughing quietly*)

STELLA. I guess you think that's funny.

STANLEY. Yeah, I thought it was pretty funny.

STELLA. Well, maybe I blinked at the wrong time, 'cuz I missed
the joke.

STANLEY. Oh, so now you're an authority on what's funny.

STELLA. I didn't say that. I said I didn't think that that was funny.

STANLEY. Well, if you know so much, why don't you show me

20
▼

what is funny.

STELLA. Look, I don't want to get twisted out of shape about it, I just didn't think it was all that funny.

STANLEY. Oh, you thought it was just a little bit funny.

STELLA. No, not even a little bit funny.

STANLEY. So, show me!

STELLA. This is ridiculous.

STANLEY. Show me what's funny.

STELLA. You want me to show you what's funny.

STANLEY. Yeah, show me funny.

STELLA. O.K., I'll show you funny ... (*Rips Stanley's sleeve*) That's funny.

STANLEY. That was not funny.

STELLA. You want funny? (*Rips off the other sleeve*) That's funny.

STANLEY. That was not funny.

STELLA. Okay. What about this? (*Rips off half of Stanley's shirt*) Or this? (*Rips off other half*)

STANLEY. That's not funny.

STELLA. I'll be right back. (*Bustles offstage and comes back with a seltzer bottle, then sprays Stanley*) That was funny.

STANLEY. That was not funny.

STELLA. I'll be right back. (*Comes back with a giant powder puff and powders Stanley*) That was funny.

STANLEY. That's not funny.

STELLA. I'll be right back. (*Comes back with a cream pie. As she nears Stanley, Stanley unexpectedly tips it into Stella's face*)

STANLEY. Now *that* was funny. (*Stanley exits. Mitch enters, pulling a curtain with a painting of a giant orchid. The Cassandra aria from* Les Troyens *comes on loudly, then fades*)

MITCH. The bell sounds and they're both middle weights. They know the rules, and they've been publicized as an even match. 'Ere, you've paid good money to see them, you want to see a battle, you want to see blood. Round One is I Love You, Round Two is You See Me For Who I Really Am. You never see a person more clearly than the first time they lay hands on you. After that, it's all up for grabs. (*To Stella*) He's gonna be back and he's gonna say he's sorry.

STELLA. (*Wiping pie from her face*) Sorry. (*Laughs*) Sorry ... sorry,

sorry. (*Laughs*) The Indian women. The Indian women, wrapping their soft bodies in thin silk the colors of a church window. Sari. (*Laughs*) I'm sorry too. It makes me laugh. They can't take it back. What the gods give they cannot take back, they can only add to what they've given, to make the gift painful to have. Cassandra! Zeus gave her the gift of the seer, and then she wouldn't have sex with him, but he couldn't take back the gift. He couldn't have her, so he made sure no one would believe her. . . . She knew all those men were in that wooden horse, but they wouldn't listen . . . (*Laughs*) That's hysterical. It was their loss, that curse! Zeus made a prophetess and then spit in her face. And just what do you think went on inside that horse? Hundreds of warlike men, spitting, smoking, dreaming death in the belly of a fake horse. . . . I dream a purple darkness . . . purple . . . the color of the sari . . . darlings. I'm in here. I'm on drugs. I'm braless, shirtless, I'm giggling, I'm lost, I'm in love. I'm stuck in the stomach of a fake horse, can you hear me? I hear you. Cassandra tell me what will happen. I promise I'll believe you! I . . . I'm in love with you Cassandra, you blonde, you seer, you whisperer . . . tell me what's going to happen . . . come here . . . let's make it happen. Please don't, blonde seer. I can't, I'm already married. Take your hands off my breasts, I'm already married. I'm in here. The horse! I'm in the belly of a horse, smoking, shirtless. I'm preparing for a war. (*She begins to strip off her house dress to reveal a tight, strapless dress*) Someone stole my woman, stole her from my house, filched her from history, and I'm here to get her back. I am a powerful warrior. (*She poses like Marilyn Monroe*) Come sweet prophetess, what is going to happen? Tell me, I'm nailed to this story. Cut me down. I'm in here. Can't you see me? I'm having sex with the fortune teller that men don't believe. Sex . . . sex! (*She sings*)

Running Wild

Running wild, lost control
Running wild, mighty bold
Feeling gay, reckless too
Carefree mind, all the time, never blue

Always going — don't know where
Always showing — I don't care
Don't love nobody, it's not worthwhile
All alone and running wild

(*Stanley has entered audience and applauds Stella loudly as piano starts intro for Stella's next song*)

Sweet Little Angel

I've got a sweet little angel
And I love the way she spreads her wings
I've got a sweet little angel
And I love the way she spreads her wings
When she spreads those wings over me
She brings joy in everything.

STANLEY. (*Clapping loudly and talking to audience*) Is she good or what? She is so good ... can you believe how good she is? (*Stella stops singing*) Any moment this dame spends out of bed is wasted, totally wasted. (*Stanley runs to Stella and drops to his knees*)

STELLA. I could smell you coming.

STANLEY. You say the sweetest things.

STELLA. Women have to develop a sense of smell. Just in general. Just as a matter of fact. Like in a war. In a war, you learn to smell the enemy. You learn to cross the street. You learn to see through their disguises.

STANLEY. I am not your enemy.

STELLA. No ... but you have many of the characteristics. Not that I go by appearances, just smell and instinct.

STANLEY. What are you looking for?

STELLA. You're tense.

STANLEY. I'm always tense. It keeps me in check, keeps me in balance.

STELLA. It's hard to watch.

STANLEY. That's 'cuz you don't know that it's leading to something.

STELLA. And are you gonna tell me what that is?

STANLEY. It's a fact of life, you figure it out.

STELLA. I already did. I don't have to spend long on the likes of you, not one as experienced as I am. I know that your tension is sexual, and it's a desire that I share in, but not for your pleasure, for my own. I'm lookin' for it, I might not find it in you, I might find it somewhere else, as a matter of fact, and there's nothing you can do about it. You don't satisfy me, you're not real.

STANLEY. Are you saying I'm not a real man?

STELLA. I'm saying you're not real. You're cute. Could be much cuter if you weren't quite so obvious.

STANLEY. Then it wouldn't be me. I am not subtle.

STELLA. Try it, just for tonight.

STANLEY. You mean put it on like clothes? I couldn't pull that off.

STELLA. No, take it off. Take it all off. I want to see what you're really made of. I want to see what it is that makes me want you. That makes me want to have you as I've never had anyone. Strip. Take it off, then we'll talk.

STANLEY. Talk is cheap.

STELLA. I want to see you naked like a baby.

STANLEY. No more talk, let's make a deal.

STELLA. We are partners in this deal. I have my part, you have yours.

STANLEY. I can live up to my end of the deal, how 'bout you.

STELLA. Put your cards on the table, I'm calling your bluff. (*Blackout*)

STANLEY. Hey, turn on the light!

STELLA. I like it in the dark.

STANLEY. I don't like the dark, I like to see.

STELLA. (*As lights slowly fade up*) You can see if you get your eyes used to it.

STANLEY. I don't want to get used to it, I'm afraid of the dark.
(*Low light reveals their silhouettes dancing as the piano player sings*)

Sweet Little Angel

I've got a sweet little angel
And I love the way she spreads her wings
I've got a sweet little angel

24
▼

And I love the way she spreads her wings
When she spreads those wings over me
She brings joy in everything

I asked my angel for a nickel
And she gave me a twenty dollar bill
I asked my angel for a nickel
And she gave me a twenty dollar bill
When I asked her for her body
She said she'd leave it to me in her will ...

Well my angel if she quit me
I believe I would die
Well my angel if she quit me
I believe I would die
If you don't love me
You must tell me the reason why.

(*Stella has pulled off Stanley's ripped T-shirt as they dance. She jumps up and wraps her body around Stanley and throws the shirt to the ground as they exit. Blackout*)

ACT 2

The stage is empty except for the large rectangular box on its side, with the painting of a tub across the front. Dim orange light comes up on Stella standing and stretching in bathtub in her slip.

STELLA. The fire is keeping me awake. It reminds me of the night Yellow Mountain was burning. All night long I could see Yellow Mountain burning on my bedroom ceiling. I was afraid that the burning debris would fall from the mountain on to our roof and burn through the ceiling. Meet up with a flicker that was already there, waiting to devour me.

MITCH. (*Light behind scrim reveals Blanche in a nightgown holding a*

cigarette and Mitch standing beside her. Mitch lights her cigarette)
There's a shadow over by the window. It's a woman. She's
smoking a cigarette. (*Blanche blows smoke into Mitch's face; he
coughs*) The smoke is coming my way. Maybe she wants me
to go with her. (*Blanche passes around scrim and crosses to center
stage, where she picks up Stanley's torn T-shirt*)

STELLA. The fire has leapt out of control. It's too late, the firemen
have all gone home to their wives. Had to hose down their
own houses, to protect them from the falling debris.

BLANCHE. (*Examining Stanley's shirt*) This shirt smells of success to
me. These elements of manhood . . . there's something about
Stanley I can't quite put my finger on. I can't put my finger
on his smell. I don't believe he's a man. I question his sexuality.
His postures are not real, don't seem to be coming from a true
place. He's a phoney, and he's got her believing it, and if she
has children he'll have them believing it and when he dies,
they'll find out. (*Crossing to Stella*) Have you ever seen him
naked?

STELLA. (*Drinking coke*) It's the sugar that satisfies me. The cool
liquid running down my throat is only temporary. It's when
the sugar hits the bloodstream, that's when my heart starts
pumping.

BLANCHE. There's something about the way he smells, something
about the way he has to prove his manhood all the time, that
makes me suspicious. I'm looking at the shape, not the content.

STELLA. (*Straddling the edge of the tub*) Don't you love that feeling
when you lean against a solid surface and you can feel your
heart beating under your body.

BLANCHE. The noises he makes, the way he walks like Mae West,
the sensual way he wears his clothes, this is no garage–mechanic
working–class boy, this is planned behavior. This is calculated
sexuality, developed over years of picking up signals not
necessarily genetic is what I'm trying to say.

STELLA. I remember leaning my abdomen against the cold sink
and feeling my heart beating between my legs.

BLANCHE. I'm trying to say, what I mean is, perhaps he was a
man in some former life. Perhaps he's just a halfway house, to
lure you into a sexual trap, a trap well laid, with just the right

flavors, just the right mood to seduce you ... what I'm trying to say is, I think he's a fag.

STELLA. The thing about coca-cola is that one sixteen-ounce bottle has more than four tablespoons of sugar.

BLANCHE. But now you have the chance to get out. To end this charade before it's too late ...

STELLA. Enough to keep you up half the night.

BLANCHE. Only someone as skilled as I am at being a woman can pick up these subtle signs.

STELLA. Enough to curb your appetite.

BLANCHE. I'm well trained, equipped. I know how to talk to him, to flirt with him, not get involved really, to decorate his arm, to aid him in his charade, to give him a passing grade.

STELLA. Sugar in a sixteen-ounce bottle.

BLANCHE. (*Grabbing Stella's hand*) I'm the real woman for you. I can show you satisfaction. A rewarding, cultural life; me and you, you and me, Blanche and Stella, Stella and Blanche. ... You were such a pretty girl. (*Stella pulls away*) What day was it that you changed? You were tipped for the top and you threw it all away. You were headed upward to the good, right life and suddenly you changed.

STELLA. Pure sugar, liquid sex.

BLANCHE. Stella, you haven't been listening to a word I've been saying.

STELLA. (*Stanley has come through the audience and is standing facing Stella and Blanche*) The fire is still burning ... my clothes sticking to my chest just like Mama's dress against her naked belly. Now why did she stay at the sink so long ... (*Walking towards Stanley*) and every day without underwear. (*She jumps into Stanley's arms*)

STANLEY. Hey! (*Stanley spins her around, then they walk offstage together*)

BLANCHE. Trouble is, Marlon Brando does look gorgeous. And I know that if I met him at the time he was in that film I'd want to lick his armpits. I don't suppose he'd be able to open himself up to that though ... surrender himself. But he does have that big shapely mouth ... I guess I'm pretty taken with this actor in the film. But what if the film was life and I could just walk right into it? I don't suppose he'd welcome me, probably give me a hard time. Just like he gave Blanche ... I mean Miss Leigh ... and what would she say if this drag queen poured out of the camera lens and blew up to size right there in front of her. Yes, well, she had to deal with Marlon Brando all day and Laurence Olivier in the evenings ... I'd say she had enough problems without me on the set. ... I feel like an old hotel. (*Piano starts prelude to "Beautiful Dream"*) Beautiful bits of dereliction in need of massive renovation. There's that record again. Have you ever had something stuck in your head for a very long time, like a record playing over and over and every time it stops there's applause, and then it starts all over again ... (*The music stops and Blanche sticks her hand in the tub*) I like a warm bath. It's the warmth I'm after, not the cleanliness. I don't even mind Stella's cheap, common soap. ... Oh I did it you know, I did lead the grand life ... chauffeurs, limos. I used to go to clubs and know I was the most attractive person there ... now I don't go to clubs.

STANLEY. (*Pulling in painted vaudeville curtain behind Blance*) Ha Ha.

BLANCHE. (*Music begins again*) Now, here it comes ... the record ... and there's a dark burgundy curtain opening on the stage, and there we are, just me and Vivien ...

STANLEY. HA HA. Did you hear what I said? I said, HA HA HA. (*Stanley exits*)

BLANCHE. (*Singing*)

Beautiful Dream

Cold wind blowing through the empty rooms
Windows broken, floors damp and rotten now
No sound in the silence
No step in the stillness
No warmth in the cold air
Only shadows moving in the half-light
Empty lockers, lines of empty hooks
Vacant showers, all deep in dust now
Just a modest price bought you paradise
No one wondered would it last

Running out of steam, now the beautiful dream
Has passed.

No one greets me as I step inside
Hot and ready for whatever comes my way
No warm body waiting for me
No pulse of a warm heart near me
No strong arms around me
No one lying warm and sweet beside me
Thought we'd party 'til the end of time
But it's over, seems so long ago now
Down the long parade, see them slowly fade
As they all leave one by one
Running out of steam, now the beautiful dream
Has gone.

So I fill the tub, rub-a-dub-dub-dub
But I still freeze up inside
'Cuz the water's cold
And the dream has grown old and died
Running out of steam
Now the beautiful dream
Has gone.

(*Lights fade, curtain is pulled offstage, Blanche moves to the tub upstage left and climbs in*) Bubbles, bawbles, bumholes ... (*Smelling soap*) Municipal, that's the word. Now I'm going under ... can't hear any noises at all ... just the odd humps and hoomps and grinds ... my hair is floating about ... whooosh ... up in the air again. (*Blanche reappears in the tub wearing bubble dress as a ukelele strums in the background*) Listen ... there it is again, the record, going around and around and then the applause. Until something replaces that song and that wild applause, I know I'll cling to it. I'll always choose applause over death.

MITCH. (*Lights behind scrim reveal Mitch in fairy costume perched on a ladder and looking down on Blanche in the tub. He is playing the ukelele and singing*)

The Fairy Song

I was sitting on my asteroid, way up in the sky
When I saw you through the window, and I thought I'd drop by
You were looking sad, bothered and forlorn
Wondering where your days of youth and beauty all had gone.

Now I don't possess a magic wand, my wings are rather small
As far as fairies go I'm nothing special at all
But still I've got that something that I know you'll just adore
That special kind of magic, gonna sweep you off the floor.

(*Chorus*)
I'm a supernatural being, I'm your sweetie-pie
And I've come here from somewhere far, away up in the sky
I'm here to play a song tonight by Rimsky-Korsakov
And if you play your cards right we might even have it off.

(*Stella mouths the words as Mitch continues singing*)
Now I was sitting in the bathtub, minding my own biz
When this vision came from outer space and now I'm in a tiz
He was gorgeous, he was handsome, he was eager just to please
And he said that he'd come here so me and him could have a
    squeeze.

I'm a supernatural being, I'm your sweetie-pie
And I've come here from somewhere far, away up in the sky
I'll take you to my fairy dell, in my fairy car
And hang a sign "Do not disturb" upon the evening star.

(*Dance break, Blanche twirls around and motions Mitch to join her.
    They dance*)

(*Blanche speaks*)
Are you sure that you're a fairy?
I'd imagined they were blonde.
And frankly I'm not leaving 'til I've seen your magic wand.

(*Mitch sings*)
My wand, alas, I left at home, you'll have to come on spec
But I promise when we get there you can hold it for a sec.

30
▼

(*Chorus*)

(*Mitch and Blanche exit. Blanche reenters with Stella and Stanley, who resets table box and holds a birthday cake*)

STANLEY. (*Sings in monotone*) Happy birthday to you, happy birthday to you, happy birthday . . . Blanche, happy birthday to you.

BLANCHE. What a lovely cake. How many candles are on it?

STELLA. Don't you worry about that right now. Why don't you tell us one of your funny stories.

BLANCHE. I don't think Mr. Kowalski would be interested in any of my funny stories.

STANLEY. I've got a funny story, what about this: There's these two faggots sitting on the sofa, which one is the cocksucker? (*Long pause*) The one with the feathers coming out of his mouth.

BLANCHE. In the version I heard it was two pollacks.

STANLEY. I am not a pollack. People from Poland are Poles. There is no such thing as a pollack. And in any case, for your information, I am one hundred percent American.

STELLA. Well, now that we're all getting along so well, why don't you blow out the candles, Blanche, and make a wish.

STANLEY. Be careful what you wish for. (*Blanche blows out all the candles. They relight. She blows them out again, but again they relight. As she goes to blow them out again, Stanley brushes her aside and sticks the candles upside down in the cake one by one. Blackout. The bathtub is removed and a painting of an oversized naked light bulb is pulled onstage*) Stella! Blanche! Mitch! It's dark. I'm afraid.

STELLA. Let's just play a game.

STANLEY. This is not funny. Stella. Mitch. (*Lights slowly fade up. Stanley is wandering around the stage blindfolded*) Don't panic . . . I feel these original sins burning into me. I feel I'm never safe. There I am at four a.m. with giant monsters spelling out my life in large slimy letters above my body, just far enough above it to heat it up. To make my skin bead in sweat starting just under my hair, above my forehead, on the back of my neck, on my chest and the back of my knees.

▼

Don't panic ... I was born this way. I didn't learn it at theatre school. I was born butch. I'm so queer I don't even have to talk about it. It speaks for itself, it's not funny. Being butch isn't funny ... don't panic ... I fall to pieces in the night. I'm just thousands of parts of other people all mashed into one body. I am not an original person. I take all these pieces, snatch them off the floor before they get swept under the bed, and I manufacture myself. When I'm saying I fall to pieces, I'm saying Marlon Brando was not there for me. (*Piano starts playing softly*) James Dean failed to come through, where was Susan Hayward when I needed her, and Rita Hayworth was nowhere to be found. I fall to pieces at the drop of a hat. Just pick the piece you want and when I pull myself back together again I'll think of you. I'll think of you and what you want me to be. (*He sings all the verses to the Frank Sinatra hit "My Way," while crawling onto the table with the birthday cake and presents on it. As he gets to his knees on top of the table, one hand breaks through a box and comes out covered in blood, the other hand goes into the cake and then into a box filled with feathers. He sings the final stanza kneeling on the cake*) WHERE THE FUCK IS EVERYBODY?! (*Blackout. After a short pause lights come up on Stella and Stanley*) What time is it?

STELLA. It's four a.m.

STANLEY. Help me make it through the night.

STELLA. Don't I always?

STANLEY. I'll be tired tomorrow, I'll be tired all day.

STELLA. Don't think about tomorrow. (*They embrace and kiss as the lights fade to black. Lights come up upstage right on Mitch stuffing cake into his mouth*)

MITCH. (*Talking with his mouth full throughout*) I think it all started to go wrong when I wasn't allowed to be a boy scout. There were more important things to be done. Vacuuming, clearing up at home, putting the garbage out. I used to get so angry putting out the garbage, I'd kick the shit out of the garbage cans in front. I thought about what I was missing. It gave me a repulsion for physical activity. Swimming was the only exception, and even then it took me a long time to learn, as I was afraid of deep water. Then one day I fell in love with a beautiful young man. He came like a messenger from another world bearing a message of simple physical desire. But it was already too late, for me everything about the body was bound up with pain and boredom. I even used to eat fast because I found it so boring. Soon the boy left. He knew better than to spend his life cooking dinners for someone with poor appetite. Then I was alone. I lived in a small room near a fly-over. I stopped going out except to go to the laundry and get groceries. At night I would lie awake on my bed, and imagine I could hear things. (*Sound of a ukelele from offstage. He opens one of the gift boxes on the table and the sound comes again. He reaches into the box and pulls out a ukelele, then sings "The Man I Love," by George and Ira Gershwin. As he sings, tap-dancing chinese lanterns — the remaining members of the cast in lantern costumes — enter and begin dancing around him. During the song the lanterns begin running into each other and floundering around the stage. The audience begins to hear them mumbling from under their costumes*)

BLANCHE. Oh, what are we doing? I can't stand it! I want to be in a real play! (*Bright light pops on as Stella drops her lantern to the floor*) With real scenery! White telephones, french windows, a beginning, a middle, and an end! This is the most confusing show I've ever been in. What's wrong with red plush? What's wrong with a theme and a plot we can all follow? There isn't even a fucking drinks trolley. Agatha Christie was right.

STELLA. Now we all talked about this, and we decided that realism works against us.

BLANCHE. Oh we did, did we?

STELLA, STANLEY & MITCH. Yes we did!

BLANCHE. But I felt better before, I could cope. All I had to do was learn my lines and not trip over the furniture. It was all so clear. And here we are romping about in the avant-garde and I don't know what else. I want my mother to come and have a good time. She's seventy-three for chrissake. You know she's expecting me to play Romeo before it's too late. What am I supposed to tell her? That I like being a drag-queen? She couldn't bear it, I know she couldn't.

She wants me to be in something realistic, playing a real person with a real job, like on television.

STELLA. You want realism?

BLANCHE. What do you mean?

STELLA. You want realism, you can have it.

BLANCHE. You mean like in a real play?

STELLA. If that's what you want.

BLANCHE. With Marlon Brando and Vivien Leigh?

STELLA. You think you can play it?

BLANCHE. I have the shoulders.

STANLEY. I have the pajamas ... O.K., let's go for it. (*Mitch and Stella exit, striking the light bulb curtain. Stanley sweeps the table with his forearm knocking the cake and presents to the floor*) I cleared my place, want me to clear yours? It's just you and me now, Blanche.

BLANCHE. You mean we're alone in here?

STANLEY. Unless you got someone in the bathroom. (*He takes off his pajama top and pulls out a bottle of beer*)

BLANCHE. Please don't get undressed without pulling the curtain.

STANLEY. Oh, this is all I'm gonna undress right now. Feel like a shower? (*He opens the beer and shakes it, then lets it squirt all over the stage, then pours some over his head before drinking it*) You want some?

BLANCHE. No thank you.

STANLEY. (*Moving towards her, menacingly*) Sure I can't make you reconsider?

BLANCHE. Keep away from me.

STANLEY. What's the matter, don't you trust me? Afraid I might touch you or something? You should be so lucky. Take a look at yourself in that worn out party dress from a third-rate thrift store. What queen do you think you are?

BLANCHE. (*Trying to get past him*) Oh god.

STANLEY. (*Blocking her exit*) I got your number baby.

BLANCHE. Do we have to play this scene?

STANLEY. You said that's what you wanted.

BLANCHE. But I didn't mean it.

STANLEY. You wanted realism.

BLANCHE. Just let me get by you.

STANLEY. Get by me? Sure, go ahead.

BLANCHE. You stand over there.

34
▼

STANLEY. You got plenty of room, go ahead.

BLANCHE. Not with you there! I've got to get by somehow!

STANLEY. You can get by, there's plenty of room. I won't hurt you. I like you. We're in this together, me and you. We've known that from the start. We're the extremes, the stereotypes. We are as far as we can go. We have no choice, me and you. We've tried it all, haven't we? We've rejected ourselves, not trusted ourselves, mirrored ourselves, and we always come back to ourselves. We're the warriors. We have an agreement . . . there's plenty in this world for both of us. We don't have to give each other up to anyone. You are my special angel.

BLANCHE. You wouldn't talk this way if you were a real man.

STANLEY. No, if I was a real man I'd say, "Come to think of it, you wouldn't be so bad to interfere with."

BLANCHE. And if I were really Blanche I'd say, "Stay back . . . don't come near me another step . . . or I'll . . ."

STANLEY. You'll what?

BLANCHE. Something's gonna happen here. It will.

STANLEY. What are you trying to pull?

BLANCHE. (*Pulling off one of her stiletto-heeled shoes*) I warn you . . . don't!

STANLEY. Now what did you do that for?

BLANCHE. So I could twist this heel right in your face.

STANLEY. You'd do that, wouldn't you?

BLANCHE. I would, and I will if you . . .

STANLEY. You want to play dirty? I can play dirty. (*He grabs her arm*) Drop it. I said drop it! Drop the stiletto!

BLANCHE. You think I'm crazy or something?

STANLEY. If you want to be in this play you've got to drop the stiletto.

BLANCHE. If you want to be in this play you've got to make me!

STANLEY. If you want to play a woman, the woman in this play gets raped and she goes crazy in the end.

BLANCHE. I don't want to get raped and go crazy, I just wanted to wear a nice frock, and look at the shit they've given me!

STELLA. (*Entering with Mitch*) Gimme that shoe! (*Piano starts "Push-over" as she grabs Stanley and sings to him*)

All the girls think you're fine, they even call you Romeo,
You've got 'em, yeah you've got 'em runnin' to and fro, oh yes
   you have,
But I don't want a one night thrill, I want a love that's for real,
And I can tell by your lies, yours is not the lasting kind.

You took me for a pushover, you thought I was a pushover,
I'm not a pushover, you thought that you could change my
   mind.

(*Mitch sings to Blanche*)
So you told all the boys that you were gonna take me out
You even, yeah you even had the nerve to make a bet, oh yes you
   did,
That I, I would give in, all of my love you would win,
But you haven't, you haven't won it yet.

You took me for a pushover, you thought I was a pushover,
I'm not a pushover, you thought my love was easy to get.

(*Mitch and Stella together*)
Your tempting lips, your wavy hair,
Your pretty eyes with that come hither stare,
It makes me weak, I start to bend and then I stop and think again,
No, no, no don't let yourself go.
I wanna spoil your reputation, I want true love, not an imitation,
And I'm hip, to every word in your conversation.

You took me for a pushover, I'm not a pushover,
You can't push me over, you thought I was a pushover . . .

STELLA. (*To audience*) Did you figure it out yet? who's who,
   what's what, who gets what, where the toaster is plugged in?
   Did you get what you wanted?
STANLEY. Hey Stella, I just figured it out. Wasn't Blanche blonde?
STELLA. That's right. And come to think of it, it was suspicious
   she didn't have a southern accent.
STANLEY. I knew it all along. The person we've been referring to
   as your sister is an imposter.
STELLA. Incredible! There's no flies on you Stanley.

36
▼

STANLEY. What did you say?

STELLA. I said there's no disguising you, Stanley. You're one hundred percent.

STANLEY. I thought you said something else ... something about flies.

STELLA. Well, come to think of it, there is something in that area I've been meaning to open up a little.

STANLEY. So, you figured it out.

STELLA. Yeah, I figured it out.

STANLEY. And in those shoes. Un–fuckin'–believable! You know what this means?

STELLA. No, what?

STANLEY. This means that you are the only thing we can rely on, because you are at least who you seem to be.

STELLA. Well Stanley, there's something I've been meaning to tell you ... (*She sings*)

You took me for a pushover (*All join in*) I'm not a pushover
You can't push me over, you thought I was a pushover.
DON'T PUSH!

(*Encore*)

I Love My Art

I've been mad about the stage since childhood,
When I roamed the sage and wildwood,
The attraction for the dazzling lights,
Caused me troublesome nights
Now I realize my one ambition
I can make a full and frank admission,
I am madly in love with my art, I love to play my part,

I love the theatre, I love it better than all my life, and just because
It's so entrancing, the song and dancing, to the music of applause,
I love the stage and all about it, it simply goes right to my heart,

I love the glamour, I love the drama,
I love I love I love my art
I love the glamour, I love the drama,
I love I love I love my art

Eye of the Gull

■

A PLAY IN TWO ACTS

BY

JANE CHAMBERS

AS REVISED BY VITA DENNIS

▼

Eye of the Gull

Jane wrote *Eye of the Gull* in 1971 as a tribute to the power and simplicity of love as she observed it in the relationship between two of her friends who were lovers and the developmentally disabled adult sister who came to live with them.

The frustration and responsibility of caring for this "child" along with the daily rigors of running Gull House and keeping a long-term relationship alive are woven into the stories of the women who visit this east coast lesbian guest house. Together they create a unique tapestry of relationships.

Once written, *Eye of the Gull* was left untouched and unpolished for twenty years. Why? Only Jane really knows.

In 1991, Vita Dennis, writer and artistic director of Footsteps Theatre Company, in Chicago, who previously produced *My Blue Heaven* and *Last Summer at Bluefish Cove*, asked might there somewhere be a Chambers script she did not know about. I responded with *Eye of the Gull*. The play needed some polishing and updating and not being a writer myself I asked Vita if she would be interested in revising it. Her response, I'm happy to say, was yes. And so with my supervision she made the necessary revisions and gave the play its first production.

Beth Allen

Eye of the Gull opened Thursday, November 7, 1991, at Footsteps Theatre, 6968 N. Clark Street, Chicago. It was directed by Robin Stanton and had the following cast:

PAT .... Phila Broich

SARA .... Elizabeth Holmes

MAGGIE .... Vita Dennis

ANNIE .... Keri Roebuck

SAM .... Theresa Carson

PEARL .... Lizanne Wilson

JESSIE .... Maggie Cain

DENNY .... Lisa Ives

LINDA .... Susan Myers

MARGO .... Patrice Fletcher

TALLY .... Julia Fabris

ROYCE .... Eileen Glenn

KATHY .... Jane deLaubenfels

CHARACTERS

PAT — about 40, suntanned, beachcomber look, a quality of strength

SARA — her sister, physically a fully blossomed 27-year-old woman, but is illiterate and reasons at the 12-year-old level; she is protected and spoiled but glows with a child's innocent approach to life; hidden deep, a grain of guts

MAGGIE — late 30s, slender but sturdy; she could be plain but her character exudes beauty

ANNIE — mid 20s, tough and sexy

SAM — early 20s, a drag butch who reminds us of Sean Penn

PEARL — late 30s, very correct, proper, sexually uptight; a spoiled housewife

JESSIE — about 40, gentle, soft woman trying very hard to be strong

DENNY — late 30s, handsome woman, intelligent, easy-going schoolteacher

LINDA — a beautiful 18-year-old who has early learned to use her pretty body as a means of exchange

MARGO — mid 40s, an actress trying desperately to preserve her star status; probably more beautiful in maturity than she was a decade before, but you'd never convince her of that

TALLY — early 30s, a production assistant grappling with the frustrating battle of keeping both Margo's and her own feet on the ground

ROYCE — mid 20s, scrubbed, cocky, energetic, ambitious and naive

KATHY — 18, corn-fed plain, pushing to make up in energy and brightness what she lacks in physical beauty; star-struck, eager for approval, she is a child in contrast to her peer and roommate Linda

PLACE

Both acts of the play take place in Gull House, a rambling, two-story frame guest house in a small beach resort area. Downstairs is a huge living room/lounge for guests, furnished comfortably with early Salvation Army chairs, sofas, and hassocks. The furnishings include a battered TV, a stereo, some books and magazines, a makeshift bar, frayed scatter rugs, and a small fireplace. The picture window stage left is spattered with seaspray. Its adjoining door opens onto a large wooden porch that fronts the living room and corners it as well, downstage on the apron. On the porch are an old-fashioned swing, rocking chairs, a bannister and steps leading to the beach. Downstage right is the office, with access to the living room. A boardwalk leads to the outside office door.

Upstairs are several small, identical rooms. Each has a lumpy shrimp-sized double bed, a mirror, a bureau, a window. The upstairs area is covered by a scrim on which appears the rough clapboard exterior of Gull House and the top half of the huge, grotesque, painted gull that decorates the side of the house. The attic window serves as the gull's eye. The gull is faded, flaking, peeling. When action occurs in the upstairs area, the scrim dissolves in lights — although the gull is always still visible.

TIME

Early Saturday morning, the beginning of a June weekend.

ACT I

SCENE I

PAT Steinberg, a handsome woman about 40, tanned, is irritably punching with one inept finger at the calculator in her office. She adds a column of figures, checks them against her ledger, attaches the strip from the calculator to the page in the ledger with a paper clip and proceeds to the next page.

Upstairs, Sara, Pat's younger sister, is cleaning the rooms and making the beds. Sara is 27, a trifle heavy and unkempt but a full-blossomed woman. She speaks, moves, and reasons, however, with the ability of a 12-year-old, stamping her foot when she encounters difficulties making neat "hospital" corners on the bed sheets. A little spoiled, demanding and irritating, Sara still exudes the innocence and vulnerability of a child. She sings "Franklin's Song" from Sesame Street *as she works.*

Offstage right in the kitchen, a teakettle whistles. Pat hits a wrong key and sends the calculator on a juggernaut of repetition.

PAT. (*Watching the damned thing take off by itself*) Son of a seahorse! (*At this moment, Maggie, late 30s, slender, sunburned, enters the office, carrying a tray of coffee and toast*)
MAGGIE. (*Also watching the machine do its thing*) What's the matter?
PAT. (*Seeing the tray*) It's about time!
MAGGIE. (*Putting the tray on the desk and confronting the calculator*) What's the matter with it?
PAT. I've been up for two hours and haven't had any coffee, that's what's the matter with it!
MAGGIE. I had to get Sara started with the linens. Can't you *stop*

it? (*It rat-a-tat-tats furiously*)

PAT. (*Ignoring the machine*) It's nine o'clock. The first ferry is docking and you're piddling.

MAGGIE. I'm not piddling! I had to get the rooms ready. (*Over the racket*) *Will you stop that thing?*

PAT. What for? Maybe it'll come up in the black for a change. (*Maggie crawls under the desk, pulls the plug. The machine shudders to a stop*)

MAGGIE. Jesus, you're helpless.

PAT. I want my coffee when I get up in the morning. When I *get up*, understand that, Maggie? (*Maggie sighs, starts to leave*) Maggie, my love, my darling, my precious partner, are you comprehending? *Coffee. When I get up!*

MAGGIE. (*Wearily, leaning against the doorjam*) I hear you.

PAT. I am running a business here. I am running a business here for profit. I am running a business here for profit so we don't have to live five flights up in the Bronx. I am running a business here for profit so —

MAGGIE. I hear you, Pat.

PAT. — I can take care of my baby sister with whom God has seen fit to saddle me.

MAGGIE. (*Chastising*) Pat!

PAT. I am also running a business for profit —

MAGGIE. (*To the heavens*) Another glorious weekend at Gull House.

PAT. — so we can get the hell out of Gull House before we all turn into a pillar of salt!

MAGGIE. We lived on macaroni for five years to buy Gull House, to live on the beach, to own our own business.

SARA. *Maggie!*

PAT. Aren't those rooms finished yet?

MAGGIE. I'm trying to let Sara take some responsibility, Pat. She's got to take some responsibility.

PAT. How the hell can she take responsibility? She's twelve years old.

MAGGIE. A twelve-year-old can take responsibility.

SARA. (*From upstairs*) *Maggie!*

PAT. Go help her! Don't put that kid through agony, Maggie. She's not capable of doing those rooms herself.

46
▼

MAGGIE. She is capable of doing them, Pat. And she's got to learn that.

PAT. Don't tell me what she's capable of, she's *my* sister. Get up there and get those rooms ready. The vultures are already pounding their way up the boardwalk. (*Maggie starts to go*) And open up the blinds, get the rooms freshened. Smells like a whorehouse up there.

MAGGIE. I thought Hitler died in Argentina. (*Starting up the stairs and calling out*) Annie! *Time to get up!*

PAT. (*Leaping from her seat and leaning out the office door*) What are you running, a wake–up service?

MAGGIE. She'll be late for work.

PAT. What do you care?

MAGGIE. *You'll* care when her rent's due. (*She calls again*) Annie! *Come on, rise and shine!*

SARA. (*Still upstairs*) Maggie!

MAGGIE. (*To Sara*) I'm coming!

PAT. (*To Maggie*) She could get up in the morning like normal people if —

MAGGIE. (*At an upstairs door*) Annie, *get your ass out of that bed!*

PAT. — She wasn't up all night carrying on! (*Annie stumbles out of her room, tousled, naked, carrying a towel and soap toward the hall bath. She's a tough but sexy girl about 25*)

ANNIE. (*Sleepy but happy*) Good morning! (*Maggie smiles back*)

SARA. (*Screaming*) Maggie!

PAT. (*To Annie, up the stairwell*) Go to hell!

SARA. (*Running out into the hallway*) What'd I do, Pat?

MAGGIE. (*To Sara*) Not you, honey. She was talking to Annie. (*Sara watches Annie's naked bottom twitch into the bathroom, a special shake aimed at Pat. Sara giggles*) Go on back to the room, Sara. I'll be right there.

SARA. (*Like a child*) I need you *now!*

MAGGIE. In a minute, honey.

SARA. *Now!*

MAGGIE. (*Forcefully*) *In a minute, I said. Get into that room!* (*Sara, pouting, does so*)

PAT. (*To Maggie*) Who the hell do you think you are?

MAGGIE. She's spoiled rotten.

PAT. She's a child.

MAGGIE. Inside. Outside, she's a grown woman and you've got to start treating her like one.

PAT. You let *me* handle my sister. You handle the whores.

MAGGIE. (*Indicating Annie in the bath*) I'd like to see *you* wake up one morning, just one morning, with that kind of smile on *your* face. (*Pat goes back into the office*) I'd like to wake up with it on *mine*, too!

SARA. (*At the doorway, whining*) Maggie . . .

MAGGIE. I'm coming, Sara, I'm coming! (*She goes into the room with Sara*) Now. What is it, honey?

SARA. (*Pointing at the window*) The blind's broken.

MAGGIE. How did you manage to do that?

SARA. I don't know. I just pulled it.

MAGGIE. Don't cry, Sara. It's just a window shade.

SARA. Pat'll get mad. The rooms aren't finished.

MAGGIE. We'll get it done. Now, look . . . (*She sits Sara down*) Look at the blind. What do you think would be the best way to fix it?

SARA. (*Staring at blind*) I don't know.

MAGGIE. Is it torn?

SARA. No. (*In the office, Pat plugs the calculator into the wall again. It takes off again. She slugs it, drops it on the desk. Nothing works. Finally, she unplugs it. Simultaneously, Sam, a masculine female stud about 22, cockily exits Annie's room, hitching up her blue jeans. She hears Annie in the bathroom, starts down the stairs*)

MAGGIE. (*To Sara*) Then we can probably fix it. Right?

SARA. Right.

MAGGIE. What if we took it down and unrolled it and rolled it back up again? (*Sara considers this, grins*) Get up on the chair and take it down. (*Maggie dusts the bureau and makes the bed as Sara climbs onto the chair*)

SARA. How do I get it out?

MAGGIE. Look at it.

SARA. It has holes at the top.

MAGGIE. Well?

SARA. I could lift it out the holes.

MAGGIE. (*Weary*) Right. (*Sara, pleased, does so. Downstairs, Sam sticks her nose into the office*)

SAM. Where'd you get the coffee?

PAT. I told you last week I don't want you around here.

SAM. I'm a guest.

PAT. You're not *my* guest.

SAM. I'm a guest of your guest.

PAT. Fifty bucks.

SAM. For what?

PAT. Fifty bucks a head a night. That's the going rate.

SAM. Better ask your tenant. I'm an innocent bystander. (*Pat glares at her*) O.K., just a bystander.

PAT. It might do you some good to try *standing* sometime.

SAM. I can do it that way, too. (*Heads for the kitchen, offstage right*)

PAT. And stay out of that kitchen! We don't serve food!

MAGGIE. (*Upstairs*) Now, unroll it all the way. Then roll it back up again and put it back on the window.

SARA. Like this?

MAGGIE. That's right. (*Maggie proceeds to the next room, Annie's room, where she makes the bed. The room is in disarray, the scene of much activity. Maggie is hungry for what this room represents. She savors it*)

PAT. (*From the office*) Maggie!

MAGGIE. (*From Annie's room*) What?

PAT. *Come here a minute!*

MAGGIE. (*Sighs*) Just a second. (*She continues to make the bed. Annie exits the bath, still nude, enters the room casually, starts to dress*)

ANNIE. You don't have to make the bed.

MAGGIE. Part of the service.

ANNIE. I never could understand why you're supposed to make a bed. You're only going to get back into it at night. (*She watches Maggie*) Thanks for waking me up. I'd never get into that damned restaurant if you didn't.

MAGGIE. It's not such a bad job, is it?

ANNIE. It stinks.

MAGGIE. Well, it's just for the summer.

PAT. (*From the office*) Maggie!

MAGGIE. (*To Pat*) Coming!

ANNIE. Yeah. Well, I had to get away. I just had to, you know?

MAGGIE. Yeah.

SARA. (*From her room*) *Maggie!*

MAGGIE. Oh, Christ.

ANNIE. Sometimes, it's too much. Like you're drowning to death, you know? (*She starts to dress*)

PAT. (*From the office*) *Maggie!*

MAGGIE. (*To Annie*) Yeah.

SARA. (*From the hall*) *Maggie!*

ANNIE. You know? (*She continues to dress*)

MAGGIE. Yeah. I know. (*Leaving the room and hollering down the stairs*) Hold on, Pat, I'm coming! (*She goes to Sara in the hall*) What is it, honey?

SARA. Is this right? (*Sara holds up the half-rolled shade*)

MAGGIE. (*Without really looking*) Fine. (*Sara is disappointed. Maggie relents*) It's really good, Sara. You're doing a fine job.

SARA. Am I?

MAGGIE. You certainly are! Just be sure to pull it good and tight.

SARA. Tell Pat, will you? Tell Pat I fixed the window shade by myself?

MAGGIE. I will.

SARA. All by myself.

PAT. (*Screaming*) Maggie! (*She glides to the office doorway on her office chair, looks up the stairs irritably. Sara sees her*)

SARA. Pat, look!

PAT. Where's Maggie?

MAGGIE. (*Starting down the stairs*) I'm coming!

SARA. Look, Pat! I did it by myself!

PAT. (*To Maggie*) Where have you been? I could have been dying!

SARA. (*Still upstairs, calling*) See, Pat?

MAGGIE. (*To no one*) I am dying.

SARA. *I did it myself!*

MAGGIE. (*To Pat*) Listen to Sara, will you?

PAT. (*To Sara*) What is it? I'm busy!

SARA. I fixed the shade by myself, Pat.

PAT. For Christ's sake, Sara, did you break the window shade?

SARA. But I fixed it, Pat.

PAT. I can't afford to be buying new shades for this whole house!

MAGGIE. Listen to her, Pat.

SARA. I *fixed* it, Pat. See?

MAGGIE. She fixed it, Pat. *By herself.*

PAT. Oh. Hey, that's real good, Sara.

SARA. Is it?

PAT. I'm proud of you!

SARA. (*Beaming down the stairs*) I'll bet you didn't think I could do it!

PAT. (*To Maggie*) That dyke is in our kitchen. Will you get her out of here? I've told you a hundred times I don't want her in this house! She'll scare off the rest of the guests.

MAGGIE. I didn't bring her into the house, Pat.

PAT. Well, the whore did.

MAGGIE. The *whore* is paying a full season's rent, Pat. We need it.

PAT. Just get the dyke out of here before the guests arrive.

MAGGIE. She's not bothering anybody.

PAT. Out!

MAGGIE. O.K. (*Maggie heads toward the kitchen, sarcastically muttering under her breath*) Here dykey, dykey, dykey, here dykey ... (*Upstairs, Annie, now dressed, sees Sara in the hall with the shade*)

ANNIE. Good morning, Sara.

SARA. Good morning, Annie. Look what I did!

ANNIE. (*Quite gently*) Let's see.

SARA. It went crooked and so I took it down and unrolled it all the way and rolled it back real tight and now I'm going to put it back on the window.

ANNIE. Aren't you smart!

SARA. I am?

ANNIE. Sure. Otherwise, you'd have to buy a new shade.

SARA. That would make Pat mad.

ANNIE. You've done a beautiful job!

SARA. That's what Pat said. (*Meanwhile, Jessie and Pearl are coming up the boardwalk toward the office, carrying their weekend bags. Jessie is attractive, strong, 40ish. Pearl is small, fluffy, frivolous, in her late 30s. They stop in front of the office*)

PEARL. (*Dramatically*) Gull House!

JESSIE. Eleven years! Every June fourteenth!

PEARL. I remember the first time I saw you. Sitting right there on the porch, under the gull's wing.

JESSIE. (*Looking up at the gull*) The old bird could use a paint job.
PEARL. So could you. (*Jessie looks at her, startled. Pearl grins*) And me too. Time marches on! (*Jessie puts down her suitcase, takes Pearl by the shoulders*)
JESSIE. Anybody looking?
PEARL. I don't care!
JESSIE. To The March Of Time! (*She kisses Jessie gently on the lips. Pat looks out the office window, sees them, flings open the door*)
PAT. You want to get me arrested before the season starts?
JESSIE. *Pat!*
PEARL. Hey! (*The three embrace, old friends*)
PAT. (*Calling into the house*) Hey, Maggie, look who's here! (*She leads them into the office*) Maggie! Guess who — (*Maggie comes out of the kitchen, smiling*)
MAGGIE. (*Before even looking up*) Jessie and Pearl!
PEARL. *Surprise!*
MAGGIE. What surprise? Every June fourteenth for eleven years! We reserve the room automatically.
JESSIE. We have to return to the scene of the crime. (*Pat hands Jessie a pen and the register book*)
PEARL. We still have to register?
PAT. Why not? You've got a record to be proud of! (*Upstairs, Annie is watching Sara put up the blind, proudly. Sam, a cup of coffee in her hand, exits the kitchen, passes the office, glances in, wanders into the living room, makes herself comfortable*)
PEARL. I'd think by now we'd be Guests of the House!
PAT. I wish I could afford it.
MAGGIE. (*Embarrassed*) Come on, I'll take you to your room.
JESSIE. (*Trying to seem unabashed*) Wow! Smell that salt air!
ANNIE. (*Bounding down the stairs past them*) Good morning!
PEARL & JESSIE. Good morning.
MAGGIE. Annie, this is Pearl and Jessie. Annie's working at the Saltbox for the season.
JESSIE. Oh, good. We'll be having dinner there tonight.
PEARL. We *always* have dinner there.
JESSIE. That's the point, isn't it? To recreate the whole thing?
ANNIE. It also happens to be the only decent food on the island. (*To Maggie*) Coffee on?

MAGGIE. Help yourself.

ANNIE. (*Passing the office, to Pat*) Morning, Smiley.

PAT. Go fuck yourself. (*As Annie goes into the kitchen*) That *would* be a change.

MAGGIE. (*In the upstairs hallway*) Sara, look who's here!

SARA. *Jessie and Pearl!* (*She hugs them exuberantly*) Come, look what I did!

MAGGIE. They'll look in a minute, Sara. Let them put their bags down first.

SARA. (*Disappointed*) O.K. but don't forget.

JESSIE. We won't forget! Promise.

MAGGIE. (*Leading them into their room*) Overlooking the surf.

PEARL. This is a glorious room! You can see the sun set in the afternoon. (*She goes to the window*) Pat's never repaired that pane of glass! (*Maggie looks quizzically, Pearl quickly adds*) The old piece of masking tape is holding up pretty well.

JESSIE. I thought this was your room, yours and Pat's. (*Downstairs, Pat gives up on the calculator, wanders outside on the boardwalk, watching for customers. She notices the painted gull, inspects its condition*)

MAGGIE. It used to be. We have the big room downstairs now.

JESSIE. I didn't know there was a big room downstairs.

MAGGIE. We knocked out a wall last winter and made a big room with a private bath. Used to be two storage rooms.

PEARL. Those two closets?

MAGGIE. Together, they're pretty big. (*Annie, a cup of coffee in hand, joins Sam in the living room, sits on her lap, kisses her playfully*)

ANNIE. Morning, stud.

SAM. The name's Sam.

ANNIE. Sam the Stud.

SAM. Nope.

ANNIE. Sam the Super Stud!

SAM. That'll do for starters.

MAGGIE. (*Upstairs, as Jessie and Pearl unpack*) Sara took to crying at night so Pat made a room big enough for all three of us.

PEARL. Sara sleeps with you?

MAGGIE. Well, in the same room.

JESSIE. Bad news.

MAGGIE. (*Shrugs*) It doesn't make much difference anymore.

JESSIE. Worse news.

PEARL. I think that's normal. You've been together fifteen years.

MAGGIE. What does that have to do with it?

JESSIE. Pearl thinks people outgrow sex.

PEARL. You think married couples carry on all their lives? (*Jessie struggles to keep her mouth shut*)

MAGGIE. I don't know.

PEARL. My mother and father stopped years ago.

MAGGIE. My mother and father only did it *once* but I don't see what that's got to do with my life.

JESSIE. (*Laughs*) I'd say it had a *lot* to do with your life! (*Maggie laughs. Sara is waiting impatiently in the doorway*)

SARA. (*Whining*) Hurry up . . .

MAGGIE. Don't rush them, Sara, that's rude.

PEARL. Sara's obviously got something important to tell us! Come on, Sara, I'll go with you. (*Sara leads Pearl to the room, shows the blind. We don't hear their conversation*)

MAGGIE. Jessie?

JESSIE. Yeah?

MAGGIE. Don't you?

JESSIE. Oh, sure. Sure, I wouldn't put up with that. We fight a lot about it but you know me, Maggie, I've got to have it.

MAGGIE. How much fun can that be if she doesn't want it?

JESSIE. You adjust. Well, sex is sex, isn't it? I just told her, "Put out, baby, or I get a mistress." I can handle her. She gets too big for her britches sometimes but I can handle her.

MAGGIE. Uh-huh.

JESSIE. You know me.

MAGGIE. Yeah.

JESSIE. Trouble is, she doesn't really seem to *need* it.

MAGGIE. Oh?

JESSIE. Yeah. Never have to worry about her fooling around. She's just not interested in sex.

MAGGIE. Yeah.

JESSIE. But I love her, you understand. Nothing's going to break us up. This one's forever.

MAGGIE. Yeah.

JESSIE. We bought a ski house this year.

MAGGIE. Oh?

JESSIE. Yeah, you'll have to come up. And we got her a little sports car. I'm still driving the Mercedes.

MAGGIE. Wow.

JESSIE. Yeah, everything's going fine.

ANNIE. (*In the living room*) Do I really have to go to work?

SAM. One of us does.

ANNIE. Why don't *you*?

SAM. You know it's tough for me to get a job.

ANNIE. You don't *have* to walk around looking like Sean Penn.

SAM. But you love it.

ANNIE. Take me dancing tonight?

SAM. You got the bread, baby, I've got the boots.

ANNIE. Come around back of the kitchen about ten and I'll slip you some supper.

SAM. Those mother-fuckers.

ANNIE. Oh, don't let them bother you.

SAM. I'd like to put me on a tux and sashay right into the main dining room.

ANNIE. You'd give twelve celebrities heart attacks.

SAM. Closet cases.

ANNIE. Not so closet if they're in the Saltbox to begin with ...

PAT. (*Calling from outside the house*) Maggie!

MAGGIE. (*To Jessie*) Come on downstairs when you're unpacked, we'll have some coffee. (*Maggie starts down the stairs. Up the boardwalk, Denny, a tall, attractive woman about 35, approaches the house. She carries no suitcase*)

DENNY. Morning, Pat.

PAT. Hi, Denny. (*Pat enters the office, leaving the door ajar. Denny follows*) I don't think she's up yet.

DENNY. I think she's afflicted with sleeping sickness.

PAT. She leads a busy life. (*Obviously familiar with the house and its inhabitants, Denny starts up the stairs, passes Maggie*)

DENNY. Morning, Maggie.

MAGGIE. Hi, Denny. She's not up yet.

DENNY. So I hear.

PAT. (*To Maggie*) That gull needs a paint job.

MAGGIE. What? (*Pat leads Maggie outside*)

DENNY. (*Tapping at the door of a room upstairs, then opening it*) On your feet, twinkle-toes!

MAGGIE. (*Outside, looking at gull*) That's going to be quite an undertaking. (*In the living room, Annie takes the coffee cups to the kitchen. Sam turns on the TV set to a soap opera*)

PAT. (*Outside, to Maggie*) You're the artistic one in the family.

MAGGIE. I'll make a deal with you.

PAT. I know your deals. *If you do the laundry, I'll let you do the dishes.* No thanks.

MAGGIE. This deal is fair.

PAT. Let's hear it.

MAGGIE. I'll outline it. You fill it in.

PAT. Paint by the numbers?

MAGGIE. Like a coloring book.

PAT. I don't know ...

MAGGIE. *Sara* could do it! Hey, that's not a bad idea!

PAT. She'd fall off the ladder and break her neck. *I'll* do it.

JESSIE. (*Coming downstairs into the living room and seeing Sam*) Hello.

SAM. Hello.

JESSIE. I'm Jessie.

SAM. Sam.

JESSIE. As in Samantha?

SAM. As in Betty Lou.

JESSIE. Oh.

SAM. My mother was a sadist.

ANNIE. (*Coming back from the kitchen, pops her head into the living room*) I'm late. See you later. (*Sam waves casually above her head*) (*To Jessie*) Have a good day.

JESSIE. Thanks. (*Annie exits via the boardwalk*)

SAM. (*To Jessie*) You know her?

JESSIE. No.

SAM. She works in the Saltbox.

JESSIE. She told me.

SAM. When?

JESSIE. A few minutes ago when I met her on the staircase.

SAM. Oh. (*Outside, Pat and Maggie lug a tall ladder and stand it upright beside the house*)

PAT. It'll reach, easy.

MAGGIE. I can't say I'm going to feel too happy on top of it.

PAT. What's that called?

SAM. (*In the living room*) This is *Beloved Hearts*.

JESSIE. What?

SAM. The soap opera. See that girl? The brunette? That's Mary Ann Thomas.

JESSIE. I've seen her in movies, I think.

SAM. (*Knowingly*) She's gay.

JESSIE. (*Not very interested*) Oh?

SAM. Yeah, I see her sometimes in the Saltbox.

JESSIE. Oh.

PAT. (*Outside*) It's not claustrophobia ...

SAM. (*Inside*) Lots of actresses are gay.

JESSIE. So are lots of other people.

SAM. You live in the city?

JESSIE. I — we — have a house in Connecticut.

SAM. That so?

MAGGIE. (*Outside*) I know what you mean ...

PAT. *Necrophilia!*

MAGGIE. That's making it with *dead people,* dummy!

SAM. (*Inside*) You commute?

JESSIE. No. I have my own business. I work at home.

SAM. What's your line?

JESSIE. I'm an architect.

SAM. Oh.

PAT. (*Outside*) Do people really do that? With dead people?

MAGGIE. Sometimes you have to take what you can get. (*As Sam and Jessie watch TV and Pat and Maggie try out the ladder, upstairs Denny leads Linda by the arm into the hallway and points her toward the bathroom. Linda is a Lolita-ish 18, wrapped in a terry robe*)

DENNY. You're supposed to be on the floor in half an hour. I've got to meet a wholesaler this afternoon.

LINDA. I'm hurrying.

DENNY. Not *enough! Hut-one-two-three!* (*Linda drags into the bathroom. Denny heads down the stairs. Sara, in the hall upstairs, sees Denny*)

SARA. Hi, Denny! (*Pearl meanwhile has returned to her own room to finish unpacking*)

DENNY. Morning, Sara-Star! How are you?

SARA. I'm good. I fixed the window shade this morning all by myself.

DENNY. Did you? Good for you! You see, you can do anything you want to, if you just try.

SARA. Could we read today? I missed *Sesame Street* this morning. I was fixing the window shade.

DENNY. I can't do it today, Sara. (*Sara looks disappointed*) I've got to do some business in town. (*Looking at Sara's face, she relents*) Well, maybe I can get back early enough — I'll come over and we'll read from the "Blue Book."

SARA. The "Blue Book"?

DENNY. I'll bet you're ready for that!

SARA. (*Delighted*) Not the "Red Book"?

DENNY. Baby stuff. You're ready for the "Blue Book"!

SARA. (*A little threatened by it*) Really? Maybe I can't do it.

DENNY. Now what have I told you, Sara? (*Sara squirms, looks at her feet; a kid in a classroom*) Come on —

SARA. I can do anything — (*She hesitates, unsure she can*)

DENNY. That's right.

SARA. I can do anything I want to.

DENNY. If?

SARA. If I try. (*Reciting*) I can do anything I want to if I try.

DENNY. But you've got to *want* to do it first, it's got to be your decision. Only Sara can make up her mind what she wants to do. It's nobody's mind but Sara's.

SARA. (*Trying to please*) Nobody's mind but Sara's.

DENNY. And when you make up your mind, *try*. Pretty soon, you'll find out that you've *done* it! (*Sara grins, pleased*) Have you been reading in the "Red Book" by yourself?

SARA. (*Shuffling uncomfortably*) I'm *very* busy. I have to make the beds and clean the rooms for Pat and Maggie. They *need* me.

DENNY. If you really want to learn to read and write, Sara, you've got to practice. *Every day*.

SARA. Pat and Maggie talk and yell all the time.

DENNY. (*Gently chastising*) Don't give me that. You can find a place to concentrate. *If*. (*They pass the office, Sara leans in to Pat and Maggie, who are coming in the door*)

SARA. Denny's going to read with me this afternoon!

MAGGIE. Good, honey.

PAT. Swell!

SARA. (*Proudly*) I've got my own private schoolteacher!

PAT. You're a lucky kid.

MAGGIE. A lucky *young woman*. (*Pearl has joined Jessie and Sam in the living room. She looks at Sam with distaste*)

PEARL. (*To Jessie*) Let's go onto the porch, get some fresh air.

SAM. Oh, is the TV bothering you?

JESSIE. No. We're at the beach, might as well get some sun.

SAM. Sure. See you.

SARA. (*Joining Sam in the living room*) What'cha watching?

SAM. *Beloved Hearts.*

SARA. Can I watch?

SAM. It's free. (*Sara sits beside Sam on the floor*)

PAT. (*To Denny*) Listen, I appreciate what you're doing for Sara.

DENNY. I've got to be some kind of nut. I teach all year and come out here for a change ...

PAT. I appreciate it.

MAGGIE. *Sara* appreciates it.

DENNY. (*Smiles*) ... and I enjoy it. (*She hollers up the stairs*) Step on it, Linda! (*On the porch, Jessie and Pearl look at the sea*)

PEARL. Who's that awful thing in the living room?

JESSIE. A guest, I guess.

PEARL. Business must be *bad*!

JESSIE. Don't be such a snob.

PEARL. I'm not being a snob, I'm being a *human*.

JESSIE. Believe it or not, *she's* human, too.

PEARL. I doubt it. (*Peers in the window*) Think so?

JESSIE. Suppose she were a millionairess?

PEARL. So what's a little eccentricity?

DENNY. (*Hollering up the stairs again*) Linda, come on!

LINDA. (*Dashing from the bath to her room*) I'm hurrying fast as I can.

DENNY. (*To Pat*) She wears about four square inches of clothing and it takes her fifteen minutes to put it on.

MAGGIE. (*To Denny*) How's Kathy?

DENNY. (*Uncomfortably*) O.K. She's working at the shop.

PAT. How's business?

DENNY. Rotten. But the season hasn't really started.

PAT. It'll pick up. I keep telling myself.

DENNY. It usually does.

PAT. Well, at least you're not dependent on it for a living.

DENNY. That's true.

MAGGIE. But Denny has to work all winter. That's just what you *don't* want to do!

PAT. Caught in my own web.

SAM. (*In the living room*) See that girl?

SARA. Which one?

SAM. Right there. The one with the black hair.

SARA. Yeah?

SAM. She's gay.

SARA. (*No discernable reaction*) Yeah?

MAGGIE. (*Calling into the living room*) Who's for coffee?

SAM. Me!

SARA. Me!

MAGGIE. (*Entering the living room*) Where are Pearl and Jessie?

SARA. On the porch. *We're* watching TV.

MAGGIE. I see that.

PAT. (*Suddenly entering the living room and speaking to Sam*) I thought I told you to get the hell out of here!

SAM. That was earlier.

PAT. I haven't changed my mind.

SAM. (*To Sara*) Sorry, pal, I got to go.

SARA. Does she have to, Pat?

PAT. She *has* to — *now! Come on, out!*

SAM. Do you object to my choosing my own exit? I'd like to take a stroll along the beach.

PAT. Pick any door. But *use* it!

SAM. (*Exiting through the front door and passing Pearl and Jessie on the porch*) So long, ladies. See you later.

JESSIE. Bye. (*Sam disappears*)

PEARL. Thank God.

JESSIE. Shh. She'll hear you.

PEARL. I don't care. *She* probably doesn't care, either.

MAGGIE. (*Appearing at the front door*) Come on in, let's have some coffee. (*Sara switches the TV to a cartoon show*)

PAT. Turn that thing off, Sara.

PEARL. (*To Maggie*) Who's the dyke?

MAGGIE. A friend of a guest.

PAT. I have to kick her out of here about twice a week. A real pain in the ass.

PEARL. Awful.

PAT. I said: *turn that TV off*, Sara!

SARA. I want to watch! Denny said it was good for me to watch!

PAT. Well, take it in the bedroom then.

DENNY. (*In the doorway*) Come on, Sara, let's take it into the bedroom. (*Denny unplugs the set and helps Sara lug it out right*) You need to concentrate, anyway. You can't concentrate with them sitting around *gossiping*. (*Sara is proud to leave the room with her buddy, Denny*)

PAT. (*Entering the living room to relax with Pearl and Jessie*) So where are the customers?

PEARL. The early ferry left early, so the late ferry will probably leave late.

JESSIE. Is that logical? (*Maggie goes to the kitchen for the coffee*)

PAT. No, but what is? (*To Jessie*) So how's life with the idle rich in Connecticut?

JESSIE. Not so idle, not so rich. A slow year.

PEARL. I didn't get a new dishwasher for Christmas.

PAT. What?

PEARL. Remember, I told you I wanted a new dishwasher for Christmas? Well, I didn't get it.

JESSIE. You'll get it, honey, give me a little time. (*To Pat*) I just bought her a sports car.

PEARL. Well, I needed it. I couldn't go anywhere without Jessie! I can't drive that Mercedes. It's too big. (*Maggie enters with the coffeepot*)

PAT. (*Indicating Maggie*) That's *my* dishwasher!

JESSIE. *That* dishwasher I'll buy.

PAT. Make an offer, it's a tight year.

PEARL. Wait a minute! Does she load from the top, have an

automatic dispenser? Is she guaranteed?

MAGGIE. (*Serving coffee*) No guarantees on used merchandise.

JESSIE. (*To Pat*) Business really that bad?

PAT. (*Proud*) Oh, not really. We just hit some unexpected expenses.

MAGGIE. Like Sara.

PAT. Last winter we moved into the city so she could go to a special school. She just cried and wouldn't go into the classroom.

MAGGIE. Well, she was fifteen years older than anybody else in the class. She should have been in a special school when she was a kid, Pat.

PAT. Yeah. But Mama wouldn't have it. She kept Sara confined to the house, her baby. Totally dependent. Now Mama's gone and there's nobody but me.

MAGGIE. Sara's doing better, though. Denny's been teaching her to read.

PAT. I'm not complaining. I love her, she's my sister. She's my responsibility. Besides, I'll still be a millionaire, sooner or later. (*She grins. Denny returns from the bedroom and starts up the stairs*)

DENNY. *Linda!*

LINDA. *I'm coming!* (*In short shorts and a tiny, tight tank top, Linda tears down the stairs into Denny's arms*) Good morning!

DENNY. How can you be so young and so slow at the same time?

MAGGIE. Denny, come in for a minute!

DENNY. We're running late! (*Denny and Linda step into the living room*)

PAT. I want you to meet our oldest friends. Denny, Linda — Jessie, Pearl. They met right here in Gull House our very first season, eleven years ago. Been together ever since.

DENNY. Remarkable. (*She shakes hands with them*) I hope longevity isn't contagious.

MAGGIE. Denny is an incorrigible roué.

DENNY. (*Indicating Linda*) Shhh!

LINDA. (*Smiling knowingly*) Oh, she had a long one once.

DENNY. (*Quickly*) Well, we're late. Nice meeting you. See you later. I promised to come by and read to Sara if I can make time this afternoon.

PEARL. Bye.

JESSIE. Nice meeting you.

PAT. Don't tear up my dunes with that damned buggy! (*Denny and Linda exit by the office door*)

JESSIE. What's that about?

MAGGIE. She's a teacher, runs a summer gift shop out here.

PEARL. She obviously has a close rapport with her students.

PAT. Yeah. She's into that.

SARA. (*Entering*) Denny!

MAGGIE. She's already gone, honey.

SARA. Oh.

JESSIE. How are you, Sara?

SARA. The cartoon's over and I don't know what to watch next.

MAGGIE. How about doing a little work? (*Sara makes a face*)

PAT. I tell you what. How'd you like to sit in the office for a while?

SARA. Play like I'm you?

PAT. Sure.

SARA. What do I do?

PAT. You just sit there. If the phone rings, answer it. You know how to do that.

SARA. What if somebody comes?

PAT. I don't think anybody will. The ferry's not due for another fifteen minutes or so, assuming, of course, that it's late.

MAGGIE. A safe assumption. (*Leading Sara to the office*) If somebody should come, you check their reservation. Remember how to do that?

SARA. In the big book.

MAGGIE. Take them to their room.

SARA. And ask for the money.

PAT. (*Hesitates*) Why not? (*Sara positions herself in the office, imitating Pat*)

MAGGIE. You certainly look *official*.

SARA. Do I?

MAGGIE. Yes, you do.

PAT. Let's go for a walk down the beach while the sun's still out. Looks like rain coming.

PEARL. Oh no!

JESSIE. Don't worry, darling, this time of year it never rains for long.

MAGGIE. Just a shower. (*They go out the front door. Sara plugs in the calculator. It does its crazy thing. She patiently pecks one by one at the keys, unsticks it. Adds up lists of imaginary figures. The phone rings*)

SARA. (*Answering*) Gull House. —— Who? —— No, Annie went to work already. —— Yes, I can take a message. Just a minute. (*She looks for a pad and pencil and gets ready*) Now, what's the message? —— Who? —— Boys. Boys. R—O—Y—C—E. Boys. —— Yes, I'll tell her. (*Officially*) Thank you for calling. (*Sara hangs up and ponders the blank piece of paper, finally draws stick figures on it*) Boys. (*She gets up and climbs the stairs to proudly slide the piece of paper under Annie's door. Meanwhile, coming up the boardwalk are Tally and Margo, carrying chic luggage. Tally is attractive, early 30s. Margo is mid 40s, quite beautiful but very conscious of her age*)

MARGO. (*Looking up at Gull House*) Already I don't like it.

TALLY. Everybody says it's a great place.

MARGO. I hate it. I hate this whole island. What if someone recognizes me?

TALLY. Just being here doesn't mean you're gay.

MARGO. It's a sizable clue.

TALLY. Well, if anyone recognizes you, they're as gay as you are.

MARGO. I don't like it.

TALLY. Will you stop being so uptight?

MARGO. I can't afford that kind of publicity.

TALLY. I give you my word you won't run into Louella Parsons.

MARGO. She's dead.

TALLY. So you won't run into her.

MARGO. What kind of people are these?

TALLY. *People* people. Just plain old homefolk lesbians.

MARGO. Plain old homefolk lesbians have big mouths.

TALLY. That's a bigoted, prejudicial thing to say.

MARGO. I have a career at stake.

TALLY. So do I! So does everybody on this island! So does everybody in that house! You think because they're schoolteachers or social workers or businesswomen —

MARGO. — or housepainters or truckdrivers!

TALLY. — *or* housepainters or truckdrivers ... they have just as much to lose as you have. *More.* They don't make a hundred grand a year.

MARGO. Two hundred.

TALLY. A million, who cares! *They* get fired, they're on the unemployment line.

MARGO. They're not celebrities.

TALLY. Did it ever occur to you that actresses are *not* the most important people in the world? Did it ever cross your mirror-lined mind that the world is full of doctors, lawyers, senators —

MARGO. File clerks.

TALLY. — professors, engineers —

MARGO. Waitresses.

TALLY. (*Shouting*) *Who make the world go round!* (*Margo glares at her*) Oh, come on. I'm sorry. Forget it. Let's don't argue this weekend. Please.

MARGO. I can't help it.

TALLY. Trust me, Margo. I *promise* you nothing terrible will happen. Just once, let's have a weekend where we can be ourselves. *Openly.*

MARGO. We could have gone to Palm Beach.

TALLY. And played straight all day with the local fags, waiting 'til midnight so we could sneak upstairs to our fancy hotel suite and make *very quiet* love, then leap up in the morning to mess up the other twin bed so the maid doesn't suspect. I'm tired of acting guilty. I *don't feel guilty.* I want you. (*Margo stiffens nervously*) For Christ's sakes, Margo, nobody's listening.

MARGO. I'm sorry, Tally.

TALLY. Please try. Just this one weekend, try. Try to love me out loud?

MARGO. Tally ...

TALLY. I can't stand any more of this.

MARGO. I'm going to lose you, aren't I?

TALLY. Like this, yes.

MARGO. I don't want to lose you. It took me so long to find you.

TALLY. I don't want you to lose me. Please? Try?

MARGO. (*Looks at the wretched painted bird*) The Gull House. (*Quietly*

▼

to Tally) All right, darling. Lead on. (*Tally opens the office door. The room is empty*)

TALLY. Hey, anybody home?

SARA. (*Rushing down the stairs*) Don't go away! Here I am! (*Tally and Margo wait in the office as Sara rushes into her official place, breathing hard*) Hi. I'm Sara.

TALLY. (*A little disconcerted*) Hi. I'm Tally. This is . . . (*she does it*) Margo.

SARA. (*With no sign of recognition*) Hi. Do you have a reservation?

TALLY. Yes.

SARA. (*Holding out the book*) Show it to me. (*Tally is bewildered*)

TALLY. (*Points*) There.

SARA. That's it?

TALLY. (*Getting irritated*) Yes, that's it.

SARA. What does it say?

TALLY. What is this? You know very well what it says. It says my name.

SARA. I know *that*. What *is* your name? (*Tally is not only irritated, she is embarrassed in front of Margo*)

TALLY. Look, this place was highly recommended to me. I came here expecting to be treated like a paying guest. I *am* a paying guest, you know.

SARA. (*Trembling*) I know. But what is your name?

TALLY. Tally Adams. *Tally Adams.* It's right in front of you! I've had these reservations for two weeks!

SARA. (*Holding up the book, stuttering*) Wh-wh-what room?

TALLY. What do you mean "what room?" *What's the matter with you?*

MARGO. Tally, let's go.

TALLY. This is supposed to be the most exclusive place on the island!

SARA. (*Trying hard to remain dignified*) What, please, is the room number?

MARGO. (*Whispering*) Tally, let's get out of here. It's *awful.*

TALLY. (*To Sara*) What's the matter with you? *Can't you read?* (*Sara bursts into tears and drops the book, running from the office into the living room just as Pat, Maggie, Jessie, and Pearl come up onto the porch*)

MAGGIE. Hey, honey, what's the matter? (*Maggie holds the sobbing Sara as Pat rushes to the office*)

TALLY. (*To Margo*) I don't understand it. Everybody says it's such a good place to come.

MARGO. I told you, darling, *all* these places are terrible! Tally, please, let's get out of here!

PAT. (*Appearing at the office door*) May I help you?

TALLY. (*Lifting her suitcase*) I don't think so.

PAT. You must be . . . (*She retrieves the register quickly*) Ms. Adams. I spoke to you on the phone two weeks ago.

TALLY. That's right.

PAT. Your room is ready. It's number four. A lovely ocean view.

TALLY. Forget it.

PAT. Did my sister do something to offend you?

TALLY. This place was highly recommended to me. The "in" place, I was told.

PAT. It is. All of our customers are word-of-mouth. We've never needed to advertise.

TALLY. Then I arrive here and this crazy woman acts like she's never heard of me . . . and my name's written right there in front of her nose!

PAT. I'm terribly sorry, Ms. Adams. My sister can't read. (*Maggie leads the sobbing Sara past the office towards the downstairs bedroom, right. Jessie and Pearl wait in the living room*)

MAGGIE. (*To Sara*) It's all right, honey, it's all right.

PAT. The ferry apparently arrived early. Or on time, I should say. I didn't expect you for another ten minutes.

MARGO. (*Watching Maggie and Sara*) What's the matter with your sister? Is she retarded?

PAT. My sister is *developmentally disabled*. It makes her feel useful to sit in the office when I'm not anticipating guests.

TALLY. I don't see how you can *anticipate* guests.

PAT. Sometimes I can't. (*There is an embarrassed silence*) I assume, however, that the kind of guests we want in Gull House would *understand*.

MARGO. (*Suddenly*) We do. We *do* understand.

TALLY. I'm sorry. I was — confused.

PAT. Do you want to stay or not?

MARGO. (*Quickly*) We want to stay.

PAT. Fine. That's two hundred dollars for the weekend. (*Margo reaches in her pocketbook and pays Pat in cash. Pat turns to Tally*) You're Tally Adams, 155 West 91st Street, the city, right?

TALLY. Right.

PAT. (*To Margo*) I'll need your name and address too. (*Margo hesitates*)

MARGO. (*Finally*) Margo Williamson, 223 East 60th. (*Tally is stunned, pleased. Pat shows no sign of recognition. She hands Margo a receipt and has them sign the registration book. Maggie appears at the door.*)

PAT. I'm Pat. This is Maggie. We own Gull House. Any problems, see us. Maggie, take them up to four, honey. (*Maggie leads them up the stairs. Jessie and Pearl watch from the living room*)

TALLY. (*To Maggie*) I feel terrible about that girl.

MAGGIE. Sara?

TALLY. Can I do something? Apologize?

MAGGIE. She'll be all right. Just leave her alone now.

MARGO. Poor thing.

MAGGIE. She doesn't need to be "poor-thinged." Every "poor thing" makes her more a child. (*Maggie opens the door to their room*) Sea view, double bed. (*Margo's eyes stay on the bed*)

MARGO. (*With a tongue-in-cheek glance at Tally*) How lovely.

MAGGIE. We don't serve food but coffee is available to guests and mixers and ice are downstairs if you've brought booze. The living room's open to everybody, the beach out front is private, guests only. The Saltbox, about ten houses down the boardwalk is the best restaurant around. Anything you need, please call us.

TALLY. Thank you. (*Maggie leaves. To Margo*) It *is* lovely. (*Tally sits on the bed, holds out her arms*) And the maid doesn't give a damn. (*Margo smiles, closes the door. Downstairs, Pearl has watched as much as she could see of Tally and Margo's entrance. Jessie is intent on watching Maggie, very tired, come down the stairs. Pat is locking up the cash box in the office*)

PEARL. (*To Jessie*) You know who that is?

JESSIE. Hmm?

PEARL. *Margo Williamson.*

JESSIE. Hmmm?

PEARL. Did you hear me?

PAT. (*From the office, to Maggie*) How's Sara?

MAGGIE. (*As she passes*) Hurt. Embarrassed. (*She pauses*) Pat, go to her. (*Pat is shocked for a moment by Maggie's commanding tone. But she goes*)

PEARL. Jessie?

JESSIE. (*Still watching Maggie*) What?

PEARL. That was *Margo Williamson.*

JESSIE. You said that. (*Maggie flops on the living room sofa*) Worn out, huh?

MAGGIE. And it's not noon yet.

PEARL. (*To Jessie*) Don't you know who Margo Williamson is?

JESSIE. No. Who is Margo Williamson?

PEARL. You saw her in *Second Avenue* on Broadway.

JESSIE. I did?

PEARL. You've seen her in a lot of shows!

JESSIE. I don't remember her.

PEARL. She always plays like second leads.

MAGGIE. (*Overhearing*) Is that woman some kind of a star?

PEARL. Not a star exactly. But to people in the know, she's a star!

MAGGIE. Well, God knows I'm *not* in the know.

JESSIE. Don't worry about it. Pearl's enough in the know for all of us. (*She starts to pour coffee for Maggie, shakes the pot, it's empty. To Pearl*) Honey, Maggie's knocked out. Why don't you make a big pot of coffee for all of us?

MAGGIE. (*Getting up*) Oh, no, I can do it . . .

JESSIE. (*Pushing her back down*) Pearl will do it. You know where everything is, don't you, sweetheart?

PEARL. (*Caught*) I guess so.

JESSIE. I'm so accustomed to your coffee, it's hard to drink anyone else's.

PEARL. (*Smug*) Jessie's so particular.

MAGGIE. I'm sorry if my coffee didn't . . .

PEARL. (*Grandly*) Oh, Jessie is just a creature of habit. She's dependent on the way *I* do things, aren't you, sweetie? (*Pearl goes to the kitchen*)

MAGGIE. (*After her*) If you need anything, holler. (*Pat enters the living room*) Sara O.K.?

PAT. Oh, yeah. Sure. (*She sprawls on the other sofa. To Maggie*) Honey, how about some coffee?

JESSIE. Pearl's doing it.

PAT. Oh. (*After a moment*) Pearl makes lousy coffee. Doesn't she? (*Maggie looks surprised. Jessie breaks into a slow grin and winks at Maggie*)

JESSIE. Shhh ... (*Maggie laughs in spite of herself*)

SCENE 2

Gull House, that afternoon.

On the front porch, stage left, overlooking the sea, Pearl has set up an easel and is painting a highly detailed portrait of a seashell.

On the downstage left porch, where it corners the house, Pat and Jessie sit in rockers, chatting.

Atop the ladder, Maggie precariously balances a paint bucket and brush and outlines the head of the gull, enclosing the attic window in its stern, omnipotent eye.

PAT. (*Calling up to Maggie*) Are you sure it's not too wet to paint, honey?

MAGGIE. It's fine. It was only a shower.

PAT. Paint won't adhere if it's wet.

MAGGIE. I know that. (*She continues painting*)

PAT. No point in doing all that work for nothing.

MAGGIE. I wiped it dry.

PAT. If it's just going to peel right off.

MAGGIE. I'm just outlining.

PAT. It's a waste of effort.

MAGGIE. *It's latex paint!*

PAT. (*To Jessie*) What does that mean?

JESSIE. I think it means "Shut up, she knows what she's doing."

PAT. *Thinks* she knows.

MAGGIE. (*Irritably*) You want to do it?

PAT. Of course not. You know I never question your judgment, darling. (*Sara comes out of the downstairs bedroom and wanders into the office, finds it empty, looks into the living room, finally wends her way to the front porch*)

JESSIE. Quite a job keeping up with this place.

PAT. Yeah. But with all my bitching, Gull House has been good to us. It's good for Sara, keeps her in contact with people — (*Maggie sways on the ladder*)

JESSIE. Watch out, Maggie!

MAGGIE. I'm O.K. Just changing my footing.

PAT. — it's kept Maggie and me together. Wouldn't you say so, hon?

MAGGIE. What?

PAT. Gull House. It's kept us together.

MAGGIE. Oh. Yes.

PAT. Someday I'm going to sell this place for a big profit — Gull House has a good name, you know. That's worth something.

JESSIE. Of course it is.

MAGGIE. Just don't tell them the building's falling down.

PAT. Oh, this old building'll hold up. It's been here fifty years.

JESSIE. Salt water's hard on a building.

PAT. (*Rapping the clapboard with her first*) Naw, she's good and sturdy.

JESSIE. And when you make your big profit, what?

PAT. Well, I'd always wanted to set Mama and Sara up in a big condo with air-conditioning, dishwasher, and a washing machine — the works.

SARA. (*On the front porch, to Pearl*) What'cha doing?

PAT. (*On the side porch*) But with Mama gone now, I guess we'll buy a house somewhere on the mainland —

MAGGIE. With, please God, a dishwasher and a *maid*!

PAT. (*Magnanimously*) — with whatever she wants.

71
▼

PEARL. (*On the front porch, to Sara*) I'm painting a picture.

SARA. Did you draw the picture yourself? (*Pearl looks puzzled*) You're not just coloring in the lines?

PEARL. Oh! No, I drew the picture myself.

SARA. (*Inspecting it critically*) It's *pretty* good.

PEARL. (*Tongue-in-cheek*) Thanks.

SARA. I mean, it's pretty *good*. (*Afraid she's offended*) In fact, it's *real good*!

PAT. (*On the side porch*) Say, Jess, did you get that contract?

JESSIE. What contract?

PAT. Last summer you were talking about a contract to design some brewery or something.

JESSIE. No. It went to a guy. Naturally. He offered me a job on the project but I'm holding out for my own jobs. I pick up a few good ones here and there. The new nursery school in Westport is mine. Crazy. They'll hire a woman to design a nursery school but not a brewery. They should only compare what I know about kids and what I know about beer. (*Pat stands up to inspect the gull*)

SARA. (*On the front porch, to Pearl*) What's that thing?

PEARL. What thing?

SARA. That *green* thing.

PEARL. (*Irritated*) Seaweed, *obviously*.

SARA. Oh. (*She inspects it*) It's a *different* kind of seaweed. I never saw any like that.

PAT. (*On the side porch, to Maggie*) You're not going to put eyelashes on that bird, are you?

MAGGIE. Why not?

PAT. Damn thing looks like a drag queen.

MAGGIE. *You think you could do better*?

PEARL. (*On the front porch, to Sara*) *You think you could do better*?

SARA. Could I try?

PEARL. What?

SARA. Could I try? Could I paint on the picture?

PEARL. Well . . . I'll tell you what. I'm going inside to get a drink. While I'm gone, you paint *just a little bit* right *here* with the green brush. O.K.?

SARA. On the seaweed?

PEARL. On the seaweed. And surprise me when I get back. (*She wipes her hands and goes inside. Sara, beside herself with artistic joy, becomes first a careful Rubens, then a free van Gogh and, at last, a mad Jackson Pollock*)

PAT. (*On the front porch, to Jessie about the gull*) What do you think?

JESSIE. Looks good to me.

MAGGIE. Thanks a lot.

JESSIE. I wish you'd get off that ladder, Maggie. You're too tired to be swaying around twenty feet in the air.

PAT. She's got a constitution like a horse. Little but mighty, right, hon?

MAGGIE. Just a regular plough horse.

PEARL. (*Leaning out of the office door*) Anybody for a beer?

JESSIE. Great!

PEARL. Not you.

JESSIE. I'm on vacation!

PAT. I'll take one.

PEARL. Does Maggie want one?

JESSIE. Why don't you ask her?

PEARL. (*Craning out*) Want one, Maggie?

MAGGIE. No thanks. I'll get something later.

PAT. She's an artist! She's concentrating!

PEARL. Pardon me. (*She goes for the beer in the kitchen, offstage right. Royce, a 25-year-old scrubbed-faced young woman approaches the house from the boardwalk, bag in hand*)

JESSIE. Who's that?

PAT. Our late guest, I guess.

MAGGIE. Pat, a customer.

PAT. I see her. I'm coming. (*She heads around the porch, glancing at Sara daubing green paint across the canvas*) Are you supposed to be doing that?

SARA. Pearl said I could. (*Pat shrugs and crosses through the living room to the office, meeting Pearl on the way. Pearl hands her the beer*)

PAT. Thanks. (*Pearl proceeds to the porch*)

MAGGIE. (*Calling down from the ladder to Royce*) That's the office. Go on in.

ROYCE. So that's the gull, huh?

73
▼

MAGGIE. I'm aiming for that effect.

ROYCE. Gull House. I've heard a lot about it. You must be Pat.

MAGGIE. Nope. I'm Maggie.

ROYCE. Oh.

PAT. (*Opening the office door*) I'm Pat. Come on in.

PEARL. (*Seeing what Sara has done to her painting*) Oh my God!

SARA. Do you like it?

PEARL. You've *ruined* it!

SARA. You said I could paint the seaweed.

PEARL. You've ruined the *whole picture*!

SARA. Seaweed grows all over everything, don't you know?

PEARL. *Ruined it!*

SARA. Seaweed would grow right over the seashell and the sand and *everything*! Don't you know anything about seaweed?

PEARL. You've ruined it!

SARA. You said I could paint the green.

PEARL. Oh, *shit!*

JESSIE. (*Overhearing and coming around the corner*) What's the matter?

PEARL. Look what she did to my picture!

JESSIE. It looks all right to me. It's a picture of seaweed, right?

PEARL. It's not *supposed* to be!

SARA. *I* painted the seaweed.

JESSIE. It *looks* like seaweed.

PEARL. It's supposed to be a *seashell*!

JESSIE. Sorry, I miss that.

PEARL. Of course you do! The dummy painted right over it!

SARA. (*Welling with tears*) I'm not a *dummy*! Denny said I wasn't a dummy! A dummy can't talk and I can talk!

PEARL. (*Holding up the canvas*) God damn it!

JESSIE. Honey, it's only a painting.

PEARL. It's the only canvas I brought!

JESSIE. So I'll buy you another one.

PEARL. I don't want *another* one! I want *this* one!

JESSIE. You're as bad as Sara!

SARA. See? (*Pearl realizes her tantrum is to her disadvantage. Maggie is listening from her post on the ladder*) I didn't mean to make you mad, Pearl.

PEARL. Forget it, Sara. Just forget it. (*Pearl starts to pack up easel and canvas*)

SARA. I color good between the lines.

PEARL. (*Handing Sara the canvas*) Here, Sara. Take this and hang it in your room.

SARA. Can I say I did it all by myself?

PEARL. You can even put your name on it.

SARA. I don't know how to write my name.

JESSIE. Show her, Pearl.

PEARL. I just put the paint *away*!

SARA. I want to put my name on it.

PEARL. (*Aggravated*) *All right*! (*She opens the metal box of paints and takes out a small brush, shows Sara how to sign the painting*)

PAT. (*In the office*) Your room's at the top of the stairs.

ROYCE. Well, I'll be staying with Annie.

PAT. She's on a season rate.

ROYCE. Can I pay for a separate room —

PAT. — and sleep wherever you want to, sure.

ROYCE. Is she going to be surprised!

JESSIE. (*On the front porch, leaning around the corner to Maggie*) Do you spell Sara's name with an H?

MAGGIE. No. No H.

JESSIE. (*To Pearl*) No H.

SARA. No H. *I told you. This* (*four fingers*) many letters.

PAT. (*In the office*) You know Annie for long?

ROYCE. (*As she signs the register*) A year. We been going together a year. (*Pat picks up her bag*)

PAT. I'm putting you in number two.

ROYCE. She's written me every week since she's been gone.

PAT. Right up the stairs. Follow me.

ROYCE. Hard for her to get work in the city during the summer, you know? The college kids pick off the best jobs. (*Royce follows Pat upstairs. Maggie has finished outlining the gull and climbs down from the ladder. Sara rushes out the office door, her painting in her hand*)

SARA. Look, Maggie, what I did!

MAGGIE. That's great, Sara.

SARA. (*Testing*) What is it?

MAGGIE. Seaweed. (*Sara beams*) Take it to the bedroom, honey.

We'll buy a frame for it and hang it up.

SARA. Really?

MAGGIE. Really.

SARA. Promise?

MAGGIE. Cross my heart. (*Upstairs, Pat shows Royce the room. Maggie is gathering her paint bucket and equipment on the boardwalk*)

SARA. (*Pausing at the office door on her way to the bedroom*) Maggie?

MAGGIE. Hm?

SARA. I color in the lines good. I'll bet *I* could paint that gull.

MAGGIE. (*In a flash*) I'll bet you could, too, Sara!

SARA. Can I try?

MAGGIE. Will you be very careful on the ladder?

SARA. Sure. I promise, Maggie.

PAT. (*Upstairs*) Bath's down the hall. We don't serve food but coffee is available to guests. Beach out front is private, for guests only. Best food in town is at the Saltbox. Where Annie works.

ROYCE. I guess that's where I'll spend most of my time.

PAT. It's expensive.

ROYCE. The good things in life *aren't* free.

PAT. Sometimes she comes home between shifts, sometimes not.

ROYCE. Do I have time for a nap? I'd like to look rested.

PAT. Sure. I'll tell her you're here.

ROYCE. Thanks. (*Royce shuts the door. Pat proceeds down the stairs as Sara has climbed the ladder and is filling in the gull's head. From the boardwalk, Maggie watches Sara. Pat catches a glimpse of Maggie as she comes down the stairs*)

PAT. Hey, Mag —

MAGGIE. Yeah?

PAT. What're you doing out there?

MAGGIE. Just getting ready to come in. (*She moves quickly to stop Pat from looking outside and seeing Sara. Maggie winks up at Sara, motions her to silence. Sara returns the motion and happily continues "filling in the lines"*)

PEARL. (*On the front porch*) How many hours have we spent on this old porch?

JESSIE. Too many. (*Pearl looks at Jessie*) I can remember our first five years here. We never sat on the porch at all.

PEARL. "When I was a child, I spake as a child . . ."

JESSIE. Honey, what's childish about making love? It's a physical *need*!

PEARL. Can't you sublimate? Relate emotionally?

JESSIE. I *can* relate emotionally! But . . . (*Jessie walks stiffly over to the steps, rocks on her heels*)

PEARL. Try cold showers.

JESSIE. I *live* with one. (*She starts down the steps*)

PEARL. Where're you going?

JESSIE. For a long walk. I think I hear a Sea Siren calling. (*In the living room, Maggie has flopped on the sofa, exhausted. Pat stacks the wood by the fireplace*)

PEARL. (*On the porch, matter-of-factly, as Jessie walks down the steps and out of sight*) If you ever cheat on me, I'll leave you. I mean that.

PAT. (*In the living room*) O.K., the firewood's done. (*She walks over to Maggie, peers down at her*) Hey, what's the matter with you?

MAGGIE. I'm exhausted.

PAT. So lie down.

MAGGIE. I am lying down. (*At the office door, Kathy, a corn-fed, plain 18-year-old, pounds energetically on the door*)

PAT. *I'm coming!* (*Maggie cringes with the shout*)

KATHY. (*Looking up at the ladder*) Hi, Sara. (*Sara looks down, puts her finger to her lips: top-secret. Kathy nods and opens the office door*) Hey, is Denny around?

PAT. (*Entering the office*) Not yet.

KATHY. She said she might come by this afternoon.

PAT. She hasn't shown yet. Come on in, Kathy.

KATHY. I can't stay long. I had to close up the shop. Linda just cut out this afternoon. Took off, can you imagine? She's not much help when she's there, anyway. If I'd known she didn't know the multiplication tables, I'd never have recommended her to Denny for the summer. Poor Denny feels stuck with her. Linda is my college roommate. I feel responsible.

PAT. Don't. At least she's decorative.

KATHY. We don't need decor! She can't *make change*! (*They go into the living room*) Hi, Maggie. (*No answer. Maggie's asleep*)

PAT. Sleeping beauty. Shhh.

KATHY. (*Quietly*) Oh.

PAT. How's business?

KATHY. Good, I guess. I've been working day and night. It's a drag. I never get to see Denny but she says I can handle the customers and Linda can't.

PAT. (*Knowing*) What does Denny do with her nights now you're working?

KATHY. You know Denny. She's a very private person. She reads and writes and stuff. She's always at the apartment when I get home.

PAT. Must be rough for the two of you when you get back on campus, playing student–teacher.

KATHY. The hardest part is keeping it from Linda.

PAT. She doesn't know?

KATHY. Of course not! She's my roomie! I mean, you know how people are ... (*Pat is fixing the bar. Kathy tags at her heels*) They think you've grown two heads and fangs and are going to attack them!

PAT. I assume you're not interested in attacking Linda.

KATHY. *What for*? *Please*!

PAT. Linda knows about *us*.

KATHY. You're not living in the same room with her.

PAT. We're living in the same *house*.

KATHY. She thinks it's all very sophisticated and glamorous and eccentric and stuff about you two and the people who come in the shop. But me and Denny? It'd blow her mind!

PAT. (*Heading back to the office*) I'm going to try to get some work done. Want to wait in the office with me and let her majesty (*indicating Maggie*) rest in peace?

KATHY. Sure. (*Kathy continues to follow Pat, chattering nonstop*) I remember when I first got involved with the theatre group at school and met my first gay guy. Oh wow! I thought he was so glamorous. I mean, that's *real the-a-tuh*, you know? And he told me how *all* the movie stars *were* and everything. What a turn-on! But if somebody had told me then that my *roomie* was one ... (*Pat pecks at the calculator*) ... I'm going to apprentice in summer stock next year. I've already applied.

Did you know you have to lay out cash for the privilege of scrubbing a flat? But you can get your union card in two seasons and that practically guarantees you a part on Broadway. Did you know I played the lead in *Star Spangled Girl* this year? Denny thought I was marvelous!

PAT. I thought Denny taught history.

KATHY. Well, *everybody* thought I was marvelous! (*At this moment, Tally and Margo are returning from their walk down the beach. They climb the stairs and encounter Pearl*)

PEARL. Hi.

TALLY. Hi.

PEARL. Great day, huh?

MARGO. The beach is *heaven!*

TALLY. Except the sand's too damned hot. Burned the soles of my feet.

MARGO. I told her to take sneakers. She never listens. (*As Pearl stares at her*) Are we disturbing you?

PEARL. Not at all. Sit down.

TALLY. (*Sitting on the steps, then jumping right back up*) Jesus, the steps are hot as the sand! I'm not going to have an unscorched inch on my body!

PEARL. Including your nose. (*Tally looks quizzical*)

MARGO. Your nose, darling, is beet red.

TALLY. Burned?

MARGO. Burned.

TALLY. Great.

MARGO. Get up here out of the sun. You're so fair-skinned.

PEARL. (*To Margo*) Did you come here with that tan?

MARGO. Am I tan?

PEARL. Very.

MARGO. Goodness!

PEARL. Becomingly so.

MARGO. I tan so easily. I can stay in the sun for hours, *days* . . .

PEARL. Me, too. Get absolutely black in an afternoon.

TALLY. I hate you both. (*Pearl laughs*) An afternoon in the sun and I'm a fluorescent shade of magenta.

PEARL. Painful.

TALLY. Agony. And a definite deterrent to other possible pleasantries of the evening. (*Margo laughs*)

KATHY. (*In the office*) ... the trouble with Linda is that she's pretty. She thinks if you're pretty, you don't have to be *anything* else! She couldn't even pass World History. Denny had to coach her.

PEARL. (*On the porch, hesitantly*) You're Margo Williamson, aren't you?

MARGO. (*Glancing at Tally*) Yes.

PEARL. I'm a great fan of yours.

MARGO. How nice.

PEARL. I saw *Second Avenue, All About Eve, Small Craft Warnings, Plaza Suite, The Women* ...

MARGO. *The Women* — That's really going back!

PEARL. You should have been a star. (*Tally can't help smiling at this*) I don't mean to imply that you're *not* a star. I told Jessie when I saw you come in that to theatre people, those of us in the know, you're a star. But you should have been a *real* star.

MARGO. (*Proudly*) I've had my moments.

PEARL. Your reviews are always good.

MARGO. Fortunately.

TALLY. Margo always *works*. (*To Margo's glance*) In a profession of hard-core unemployed, I think you've done remarkably well.

MARGO. (*Coolly*) Thank you, dear.

PEARL. My name's Pearl. My friend Jessie is walking on the beach, you may have seen her.

MARGO. I didn't see anyone. I was engrossed in anointing Tally's singed feet with sea water.

TALLY. It was nice of you. They really *did* burn.

PEARL. (*To Tally, politely*) What do you do?

TALLY. I'm the associate producer of a TV show.

MARGO. Assistant to the producer, darling, is the way your credit reads.

PEARL. You must know a lot of stars!

MARGO. (*To Tally*) Do you, dear?

TALLY. (*To Margo*) *Intimately*.

PEARL. (*Changing the subject*) It's so great to find out that a star — well, like *you* — (*Margo smiles*) is one of us. (*The smile subsides*)

MARGO. Tally, darling, would you make me a drink?

TALLY. My feet burn. (*Margo looks at Tally. The look is an order*) O.K. Where's the liquor?

MARGO. In the bottom of the case. (*Tally enters the living room, gingerly on her tender feet. She observes Maggie asleep on the sofa, heads for the stairs and their room*) My late husband told me about this place, you know. It wasn't always — exclusively — well, you know. I have no prejudices, being in the theatre as long as I have, one meets all kinds of people. It's good for the soul occasionally to get out and see how other kinds of people live.

PEARL. (*Confused*) Oh.

MARGO. Yes, this particular resort used to be primarily theatrical rather than, well, homosexual.

PEARL. I didn't know that. I've been coming here for *years*.

MARGO. Time passes quickly.

KATHY. (*In the office*) I don't see anything wrong with loving anybody you want to. I mean, what's the difference? Once I went with a guy named Cowboy Horst, that's really his name, he's on the football team.

PAT. (*Trying to concentrate on the calculator*) Denny was probably on the football team in her day.

KATHY. You *know* what I mean!

PAT. Kathy, I don't want to seem rude but you're *driving me up the wall!* Go sit on the porch or something, will you? I'm trying to *work!* (*Kathy, slightly wounded, wanders into the living room, stares at Maggie sleeping. Annie runs up the boardwalk, playfully being chased by Sam. Pat sees them from the office*) Outside! How many times have I got to tell you, *stay outside!*

ANNIE. (*Entering office*) She's with me.

PAT. Not in *my* house!

ANNIE. (*To Sam*) It's O.K. I'll just be a minute. (*Sam sits on the boardwalk, watches Sara paint. Pat watches Sam, gets increasingly irritable, sets the calculator into another tangent, jerks out its plug, and storms offstage into the kitchen*)

PAT. (*As she goes*) Now she's sitting out there like a goddam billboard!

ANNIE. (*To Pat as she runs up stairs*) We won't be long! (*Annie passes Tally on the stairs*)

ANNIE. (*Noticing with interest*) Hi . . .

TALLY. (*Oblivious*) Hi.

ANNIE. (*To Tally's back, as she proceeds down stairs*) Bye. (*Tally approaches the bar, quietly, to mix Margo's drink. Everytime she clinks an ice cube, she winces for fear of disturbing Maggie*)

KATHY. (*Appearing from the corner*) Hi.

TALLY. (*Indicating Maggie*) Shhh. (*Upstairs, Annie opens her door and finds Sara's note under it. Looks at it, holds it up, can't interpret it, stuffs it in her halter*)

SAM. (*On the boardwalk, to Sara*) What'cha doing?

SARA. Coloring in the lines, can't you see?

SAM. What's it supposed to be?

SARA. The eye of a gull.

SAM. A gull?

SARA. A sea gull.

SAM. How about that.

SARA. Don't disturb me, I'm concentrating. (*Upstairs, Annie changes clothes, goes into bathroom*)

SAM. (*On the boardwalk*) Anybody ever tell you you've got good legs?

SARA. No.

SAM. Well, you have. (*Sam stretches out on the boardwalk to better admire the view*) That's good.

SARA. It is? (*Tally heads for the porch with a drink for Margo and one for herself. Kathy watches her*)

MARGO. (*On the front porch, to Pearl*) Tally and I just worked on a television show together. Terrible! Worked twelve out of twelve, well, I was just exhausted! Michael Canan, do you know him?

PEARL. He plays Sam on *Mystery Tonight* . . .

MARGO. Yes, that's right. Well, Mike and I (*Kittenish*) have an *understanding*. Usually I would have come with him but the poor dear is on the road, one of those awful personal appearance tours, and I just had to get away. (*Tally, in the doorway, listens to this. She steps onto the porch and hands Margo a drink*)

TALLY. (*Disappointed in her*) Oh, Margo . . .

MARGO. Thank you, dear. I was just telling the lady —

PEARL. Pearl —

MARGO. I was telling Pearl —

TALLY. I heard you.

MARGO. (*Changing the subject rapidly*) How are your poor feet?

TALLY. My poor feet are *hot*.

PEARL. It's getting hot out here.

MARGO. The midafternoon sun.

PEARL. If you'll excuse me, I think I'll go upstairs and catch a nap before cocktail time. (*She smiles at Margo's drink*) That's starting a little early for me. (*Pearl enters the living room, leaving a bewildered Margo and Tally on the porch*)

PEARL. (*To Kathy*) Hi.

KATHY. (*Indicating Maggie*) Shh. (*Pearl goes upstairs. Kathy creeps nearer and nearer the front door, listening to Tally and Margo*)

SAM. (*On the boardwalk*) That window is supposed to be the gull's eye? That the idea?

SARA. I can see right into the attic. I've never been in the attic. It's *big*.

SAM. That so.

SARA. A person could live up there, I'll bet. It's really *big*.

SAM. (*Bored*) Interesting.

TALLY. (*On the porch*) "Mike and I have an understanding ..." You check into a hotel with another couple and segregate the sexes *behind* closed doors!

MARGO. I told you I'd be recognized in a place like this.

TALLY. *So what*?

MARGO. I can't afford the publicity!

TALLY. There's not going to be any publicity, Margo. You're a damned good working actress but you're *not* a star!

MARGO. My name is on the marquee. I have fans.

TALLY. Theatre buffs. Your fans are the same people who brought back Judy Garland. You know who *they* are, don't you? Margo, you're not exactly a household name in Milwaukee.

MARGO. (*Standing up*) I don't think that was necessary, Tally.

TALLY. I'm sorry that it *was*. (*She goes to Margo*) Don't you understand that I don't *care* if you're a school crossing guard! You don't *have* to be a star for me. I care about *you*, the *person* you are.

MARGO. That is part of the person I am. (*She eyes Tally icily*)

TALLY. Margo, be honest with yourself, for once!

MARGO. (*Detached*) I don't know what I'm doing here. (*She looks at Tally as though she has never seen her before, turns and walks down the steps, onto the beach*)

TALLY. Margo ... (*Margo doesn't turn*) Don't you know ... (*Margo disappears, quietly*) I love you. (*Tally watches Margo for a while, finally lies down on the porch swing. Upstairs, Annie bolts from the bathroom to bump into Royce, heading for the same room*)

ANNIE. Royce!

ROYCE. Annie, baby! (*Royce grabs her fiercely, swings her around*)

ANNIE. I didn't know you were coming.

ROYCE. I left a message for you.

ANNIE. I never got it.

ROYCE. I called this morning.

ANNIE. Well, how are you? Are you here for the whole weekend?

ROYCE. The *whole* weekend. All yours.

ANNIE. I have to work, you know.

ROYCE. So I'll sit around and watch you.

ANNIE. I wish I'd known you were coming.

ROYCE. I've missed you.

ANNIE. I'm due back for the second shift in a few minutes.

ROYCE. (*Pulling her into the room*) Be a little late.

ANNIE. Royce, I really haven't got the time ...

ROYCE. It's been a whole month ... (*She pulls Annie inside, shuts the door. Jessie returns from her walk, slowly mounts the stairs, paying no attention to Tally in the swing. As Jessie enters the living room, Kathy, who has been watching Margo walk on the beach, bolts suddenly past her toward the porch*)

JESSIE. Hey!

KATHY. 'Cuse me. I'm going for a walk. (*She bounds across the porch, down the steps and out of sight. In the living room, Jessie looks at Maggie asleep on the sofa. Finally, she sits beside her softly*)

JESSIE. Hey ...

MAGGIE. (*Asleep*) Hmmm ...

JESSIE. You O.K.?

MAGGIE. (*Waking*) I guess so. (*She looks quickly at her watch*) I hope I didn't snore!

JESSIE. Not that I heard.

MAGGIE. (*Sitting up, smiling*) Pat snores like a steam engine.

JESSIE. So do I.

MAGGIE. I don't think I do. At least, nobody ever told me I do. But then, who'd tell me? We both have to stay awake every night (*Sara is climbing down the ladder to get fresh paint. Sam is admiring the view. Sara overhears the conversation inside*) until Sara's asleep. Then Pat's out like a light. Nobody's awake when I'm asleep. There's nobody to hear me snore!

JESSIE. Why don't you get out of here?

MAGGIE. What?

JESSIE. You're unhappy.

MAGGIE. Just tired.

JESSIE. What kind of life is this? You're worn out, you're —

MAGGIE. It's the life I chose.

JESSIE. Choices aren't irrevocable.

MAGGIE. I can't leave her, Jessie. I didn't know when we started out that we'd be stuck — that we'd inherit Sara, that she'd be so costly, that Pat's first obligation would be to her, not to me. But it happened. Sometimes I hate Sara so much — I lie there at night, waiting for her to go to sleep, praying she'll go to sleep before Pat's too tired — that maybe, just once, Pat will turn to me again. I keep telling myself I can teach Sara to stand on her own and things will be like they were again, Pat and I can be together again. Then I wonder: did I put her up on that ladder out there so she could gain a sense of responsibility? Or am I hoping she'll fall and break her neck? I don't know. I just go from day to day, hanging on, waiting for — something.

JESSIE. You can't just give up your own life.

MAGGIE. But this is my life, Jessie. Fifteen years of my life. There's nothing to go back to — or on to.

JESSIE. I know.

MAGGIE. I know how she likes her coffee and how she likes her steaks and what kind of presents please her. I know the smell of her skin and the texture of her hair and I could pick out her little toe from a lineup of a thousand other women. I know every morning she's going to leave the coffee cup on top of the television set and every night she's going to kick her underwear under the bed. She always leaves soap in the washcloth and hangs her towel over the shower rod. She has a birthmark behind her left ear, a bump on top of her head from a childhood fall, and a piece of pencil lead imbedded in her right palm from the sixth grade. She chews the little fingernail on her left hand when she's uptight and on her right hand when she's happy. She has a funny, crooked bottom tooth and she won't admit to anyone, even me, that she *enjoys* watching cartoons with Sara. She wants to own the world and she'll never get it —

JESSIE. And —

MAGGIE. — and if she never makes love to me again in our lives, I love her. I still love her. (*Sara, listening on the ladder, climbs to the top and continues to paint, slowly, thoughtfully*)

JESSIE. (*Looking out the window*) Pearl's very religious, you know. She thinks sex is only for procreation. (*Goes to the bar, pours a drink*) Beats hell out of me why she ever got mixed up with a *woman!* (*To Maggie*) Want one?

MAGGIE. No, thanks. It'll make me sleepy. I'd like to stay awake to see you a *few* hours while you're here.

JESSIE. Maggie? (*Maggie looks up at her*) You're a very beautiful woman.

MAGGIE. *All* women are beautiful when they first wake up. It's an aura of something ...

JESSIE. (*Flatly*) Senuousness. (*Jessie pulls her gaze from Maggie back to the window*) Who's the kid out there with our movie star?

MAGGIE. (*Peering over the sofa, out the window*) That's Kathy. Denny's girl.

JESSIE. I thought Denny's girl was Linda.

MAGGIE. Kathy thinks it's Kathy, Linda thinks it's Linda. Very confusing.

JESSIE. I could never understand how people manage that. I have enough trouble dealing with one at a time. (*Upstairs, the door to Annie's room opens*)

ANNIE. I've got to get to work, Royce.

ROYCE. But I haven't told you the really big news, yet!

ANNIE. (*Impatiently*) What is it?

ROYCE. I'm assistant manager. I got a promotion.

ANNIE. Great.

ROYCE. And a raise.

ANNIE. That's nice.

ROYCE. And (*Enticing*) if you really want to go back to school, I think I can swing it this year.

ANNIE. *Really?*

ROYCE. Really.

ANNIE. Can we get a car?

ROYCE. Not much of one. Maybe a used car.

ANNIE. *Royce!*

ROYCE. And, I heard about a rent-controlled apartment on the East Side . . .

ANNIE. *Royce!*

ROYCE. *Six* rooms!

ANNIE. *I love you!*

ROYCE. (*Kidding*) Stick with me, baby . . .

ANNIE. You comb your hair, darling, and come on to work with me. If the manager says anything, I'll tell him to fuck off. I'll be downstairs. (*Royce goes back to her own room and Annie dashes down the stairs, through the office, to the door. Quietly*) Sam, listen, something's come up. You know I told you I live with somebody . . . (*Sam looks up*) Well, she arrived unexpectedly.

SAM. That's a hell of a thing to do!

SARA. I left a note for you, Annie, didn't you get it?

ANNIE. (*Holding up paper*) This?

SARA. See? Boys. (*Annie breaks up*)

ANNIE. They do look like boys. But her name is *Royce*, Sara.

SARA. I didn't know how to draw *that.*

SAM. I thought you hated her.

ANNIE. I can't just leave her roaming around loose . . . she doesn't know about you.

SAM. What am I supposed to do?

ANNIE. Entertain yourself for the weekend. She'll be gone on Monday. (*Annie runs back into the house. Sam lies back down on the boardwalk*)

SAM. Let me give you some advice, Sara. Never trust a woman.

JESSIE. (*In the living room*) Movie Star certainly looks interested in whatever the kid's saying.

MAGGIE. I don't think she's a movie star, Jessie.

JESSIE. Whatever kind of star she is, she's twinkling.

MAGGIE. Kathy wants to be an actress.

SAM. (*On the boardwalk*) The whole damned weekend. What am I supposed to do for the whole damned weekend? I haven't got any money!

SARA. I have.

SAM. Well, I haven't.

SARA. I have thirty dollars of my own. I got it for Christmas to buy anything I wanted. I haven't decided what I want yet.

SAM. (*Sitting up, adjusting her clothing*) Could I interest you in a slightly used . . . (*Pat appears at the office door, steps out onto the boardwalk*)

PAT. (*To Sam*) I'm not going to tell you again to get out of here!

SAM. God, you're boring.

PAT. What do I have to do, have you arrested for trespassing?

SAM. Save your breath, you need it at your age. (*Sam starts to get up. Pat suddenly looks up, sees Sara*)

PAT. Sara, what are you doing up there? (*To Sam*) Are you crazy letting her get up there? She'll *kill herself*!

SAM. She was there when I got here.

PAT. *Sara, get down from there*!

SARA. I'm filling in the lines, Pat. I haven't gone out of the lines *once.* (*In the living room, Maggie hears the commotion and she and Jessie run to the porch window*)

PAT. *Get down from there, do you hear me? Right now*!

SARA. I haven't finished!

PAT. *Now! Right now*!

MAGGIE. Pat . . .

PAT. You stay out of this! Come on, Sara, climb down. *Careful*! (*Sara climbs down*)

MAGGIE. Pat, listen . . .

PAT. Will you shut up and stay out of this! (*As Sara touches ground, Pat grabs her, shakes her, a mixture of anger and relief*) You *idiot*! You could have killed yourself! You think I don't have enough to worry about without you climbing up twenty-foot ladders? Do I have to watch you every minute? I can't trust you by yourself in our own front yard? You'll drive me crazy! You're a full-time job! Goddamit, Sara, you're eating up my life! (*Sara bursts into tears, races through the house into the downstairs bedroom. Margo and Kathy come up the porch steps. Margo sees Tally, ignores her, sits on the steps beside Kathy who is both awe- and star-struck. Tally watches*)

KATHY. I never thought I'd ever meet a *real* star.

MARGO. (*All for Tally's benefit*) Stars aren't any different from other people. *You* (*She cups Kathy's face in her hand*) may be a star yourself someday.

KATHY. Oh, I know I will. Knowing somebody like you, I know I will. When I come to New York, will you help me?

MARGO. (*It's getting a little sticky*) Well, I'll do what I can, Kathy . . .

KATHY. Imagine. A real star. (*Margo basks, making sure Tally sees. Annie and Royce dash down the stairs*)

ANNIE. (*To the living room, without looking in*) We're off! See you later! (*No one in the living room answers but Annie and Royce don't notice as they run gaily from the house, down the boardwalk, out of sight*)

MARGO. (*On the porch, dramatically*) The vast and ever-changing sea.

KATHY. Is that Shakespeare?

MARGO. No. (*Tally smiles*)

MAGGIE. (*Coming now into the office*) Pat, I told her she could paint the gull. I thought it would be good for her.

PAT. You've got no business telling her anything! She's *my* sister!

MAGGIE. I'm sorry. I thought I was *helping*.

PAT. Stop helping! (*Maggie moves toward the bedroom*) And don't go running to her! She's got to grow up sometime! (*To Sam*) And you, you son of a bitch, *get off my property*! (*Sam runs off*)

JESSIE. Come on inside, Pat, have a drink.

PAT. She's driving me insane!

JESSIE. Come on . . .

PAT. (*To Maggie*) And you're just as bad!

JESSIE. Come on, Pat, come on. Sit down. (*Jessie leads her to the living room, fixes her a drink as Maggie sits on the arm of the chair, comforting Pat*)

PAT. Do I have to shoulder *all* the responsibility in this family? Can't you see I'm exhausted?

MAGGIE. We're both exhausted, honey. (*Maggie holds her tightly as from the back bedroom, Sara, dressed in her best dress, carrying a little girl's plastic pocketbook, tip-toes past the living room, unseen. Quietly, she lets herself out the office door and disappears down the boardwalk*)

ACT 2

Late that evening in Gull House. The ladder still stands but the house is empty except for Pat and Maggie who lie on separate sofas, watching an old movie on TV.

In the movie, the heroine emits a piercing scream: "Call the police!" Then the sound of a chase, gunfire, sirens.

In maybe thirty seconds Pat, who has been fidgeting nervously, leaps to her feet.

PAT. I'm going to.

MAGGIE. Going to what?

PAT. *Call the police!*

MAGGIE. It's only ten o'clock, Pat.

PAT. She's been gone since four this afternoon!

MAGGIE. They'll think you're crazy.

PAT. (*Over the gunfire*) What?

MAGGIE. *They'll think you're* (*She snaps off the TV*) crazy.

PAT. Why? She's a *missing person!* (*Maggie moves to calm her*)

MAGGIE. Honey — she's *twenty-seven years old.* It's not *unusual* for a twenty-seven-year-old to be out at ten o'clock on a Saturday night.

PAT. She's never been out at night by herself before!

MAGGIE. She's probably sitting at the Dairy Queen, drinking

90

chocolate sodas, feeling very sorry for herself and very homesick.

PAT. And getting short-changed.

MAGGIE. She'll be back, honey.

PAT. Maybe she doesn't know *how* to get back!

MAGGIE. Pat, she knows her *address*! Everybody in town knows this house.

PAT. I should have gone after her this afternoon.

MAGGIE. You're the one who said, "she's got to grow up sometime."

PAT. *You*'ve been saying that for two years! (*There is a momentary silence*)

MAGGIE. This may be the best thing that ever happened to her.

PAT. Or to *you*! Suppose she got into a car with some nut ...

MAGGIE. She knows better.

PAT. *You*'d be happy if she *never* came back! You'd have me all to *yourself*! (*Maggie doesn't answer*) If anything happens to her, *you*'re to blame. You *want* it to happen!

MAGGIE. (*After a silence*) That's not true. I can stand *sharing* you, Pat, but I can't cope with *losing* you.

PAT. You haven't lost me. I'm here. God knows, I'm here *all the time*! And you can thank Sara for that!

MAGGIE. You're here and I'm here. *We're* gone.

PAT. All right! I promised you a cottage by a waterfall and didn't deliver. I *couldn't* deliver!

MAGGIE. I know that.

PAT. Mama and Papa had her for twenty-five years! How do you think *they* felt?

MAGGIE. I *know* how they felt.

PAT. Why don't you just leave? Find somebody who can give you what you want.

MAGGIE. *You*'re what I want. (*Pat heads for the office, slams the door behind her, lifts the phone. Maggie opens the door, stands in the doorway*) I'm married to you. Oh, we didn't have a ceremony and God knows, no cheering relatives. We didn't cut a cake or throw a bouquet and our honeymoon was a stifling Fourth of July weekend in a five-flight walkup but fifteen years later, here we are: married. *For better or worse*, isn't that what they say?

PAT. (*Putting down the phone*) You had plenty of reason to leave *before* Sara came along.

MAGGIE. Not good enough reason.

PAT. (*Attacking*) For three summers, I had an affair with Mona — remember her? — the hostess at the Saltbox? — right there in number six. Right under your nose! And Aggie and Jackie and Sandra and a hundred weekends right in this house! I even had an affair with frigid Pearl! (*That is a shock*) Long before Sara. You can't blame Sara.

MAGGIE. I don't.

PAT. Why didn't you leave?

MAGGIE. Summers always end. (*Pat turns from her, buries her head in her hands*)

PAT. You're the best thing that ever happened to me. Maggie, don't let me drive you away.

MAGGIE. (*After a moment*) Stop trying so hard. (*Maggie turns and goes into the living room as Denny and Linda come up the boardwalk. Denny opens the office door*)

DENNY. Is she back?

PAT. Not a word.

DENNY. We just had dinner at the Saltbox. She wasn't there.

LINDA. Maybe she went to a bar. (*Pat looks surprised*) To pick somebody up. After all, her *body*'s grown up.

PAT. (*Defensively*) Sara wouldn't think of going to a bar!

LINDA. Maybe she met somebody who thought of it for her. (*Linda prances sexily up the stairs*) Come on, Denny.

PAT. Sara wouldn't go into a bar!

DENNY. Nobody'd be that rotten. Most of the *girls* know Sara.

LINDA. (*From the stairs*) Who said anything about *girls*?

PAT. (*Standing suddenly*) God! I never thought of that!

LINDA. (*Wiggling her ass*) *Come on*, Denny!

PAT. (*Starting for the door*) If some son-of-a-bitch knocks her up . . .

DENNY. Where're you going?

PAT. To every bar on the island.

DENNY. I'll go with you. We can make better time in the buggy.

LINDA. *Denny!* (*As Pat and Denny head down the boardwalk, out of sight, Linda pouts for a moment, then comes down the stairs and*

92
▼

enters the living room. To Maggie) They've gone to the bars.

MAGGIE. What?

LINDA. Looking for Sara.

MAGGIE. In bars? Sara doesn't drink!

LINDA. Bars aren't just for drinking. She's *human*, isn't she? (*Linda heads for the bar*) With that pair of knockers, she won't have to wait long. — Mind if I help myself? (*Without waiting for an answer, she pours a drink*) Did you ever tell her about the birds and the bees? (*She looks up at Maggie, who doesn't answer*) Not everybody can stand a long drought, you know. (*She stirs the drink, sips it*) Celibacy is for the very religious. Or the very frightened. (*Maggie goes to the window, looks out*) Are you religious, Maggie? (*Jessie and Pearl are coming up the boardwalk*)

MAGGIE. Go to hell.

LINDA. Then you must be frightened. (*Maggie doesn't answer*) It'll take them *hours* to cover all the bars on the island. (*Maggie is watching Pearl as though she's seeing her for the first time*) And I'm not the least bit sleepy.

MAGGIE. (*Just as Jessie and Pearl come in the door*) Why should you be? I'm sure Mommy put you to bed for your afternoon nap, didn't she? (*Jessie and Pearl enter the living room*)

JESSIE. Did Sara come home?

PEARL. We checked all the stores on the boardwalk, not a sign of her. (*It's hard for Maggie to deal with Pearl's presence*)

MAGGIE. Pat and Denny are out now, looking.

LINDA. I'm sure they're *looking*. Let's hope it's for *Sara*.

JESSIE. Where'd you find the smart–ass kid?

MAGGIE. I'm changing the sign tomorrow to Sea Gull Nursery School.

JESSIE. (*To Pearl*) Make us all a nightcap, honey.

MAGGIE. (*To Jessie*) Do you think Sara would go off with a *man*?

JESSIE. Women have been known to do that.

PEARL. (*Dramatically*) A *man*? Where did we fail? (*Jessie and Maggie don't think that's funny. Linda, who is no more concerned than Pearl about Sara, laughs*)

MAGGIE. I can't believe that any *woman* would take advantage of her ...

LINDA. Why not? They all look at her. Does "a stiff prick has no conscience" exclude women? (*Maggie glances at Pearl and Linda*)

MAGGIE. *Most* women.

LINDA. Haven't you learned by your age that lust is a mighty motivation?

JESSIE. (*To Linda*) Or means of profit.

LINDA. (*To Jessie, smiling*) Or weapon. (*There is a moment of silence. Pearl is acutely uncomfortable as she serves the drinks*) Most of us are, after all, *normal* human beings.

PEARL. (*Suddenly*) Sam!

MAGGIE. What?

PEARL. Maybe Sara ran off with Sam!

LINDA. Sam *is* remarkably *human*.

JESSIE. I'm sure you can bear witness.

PEARL. (*Making light*) Well, she won't get pregnant!

LINDA. (*Forming a camaraderie with Pearl*) Don't underestimate Sam.

MAGGIE. (*Hopefully*) If she's with Sam, they'll be in a bar. Sam has no place to go. (*The office door bangs open and shut*) Sara? (*It's Kathy*)

KATHY. No, it's me. (*As she enters the living room*) Hasn't Sara come back yet? It's all over town that she's out. The whole island is a self-appointed posse. (*She sees Linda*) Where's Denny? I closed up shop and went to the apartment but she's not there.

MAGGIE. She and Pat are out looking for Sara.

LINDA. In the *bars*. They assigned less fortunate volunteers to coffee shops and filling stations.

KATHY. Denny doesn't even know where the bars *are*!

LINDA. Want her itinerary? She checks them out every night. (*Kathy has no intention of believing this*) She's an undercover agent for the vice squad.

PEARL. (*To Kathy*) Want a drink?

LINDA. She doesn't drink. It might make her skin leathery. And she does have good *skin*. Kathy has to protect her assets.

KATHY. (*Defensively*) Where were you today? You've got no sense of responsibility!

LINDA. I haven't heard Denny complain. She *is* the boss.

KATHY. She feels sorry for you! Even *I* feel sorry for you! Did anybody ever tell you that you have blank eyes? Like looking in a plate glass window.

PEARL. (*On Linda's side*) Ah, but what's in the display case? (*Linda smiles, victorious*)

JESSIE. (*Helping Kathy*) A going–out–of–business sale.

KATHY. Sara's gone, it's practically a national emergency and you stand there, Linda, preening yourself like a cat!

LINDA. (*With graceful dignity*) It's a terribly warm night, don't you think? And getting quite sticky in here. (*To Pearl*) Care to join me for a breath of fresh air? (*Quite grandly, Linda leads Pearl onto the front porch*)

KATHY. (*Apologizing to the rest*) She has no sense of responsibility. (*Kathy comforts Maggie, taking over dramatically*) Don't worry, Maggie, we'll find Sara. We'll take the island apart, piece by piece —

JESSIE. *That*'ll be a job.

KATHY. — every nook and cranny, under trees and rocks, behind every sand dune —

MAGGIE. (*Suddenly*) Has anybody looked on the beach?

LINDA. (*On the porch, to Pearl*) You remind me of my mother.

KATHY. (*In the living room*) Of course, the *beach*! (*She heads for the front door*) If she's out there, I'll find her. I know that beach, every pebble, every grain of sand . . .

LINDA. (*On the porch*) I'll bet you have a house in the suburbs, two dogs, two cars and a maid. (*Kathy races across the porch and down the beach, out of sight*)

PEARL. (*Pleasantly*) Wrong! No maid.

LINDA. You drink a martini before dinner every weekday and two on weekends. After dinner, two brandies. (*Pearl holds her brandy snifter uncomfortably*) Are they integrating your neighborhood? Is the value of your property decreasing?

PEARL. Yes, as a matter of fact, it is.

LINDA. I'll bet your house is impeccable. You could eat off the floors. (*In the living room, Maggie is looking out at the window at Kathy*)

PEARL. (*Proudly*) Yes. It *is* impeccable.

LINDA. Do you collect crystal or pewter?

PEARL. (*Slightly irritated*) Crystal.

JESSIE. (*In the living room, to Maggie*) She'll be back, you know. Sara.

MAGGIE. I know. Tonight may even have been good for her — if only something hasn't happened . . .

JESSIE. Maggie. What could happen to her on this island?

MAGGIE. Sam. A man.

JESSIE. Is either one so bad?

MAGGIE. (*Smiles*) No.

LINDA. (*On the porch*). You have two affairs a year. One in the country and one in the city. (*Pearl is getting the drift. She stiffens in defense*) Just like my mother.

PEARL. Jessie and I have been together eleven years.

LINDA. She'd never believe it, would she? You're the Virgin Mary. Maybe once a month — (*She considers Pearl*) — no, a couple of times a year, you condescend to lay back. (*Stalking Pearl now*) Keep 'em guilty. Animal lust! My great grandmother knew *that* one. Amazing, Jessie doesn't see through it.

PEARL. (*Self-righteously*) I'm attractive, compatible, an excellent housekeeper, a perfect hostess.

LINDA. And all her property and stocks are in your name.

PEARL. *Jointly*. That's only sensible. (*In the living room, Jessie slowly approaches Maggie at the window*)

JESSIE. Maggie? (*Trying to sound casual*) I'm out this way nearly every week on business. Why don't we get together (*Maggie looks at her*) for lunch. (*Maggie looks at the floor*) Or a drink.

MAGGIE. No.

JESSIE. Who would it hurt?

LINDA. (*On the porch*) I'll bet you haven't worked a day in eleven years.

PEARL. It's not necessary.

JESSIE. (*In the living room*) I don't want to break up my relationship, Maggie. I like my home. My martinis are chilled and ready at four o'clock and my bath is drawn and waiting. Pearl has excellent taste. We have the best furniture, the finest rugs and drapes. We're putting a pool in the back yard next summer. We go to Europe every other year. My dinner guests are always served beautifully prepared food and drinks at a perfectly appointed table. My clothes are cleaned and laundered. I haven't packed a suitcase in eleven years. Pearl is charming and gracious and dignified and *never* obvious with my business clients, they adore her. My family thinks she's a delightful "roommate." Every penny I've ever made is in both of our names.

LINDA. (*On the porch*) If you had to choose between Jessie and a maid . . . (*Pearl glares, walks away to the side porch*) Why didn't you pick on a *man*? (*Pearl sits on the side porch. She can hear Jessie and Maggie inside*)

JESSIE. No one would know. Pearl would leave me if she knew.

MAGGIE. I don't think she would.

JESSIE. My life is exactly like I want it. All I need . . .

MAGGIE. All you need, Jessie, is a mistress. (*Without malice*) A little something on the side. (*Tally and Margo are coming up the boardwalk. They wave to Pearl, call out "Hello, Good evening," distracting her from the rest of the conversation inside*)

JESSIE. That's what you need, too.

MAGGIE. No, Jessie, I need much more than that. (*Tally and Margo enter the living room*)

MARGO. I assume Sara's back and none the worse for wear.

JESSIE. You're a positive thinker.

TALLY. She wasn't at the Saltbox.

MARGO. God knows everybody else in the world *was*. (*Kathy bounces up the front steps, stomps sand off her feet, takes off her shoes and shakes them, ignores Linda. Jessie sees her*)

MARGO. Tally, I really need a drink.

TALLY. That's bad. To *need* a drink.

MARGO. (*To Tally*) Sorry God, I didn't notice the burning bush.

JESSIE. (*At the door*) Any sign of her, Kathy? (*Jessie, anxious to get away from Maggie's presence, steps onto the porch*)

KATHY. Nowhere. The beach is absolutely deserted. (*Kathy comes into the living room. Jessie remains on the porch with Linda. Kathy sees Margo and beams*) Hi! I told you I'd come by after I closed the shop.

TALLY. So you did.

MARGO. It's a lovely little shop, Kathy.

KATHY. It's not mine. I only work there. It belongs to Denny

Tate. (*Tally stops pouring*)

TALLY. Who?

KATHY. Denny Tate. Do you know her? (*Tally is stunned, tries to cover her reaction. Margo looks at Tally's face, a grim smile on her own*)

MARGO. (*After a moment*) Denny is an old friend of Tally's. Isn't that so, dear?

LINDA. (*On the porch, to Jessie*) The beach is absolutely deserted. Kathy said that, so it's honor bright.

MARGO. (*In the living room*) A *very* old friend.

KATHY. She'll be back here later. She's out with Pat, looking for Sara. (*Kathy helps herself to a large handful of potato chips, crunching loudly*)

MARGO. (*Irritated by the noise but playing mentor*) Ah–ah, dear, bad for the complexion.

LINDA. (*On the porch*) Hardly any moon. A perfect night for a long walk. Of course, it wouldn't be much fun alone. (*She looks at Jessie and starts down the steps. Jessie considers and follows, out of sight. Pearl, hearing Linda's voice, gets up to see that she's gone. Far down the beach, she sees Linda — with Jessie. Frightened, she sits on the steps to watch*)

MARGO. (*In the living room*) So Denny Tate is coming here tonight. I'm anxious to meet this paragon.

TALLY. (*Trying to sound casual*) Is she still teaching?

KATHY. That's how I met her. I'm a student of hers.

MARGO. (*Turning the knife*) Doesn't sound like she's changed much, Tally.

KATHY. *Tally?* Are you Tally Adams? (*She looks at Tally in a different light*) Denny's talked about you. A lot.

TALLY. (*Lightly*) In her sleep, no doubt. Nightmares.

KATHY. You lived together seven years!

TALLY. (*Handing Margo her drink*) Six.

KATHY. Denny says seven.

TALLY. Denny was always inclined to exaggerate.

MARGO. Oh, a matched pair!

KATHY. You had a house together and everything.

TALLY. It was a costly — divorce. For both of us.

MARGO. Tally!

TALLY. I'm tired of playing games, Margo.

KATHY. (*Innocently*) Are you two together long? (*Margo hesitates, is saved from answering by Pearl who, having seen Jessie and Linda embrace somewhere down the beach, turns with a muffled cry and runs into the house, through the living room and upstairs to her room*)

MAGGIE. (*To Pearl*) Hey ... (*She leaps up and follows Pearl to the stairs*) What's the matter? (*Maggie runs partway up the stairs after Pearl*) Pearl!

PEARL. *Just leave me alone!* (*She slams the door closed. Puzzled, Maggie stands on the staircase*)

KATHY. (*A bad Garbo*) She vants to be alone.

MARGO. Ah, a little drama. Always, a little drama.

KATHY. All lesbians are actresses.

MARGO. (*Coldly*) It does not follow, however, that all actresses are lesbians.

KATHY. (*Honestly*) They ought to be. Everybody ought to be. (*Maggie is still looking up the stairs. Tally goes to her*)

TALLY. Is there anything I can do?

MAGGIE. (*Helplessly*) I don't think so.

MARGO. (*Uncomfortably, to Kathy*) Here I am at the seashore, inside, leaning on a bar. Doesn't make much sense, does it? (*She walks to the front door. Loudly for Tally's benefit*) Smell that air! (*But Tally is truly concerned about Maggie, who is leaning on the bannister in a daze*)

TALLY. (*To Maggie*) Are you all right?

MARGO. (*Again loudly*) Beautiful night!

MAGGIE. Sure. (*But Tally watches as Maggie descends the stairs slowly. Margo, feeling ignored and already threatened by the mention of Denny, turns quickly to Kathy*)

MARGO. Let's go out in the air, Kathy. You can tell me all about you and Denny Tate. (*Tally leads Maggie to a sofa, looks up surprised to see Margo gone*)

TALLY. You're really worried about the girl, aren't you?

MAGGIE. (*Shivering*) Among other things.

TALLY. I'm sure she'll turn up. (*Calls*) Margo!

MARGO. (*From the porch*) We're out here.

MAGGIE. (*Still shivering*) Is it cold in here?

TALLY. No.

MAGGIE. I'm terribly cold.

TALLY. I'll get you a blanket. (*She gets a comforter off the other sofa, spreads it over Maggie. She's torn between going to Margo and helping Maggie*) Would you like me to build a fire?

MAGGIE. Don't bother.

TALLY. It's no bother. If you're cold ... (*Maggie doesn't want to be alone*)

MAGGIE. A fire would be nice. (*Tally pulls a piece of newspaper from the stack beside the fireplace, wads it up*) Thank you for doing this.

TALLY. It's no bother. (*But Tally's eyes and ears are glued to the front porch*)

MARGO. (*On the porch*) Have you and Denny been friends long?

KATHY. A year and a half. Since the second semester of my freshman year. She's World History. Required.

MARGO. How convenient.

KATHY. She's a good teacher.

MARGO. I'm sure she is.

KATHY. (*Defensively*) She doesn't go around seducing students, if that's what you're thinking. It's not like that.

MARGO. It's not? (*Inside, Tally, straining to hear, reacts to this*)

KATHY. Everybody likes her class. It's fun. Can you imagine World History being fun?

MARGO. It strains my credibilities.

KATHY. Practically everybody gets a crush on her. She could have any student she wanted. A whole bunch of us used to hang around after her class every day, sit on the desk, talk and stuff. Sometimes she'd have to take us to the lounge for coffee to get rid of us.

MARGO. But *you* were special.

KATHY. No. Persistent. Before anything ever happened, I used to call her at home every night. One time she told me never to call her again. I cried all night. Then I wrote her letters: every morning, between every class, at lunch, at supper, before bed. I wrote forty-four letters. I had to give up smoking to pay the postage.

MARGO. What on earth did you *say* in *forty-four* letters? (*Tally, still straining to hear, is making the fire. Maggie is curled comfortably on the sofa)*

KATHY. That I loved her.

MARGO. Well, that's laying it right out front.

KATHY. Finally, she came to the dorm one night. Linda, my oversexed roommate, was out screwing around. Denny brought back all my letters and dumped them on the bed. She said she *was* but she couldn't get involved with a student. It was wrong. (*Annie and Royce, slightly high, come up the boardwalk and enter by the office*)

ANNIE. (*Happily*) That was too much money to spend, Royce!

ROYCE. What's money? Just a means to an end.

KATHY. (*On the porch*) How could anything so beautiful be wrong?

MAGGIE. (*In the living room*) Hi, Annie. Come on in.

ANNIE. Twenty-five people must have asked me about Sara tonight. (*She comes in, looks at Maggie*) She's not back yet.

MAGGIE. (*Shakes her head*) Want a drink?

ROYCE. One more and I'll capsize.

ANNIE. I can always make room. (*To Maggie*) Oh, Maggie, you haven't met Royce. (*They shake hands*)

MARGO. (*On the porch*) The world says it's wrong.

KATHY. The world is wrong about a lot of things.

TALLY. (*In the living room, offering her hand to Royce*) Tally.

MARGO. (*On the porch*) The world can be a vicious enemy.

KATHY. I guess I'll have to learn to be vicious back.

MAGGIE. (*In the living room*) Annie . . . do you think Sara might be with Sam?

ANNIE. (*Faking very well*) Who's Sam? (*Annie has poured herself a drink. To Royce*) Sure you don't want one, darling? (*Royce nods no*)

MAGGIE. Maybe I ought to call the police.

ANNIE. (*To Royce*) Is there anything you want? (*Royce smiles. Denny comes up the boardwalk, alone, enters the office*)

MAGGIE. (*Hopefully*) Pat?

DENNY. No. It's me. (*Royce guides Annie and her drink towards the stairs*)

ROYCE. You'll excuse us, we've had a busy day.

MAGGIE. (*Calling*) Where's Pat? (*Royce and Annie go up the stairs as*

Denny enters)

ROYCE. Early to bed and early to rise and so forth ...

DENNY. (*To Maggie*) Not a trace of Sara. But no trace of Sam, either. Pat insisted on checking out the boarding houses on either side. (*Denny sees Tally*)

TALLY. Hello, Denny.

MAGGIE. Should I call the police, Denny?

DENNY. (*Without taking her eyes off Tally*) Yes, why don't you do that? (*Maggie is aware of the encounter taking place. She goes to the office, sits at the desk and contemplates whether or not to call*) What are you doing here?

TALLY. I didn't know *you* were here.

DENNY. I thought you were off to Hollywood with some movie star.

TALLY. I haven't been to Hollywood and she's not a movie star.

DENNY. You look the same. Your hair's lighter. Have you been putting that stuff on it again?

TALLY. It's the sun. (*An awkward moment*) How are you?

DENNY. Fine. Same as always. Are you still with her? Is she here? Are you happy?

TALLY. (*Honestly*) I don't know. Are you?

DENNY. I guess I've always needed to be free. I'll never tie myself down to anyone again. I learned my lesson. Do you love her?

TALLY. I'm trying to.

DENNY. I guess you'll set up house again, huh? You're the domestic type. Not me. I'm not domestic and I'm not monogamous.

TALLY. I'm not sure anybody really is. (*They look at one another*) That's the lesson *I* learned.

DENNY. (*Lightly*) You know it took me months to match up the black socks and the brown socks? You're right, I *am* color-blind.

TALLY. You're right, too. I can't carry a tune. (*Margo and Kathy have entered the living room. Kathy dashes into Denny's arms, uninhibited, exuberant*)

KATHY. I was worried about you!

TALLY. Margo — Denny. (*Margo approaches with all the pleasant dignity she can muster. She extends her hand*)

MARGO. No, she can't carry a tune.

KATHY. (*Still hugging*) You weren't home when I got there. (*Denny tries to placate Kathy and carry on a conversation with Margo simultaneously*)

MARGO. She inflicts unpardonable pain on the neighbors every time she takes a shower.

KATHY. You're *always* home when I get there!

DENNY. No, I'm not.

MARGO. Kathy tells me you're a fine teacher.

DENNY. I try to be.

KATHY. You *are* always home when I get there.

DENNY. Don't start that, Kathy. I don't punch a time clock. (*To Margo*) You're in the theatre?

MARGO. Yes.

KATHY. You have a responsibility —

DENNY. I don't know a damn thing about the theatre but if you'd like to discuss the political implications of the sinking of the Maine —

KATHY. — you have a responsibility to me! (*Denny pushes Kathy away, irritably*)

DENNY. *Will you stop crawling all over me?* I'm trying to carry on a conversation! (*Kathy bursts into tears and runs into the kitchen*)

TALLY. (*A little sarcastically*) Oops.

DENNY. (*Looking after Kathy*) She's right. (*To them*) I'm sorry. I do have a responsibility — (*She looks at them, justifying*) — I *feel* responsible — for her. (*Without much enthusiasm, Denny goes after Kathy*)

MARGO. (*After a moment, to Tally*) She's very attractive.

TALLY. Yes.

MARGO. And bright.

TALLY. Very.

MARGO. And you wish you were with her.

TALLY. I only wish I'd known then —

MARGO. (*Brightly, defensively*) We always learn too late. (*She walks away from Tally, unable to look at her, sits on the arm of a chair, its back to the audience*)

TALLY. The fates are clever devils. They send you to school, offer you a lesson and if you learn it well, they give you a chance to use it.

MARGO. You make life sound like a manpower training center.

TALLY. I think I learned my lesson.

MARGO. So have I, Tally. Too late. But it's not too late for you. Go while you still have time. Go to her. (*Quietly, Tally comes to Margo, kneels by her side*)

TALLY. I think my chance is *you*. (*Unbelieving, Margo doesn't dare to move*) I love you. (*Margo still doesn't respond*) If you feel it, Margo, say it. Please *say* it. (*Finally Margo looks at her, touches her hair gently*)

MARGO. (*Quietly, it is not easy*) I love you. (*She holds Tally's head close to her. To no one, to the world*) How can anything so beautiful be wrong? (*Slowly, her hands in her pockets, Pat moves up the boardwalk. She stands outside Gull House for a moment, looking around. No sign of Sara. Maggie sees her through the office door, rises, comes to the door, opens it*)

PAT. (*To Maggie*) No. (*Maggie puts a comforting arm around Pat*) Is Denny back?

MAGGIE. She's inside. (*Pat pulls away from Maggie preoccupied, enters the house*)

PAT. (*Calling*) Denny! (*Margo and Tally are in the overstuffed chair together*)

DENNY. (*From the kitchen*) Yeah! (*Above, in the eye of the gull, a light snaps on in the attic window. Denny comes into view from the kitchen, followed by a comforted Kathy*)

PAT. Anything?

DENNY. Nothing. You?

PAT. I found Sam. Shacked up with some dame two houses down.

KATHY. It wasn't Sara?

PAT. No, *it wasn't Sara!*

MAGGIE. Maybe we had better call the police, Pat.

DENNY. Is there anything else I can do?

PAT. No. Thanks, Denny. (*Denny and Kathy start down the boardwalk. Pat enters the office, is dialing the telephone, when we hear a tap-tap-tap*) What's that? (*It becomes a bang-bang-bang. Pat hangs up the phone, looks around*)

MAGGIE. I don't know. (*Maggie steps outside to look just as we see a paper window shade pulled down, then up, in the attic window, the gull's eye. In the open window, Sara looks up at the working window shade and smiles with satisfaction. Maggie sees her)* Sara! Pat, it's *Sara!*

PAT. *(Racing out of the house and looking up)* Sara! What are you doing up there? *(Pat starts to climb the ladder immediately. Sara's voice stops her midclimb)*

SARA. *(Simply)* I'm fixing up my room.

PAT. You're *what?*

SARA. Fixing up my room. I bought a window shade because if it breaks, I know how to fix it.

PAT. What are you doing in the *attic?*

SARA. I told you, I'm fixing up my room.

PAT. In the *attic?*

SARA I didn't know it was here. You never told me it was here.

PAT. The attic's for *junk*, Sara.

SARA. No! It's my room.

PAT. It's dangerous up there —

MAGGIE. Pat —

PAT. It's not insulated —

MAGGIE. *(More persistently)* Pat —

PAT. Sara, *come down from there!*

SARA. *(Firm)* It's my room.

MAGGIE. *(Pleading)* Listen to her, Pat . . .

SARA. I saw it today when I was filling in the lines. It's a *big* room and it has this many bureaus *(four fingers)* and *two* beds and this many *(nine)* lamps. So I went downtown and I spent my thirty dollars. You said I could buy anything I wanted. And I bought a window shade.

PAT. For *thirty dollars?*

SARA. No. I bought two submarines for supper. I've got half a one left, you want it? *(Generously, Sara tosses half a sandwich wrapped in aluminum foil to Pat on the ladder)* It's got olives in it. And I've got this much *(She displays a wad of dollar bills)* left and I'm going to have even more.

PAT. Sara, come down, please. We'll talk about it *down here.*

SARA. Mrs. Bowles at the dime store where I bought my window shade said I could come in every day at five o'clock and sweep the floor. She's going to pay me twenty-five dollars every week and by September I can buy my own TV set to put in my room.

PAT. Sara, you can't crawl up and down this ladder, you'll — *it's too dangerous!* There's no insulation, you'll freeze to death this winter. Now, *come on down!*

SARA. (*Steadfast*) I have to have a room of my own so I can concentrate, like Denny says.

PAT. We'll fix up another room for you. One of the guest rooms, right, Maggie?

SARA. I want *this* room. I found it myself. It's nobody's room but Sara's. It's in the eye of the sea gull and I can look at the ocean if I want to, and the boardwalk if I want to. I can see *everything* that happens. *If* I want to.

MAGGIE. Sara, how did you get up there without us seeing you? We've been worried sick all night. Pat's been all over the island looking —

SARA. I just climbed up the ladder. You were having supper in the kitchen. I don't have to be a bother to anybody. I have my own room. I found it myself. It's nobody's room but Sara's. (*Pat looks helplessly at Maggie*)

MAGGIE. (*To Pat*) We can build steps from the second floor to the attic. Insulation comes in sheets. I'll bet Sara could put it up herself.

SARA. I *can* do it myself. It's my room. ... It'll be *easier* if you show me *how*.

PAT. I'll show you how. Tomorrow. You better go to bed now, Sara, it's late.

SARA. I've *been* asleep for hours. Shopping wears you out.

PAT. It's late, past your bedtime.

SARA. I don't have to go to sleep until I want to. I have my own room. I found it myself. And it's nobody's room but Sara's. (*She firmly pulls down her blind. The light shines through it. Pat backs slowly down the ladder*)

PAT. (*To Maggie*) I've got to talk to her first thing in the morning.

MAGGIE. (*Amused*) About what?

PAT. Well — about the birds and the bees. I can't let her go off by herself into town every day, not knowing anything. I've got to have a *firm* talk with her.

MAGGIE. Right, darling. First thing in the morning. (*They both look up at Sara's shadow moving back and forth busily behind the shade*) Pat — I think Sara grew up tonight.

PAT. Sara — and me. (*She turns to Maggie*) Thank you for waiting. (*Maggie approaches the door, extends her hand to Pat*) Crazy. I'm nervous. Like our first night together.

MAGGIE. You weren't nervous.

PAT. Oh, yes, I was. Walking home at dawn through Washington Park. You took off your shoes and waded in the fountain. I just watched you. I didn't say a word.

MAGGIE. Yes, you did. I held out my hand and you took it (She does) and said, "Hey, Lady, I think I love you." (*They look at one another for a long moment*)

PAT. I don't want to erase fifteen years. I want to use them. (*Quietly, deeply*) Hey, Lady ... (*Pat and Maggie enter Gull House, their arms around each other. Gull House is dark now except for the eye, Sara's room, which continues to blink as Sara's shadow moves back and forth across it*)

One Tit, A Dyke, & Gin!

■

A ONE-ACT PLAY

BY

PENNELL SOMSEN

▼

One Tit, A Dyke, & Gin!

One Tit, A Dyke, & Gin!, my first play, was conceived in a doctor's office, born in E. Katherine Kerr's acting class at Playwrights Horizons, and developed in Stuart Spencer's playwriting class at Ensemble Studio Theatre. It was written in the Chelsea Hotel.

I wanted to write a play that included lesbian characters but was not necessarily about being lesbian. In that sense I came to *One Tit* through the back door. I was in a doctor's consulting room, undressed but for my "modesty" gown, waiting for the doctor to appear. I wondered whether the doctor and staff ever forgot a patient and went home. I didn't think it impossible or even unlikely.

As I waited, I created a character, Louise, who gets left in a doctor's office. She's trapped not only by the situation but also by something within herself. Someone else enters. Who? A security guard. A female security guard. A lesbian. And from there the characters took on a life of their own.

Initially I thought a romance might develop between Louise and Rosemary, but Louise turned out to be an incurable heterosexual. Gina and Miss Tate didn't appear in the original version of the play, although Louise and Rosemary mentioned them. I decided to bring them onstage to see what would happen. I didn't know Miss Tate was a lesbian until she appeared. Someone commented that it's unbelievably coincidental that Miss Tate is a lesbian. Perhaps so, but isn't it an extraordinary coincidence that almost all the characters in mainstream theatre just happen to be heterosexual?

Writing and going through a workshop production of *One Tit*, I learned what a collaborative effort playwriting is. Nomi Tichman, the extraordinary actress who created the role of Rosemary, read an early version of the script with me in

E. Katherine Kerr's acting class. Nomi, Katherine, and the class all contributed support and suggestions. Stuart Spencer, my playwriting teacher, worked through the play with me beat by beat.

When I had gone as far as I could go without a director and actors, Stuart encouraged me to try to get the play produced. I submitted *One Tit* to John Bale, who was in charge of Playwrights Horizons Theatre School Summerfest '91, and he included it in the festival.

Catherine Coke, a director I had worked with as an actress and admired, liked the play and agreed to direct it. When Catherine and I began working on the script we agreed so consistently with what needed work and what to do about it that I knew I had chosen a director I could trust with my firstborn. My trust was well placed.

The show worked! People came (two of the nights in a rainstorm), paid money, watched the show, and laughed. Even though I knew all the lines, I laughed too. Catherine and the cast brought things to the play that I'd never imagined.

One Tit would never have gotten off the page without the support of the following people, most of whom volunteered their time and talent: Lauren Andersen, John Bale, Gary Matthew Binnie, Anthony Ciccotelli, Catherine Coke, Sid Curl, Sarah Ford, Graeme F. McDonnell, Judith Morse, Liz Pierrotti, and Nomi Tichman. Carol Estey, Leila Holiday, Madlyn McKendry, John McCormack, and Dan Varrichione joined *One Tit* for its second workshop production at Playwrights Horizons Theatre School.

Friends and family who read *One Tit* as it grew and contributed encouragement and suggestions include Katherine Chew, Susan Martin Cohen, Mark Conway, Sara Diel, Vicki Falco, Kevin Fisher, David Fobair, Mary Fogarty, Gil Gold, Brendan Huhn, Floyd King, Robyn Cronulla Lee, Glenda Mace, Bruce Rise, and Henry Somsen.

I especially want to thank Terry Helbing, who asked for submissions to this anthology. I appreciate Terry for taking the time to read and consider a play by an unknown playwright, and for trusting himself enough to choose it.

Pennell Somsen

One Tit, A Dyke, & Gin! was given its first professional production January 15, 22, 30, 31, February 1 & 2, 1992, by The Vortex Theater Company, Robert Coles, Artistic Director. It was directed by Catherine Coke and performed by the following cast:

NURSE/MISS TATE .... Jan Owen

NANCY/GINA .... Lauren Andersen

LOUISE .... Carol Estey

ROSEMARY .... Nomi Tichman

VOICE OF DR. SEVERT .... Madlyn McKendry

The lighting was designed by Mary Ann Hoag, the set was designed by Diana Schlenk, and the stage manager was Diane B. Greenberg.

The second production of *One Tit, A Dyke, & Gin!* was performed in Washington, D.C., in 1992 at Source Theatre Company's Twelfth Annual Washington Theatre Festival, Pat Murphy Sheehy, Producing Artistic Director and Keith Parker, Festival Director.

CHARACTERS

Nurse — An older woman still very interested in men; doubles as Miss Tate

Nancy — A receptionist; trashy in an endearing way, very scatterbrained; doubles as Gina

Louise — Elegant hairstyle; good pants or skirt and shoes; obviously wealthy; wears only a paper modesty gown on top for most of the play; is clearly missing one breast; has a thin veneer of rich attitude over an insecure little girl

Rosemary — Wears a security guard uniform; butch; tough; socially clumsy but kind

Gina — Rosemary's lover; beautiful in a very feminine way; as hot-tempered as she is affectionate

Miss Tate — Appears to be the prototypical "old maid"; at least sixty, a little fussy looking; undoubtedly carries a lacy handkerchief with her

Voice of Doctor Severt

PLACE

A doctor's waiting room. A receptionist's desk with phone, a couch or some chairs, a prominently displayed "No Smoking" sign. There are numerous magazines. Ideally they should all be superspecialty magazines that are of little interest to the average person. Down right or left is a tiny cubicle with a stool and a curtain or door that separates it from the rest of the stage. There are three doors; one to the rest of the building, one to the interior room in which Louise's clothes are locked, and one to the bathroom.

THE PLAY

*ALL lights come on in all areas. Louise is sitting on a stool in the
cubicle, wearing pants, shoes, but only a paper modesty gown
on top. She is paging through* Tennis *magazine or some other
specialty magazine that few people want to read. She glances
frequently at her watch. In the waiting area a nurse and receptionist are getting their things together in preparation for going
home. Louise cannot hear their conversation.*

NURSE. Are you ready, Nancy? I want to get to Tweedle Dum's
before happy hour's over.
NANCY. No, you go ahead. I can't find my nail polish and I've got
to do my nails tonight. I'll lock up.
NURSE. If you're sure you don't mind. ... If I don't get there
soon all the good men will be taken.
NANCY. No, its fine. I really want to find that polish. My nails are
chipped and I didn't get a chance to do them at work today. I
guess I'll just have to do them at home.
NURSE. If you're sure. ... Good–night. See you tomorrow. (*Exits*)
NANCY. (*Calling after her*) Get lucky. And catch one for me. (*The
door closes behind the nurse*) Shit! Where the hell is it? If Benita
borrowed it, I'll have her head. You can't even buy Fiery Wet
Dreams any more. (*She continues to search for polish, finds it, and
exits. After she exits the stage all the lights go out at once as if a
master switch has been pulled. We hear the sounds of a door closing
and being locked. The only light onstage comes through the slats of a
venetian blind. The minute the lights go out Louise jumps up from
her stool and yells, "Hey!" When she gets no response she peeks out
the door into the waiting room*)

LOUISE. Hey, what happened to the lights? Hello? Nurse? Hello? The lights went out! (*She leaves the cubicle and heads toward the light coming from the blinds*) Hello? Is anybody here? Nurse? Dr. Severt? This is ridiculous. Now where . . . (*She tries to raise the venetian blinds and they crash down*) Oh my God! Where is everybody? Nurse! Dr. Severt! Nurse! (*She ineffectively tries to replace the blinds, but gives up quickly as she remembers*) Oh no! My clothes! (*She runs to a door, rattles the knob, bangs and kicks at the door*) Please open, please! C'mon, just be jammed . . . (*She moves to the receptionist's desk and starts frantically going through the drawers*) Keys . . . If I were a key, where would I be? (*She finds a pack of cigarettes, takes one out, starts to light it, looks guiltily at the "No Smoking" sign, then lights the cigarette anyway. She picks up the phone, punches several buttons until she reaches an outside line and finally dials*) Hello, Harold? —— I'm not calling about the divorce. I know the lawyers —— Harold, I need a favor . . . I'm at Dr. Severt's. They apparently forgot I was waiting and left. My clothes are locked up. I need —— I can't call anyone else. I don't even have my bra —— its locked up. —— How could I have —— But, I don't have my bra! Please —— (*The lights jump on, the door to the hall bursts open, and Rosemary enters. She has a gun pointed at Louise*)

ROSEMARY. Freeze! Put out that cigarette!

LOUISE. I can't do both!

ROSEMARY. What?

LOUISE. I can't freeze and put out my cigarette at the same time.

ROSEMARY. Put out the cigarette but don't make any fast moves.

LOUISE. (*She looks around for someplace to put out her cigarette. Can't see any*) Where?

ROSEMARY. (*Backs into bathroom, keeping her gun pointed at Louise*) You should have thought of that when you lit it. I have you covered, so don't try anything (*Sound of running water. She returns with a urine cup half filled with water. Hands it to Louise who drops her cigarette in it*)

LOUISE. Please stop pointing that gun at me.

ROSEMARY. Are you a patient?

LOUISE. Yes, I'm —

ROSEMARY. Then what the hell are you doing in here? It's after hours.

LOUISE. Please stop pointing that gun at me.

ROSEMARY. Just don't make any fast moves. (*Puts gun in holster. Louise crosses her arms in front of her chest and remains that way until further notice*) So what are you doing here after hours?

LOUISE. I got left here. In that room. My clothes are locked up in there. Are you the security guard? You must have keys.

ROSEMARY. They just left you? Forgot you?

LOUISE. Yes, they just left me. Forgot me. Just get my clothes, will you?

ROSEMARY. I don't have keys to any of the rooms in here. Just to the main door.

LOUISE. I'd be glad to pay you if you'd just get my clothes for me.

ROSEMARY. But I don't have the keys.

LOUISE. I said I'd pay you. I have at least a hundred dollars in my purse.

ROSEMARY. Look, I don't have the keys. Your money doesn't change that.

LOUISE. That's ridiculous. You're the guard. You should have the keys.

ROSEMARY. Well, I don't.

LOUISE. Certainly you must know where they are. I have to get out of here. I have to meet someone.

ROSEMARY. I don't have keys. I don't know where they are. I can't get your clothes for you.

LOUISE. But, what am I going to do?

ROSEMARY. Why are you asking me? I don't know. Try to call your doctor.

LOUISE. I don't know her home number.

ROSEMARY. (*She begins searching the desk*) It's probably around here someplace. I bet you have a fur. If you didn't have a fur, they wouldn't have locked up your clothes. (*She pulls a card from a rolodex, hands it to Louise*) Here.

LOUISE. (*Takes the card*) Thank you. (*She tries to dial the number, has a great deal of trouble with the buttons on the machine*)

ROSEMARY. All you do is push nine to get an outside line. (*Rosemary does it for her*)

LOUISE. (*To Rosemary*) Thank you. (*Into phone*) Hello? —— Could

I speak with Dr. Severt, please? —— Oh, I see. —— Do you have her home number? —— But, it's an emergency. —— Then, would you please tell her to call her office? It's urgent. —— I see. —— Louise Penniman. —— That's Penny with an "i", man. Thank you. (*She hangs up*) I just got her service. They don't know where she is and they wouldn't give me her home number. She might not call back for hours. If at all.

ROSEMARY. Well, don't you have a friend you could call to bring you some clothes?

LOUISE. Actually, no.

ROSEMARY. You don't have any friends?

LOUISE. Of course I have friends. A great many friends. But I called them already.

ROSEMARY. So, what's the problem? Your friend brings you some clothes. Tomorrow you come back and pick up your other ones.

LOUISE. None of my friends are home. I left messages, but I'm not sure how long it will be until someone gets back to me.

ROSEMARY. I guess you'll have to wait then. You can't go out on the streets like that.

LOUISE. Thank you for reminding me. Believe me I'm even more aware of my deformity than you are. I know I can't go out like —

ROSEMARY. I didn't say anything about any deformity. It's cold outside. You can't go out like that in twenty degree weather is all I meant.

LOUISE. Oh.

ROSEMARY. And I wouldn't call it a deformity either. So they took away part of you. In that stupid gown you still look better than I do on my best days. (*Louise gradually begins to unlock her arms from her chest*)

LOUISE. Do you have a jacket I could borrow? Just to —

ROSEMARY. It would be too big for you.

LOUISE. I wouldn't mind. Just anything to get me out of here. I'd return it tomorrow.

ROSEMARY. It would be way too big.

LOUISE. But I don't care! I'm stuck here! I have to get out!

ROSEMARY. Don't get all excited! One of your friends will call.

(*Phone rings. Louise goes toward it. Rosemary draws her gun*)

LOUISE. Well, answer it! It could be Dr. Severt.

ROSEMARY. Just hold your horses! (*Phone rings twice and stops. Rings again. Rosemary picks it up*) Hello? —— Gina, I was just about to call you. —— I got hung up. —— No, I didn't stop off at the bar. I came straight to work. —— What do you mean, tonight of all nights? —— Oh, shit! Gina, honey, I'm sorry. I thought this year I'd get it right. Remember. —— What else can I say? —— We'll do something really special tomorrow night. —— No, I can't possibly leave tonight. —— Gina, give me a break. —— I'll make it up to you. I promise. Gina? (*Hangs up phone*) Shit! Goddam! ... Look, I have to check the rest of the building. Maybe you should try your friends again. I'll leave the lights on. (*She stomps out*)

LOUISE. (*Lights cigarette. Dials phone*) Bergdorf's please ... Manhattan. (*Dials again*) Plaza Collections, fourth floor, please. —— Hello, Miss Tate? —— This is Louise Penniman. —— I'm fine, how are you? —— I'm glad to hear it. —— Miss Tate, I'm in an unusual situation. I'm at the clinic up the street from you and my appointment ran overtime —— No, just routine —— I don't have the appropriate clothes with me for my dinner date this evening —— I was wondering if you would be so kind as to pick something out for me and have it sent over here by messenger. You could just charge it to my account —— Yes, I'll speak with him —— Hello, Mr. Teitel? —— There must be a mistake. We've always been prompt with our bills —— He's taken me off the account? —— I see —— Well, I'll open my own account then —— Over the phone, of course. I simply don't have time to come in today —— I see —— There isn't any way? This really is an emergency. I could come in tomorrow and —— I see —— Miss Tate? —— Please don't blame yourself. It's not your fault —— I'll work something out —— Thank you Miss Tate. (*She hangs up. She tries once more to break down the door of room her clothes are in*) Shit! Shit! Goddammit! (*She keeps hitting door, screaming and crying*)

ROSEMARY. (*Enters. Pulls out her gun. Grabs Louise's cigarette and puts it out*) Freeze! Hands over your head! What the hell do

119
▼

you think you're doing?

LOUISE. I was just trying —

ROSEMARY. Are you really a patient?

LOUISE. Why do you think I'm wearing this stupid gown?

ROSEMARY. Did you hide out here on purpose, trying to get your hands on some drugs?

LOUISE. Do I look like a drug addict?

ROSEMARY. Forget looks. I've heard about you rich women and your tranquilizers.

LOUISE. Would you please stop waving that gun at me.

ROSEMARY. Just don't —

LOUISE. Make any fast moves. I know. I won't. I won't. I did not hide here on purpose. I don't want any drugs. All I want to do is get some clothes, get out of here, and have a cigarette.

ROSEMARY. Nicotine is a drug, you know. All right, I believe you. But I can't let you tear the place down. You may not understand, but I need this job. I can't afford to lose it because you have a tantrum.

LOUISE. Did I do any damage? I'll pay for it.

ROSEMARY. What is it with you and money? Like giving people money is going to solve everything.

LOUISE. I simply offered to pay for any damages I might have caused.

ROSEMARY. I guess you didn't really damage anything. Except the air, with your smoke.

LOUISE. I'm cold. Can't I borrow your jacket? Just to wear here.

ROSEMARY. No, I told you it would be too big for you.

LOUISE. Well, is it all right if I look for a blanket or something? If I don't make any fast moves?

ROSEMARY. Sure. Make yourself at home. But if the phone rings, let me answer it.

LOUISE. (Goes into cubicle, finds sheet. Drapes it over herself like a shawl) What if the phone rings and you're not here?

ROSEMARY. Just don't answer it.

LOUISE. But I'm expecting a call.

ROSEMARY. I'll be here. This is the only warm place to hang out between rounds.

LOUISE. Warm? You're kidding. Wait, do you mean you're going to stay in here? In this room?

ROSEMARY. Don't have much of a choice, do I? Look what happens when I leave you on your own.

LOUISE. (*Gets out cigarette. Rosemary glares at her, touches her gun. Louise puts cigarette back. Rosemary turns on radio, changes from an easy listening station to a country one. Louise gets a magazine, sits down to read. Silence*) Being a security guard is an unusual job for a woman. How did you get into it?

ROSEMARY. I'm an unusual woman.

LOUISE. Oh. Well, how long have you been a security guard?

ROSEMARY. Not long. It's a second job.

LOUISE. Oh. What's your other job?

ROSEMARY. I teach.

LOUISE. Physical education?

ROSEMARY. Home economics. What is this, an interview?

LOUISE. I was just trying to be friendly.

ROSEMARY. What for?

LOUISE. What do you mean, what for?

ROSEMARY. We're not very likely to become friends, so why be friendly?

LOUISE. We're stuck here together. We might as well be nice to each other.

ROSEMARY. Well, I don't like small talk.

LOUISE. Well, I don't like sitting here. Waiting. I'm sorry I bothered you.

ROSEMARY. Look, you want to play some cards? As long as we're stuck here together? Just until one of your friends calls?

LOUISE. That's all right. You don't have to entertain me.

ROSEMARY. I know that. I'd just rather play cards than talk.

LOUISE. I understand. You don't have to talk to me. I'll just read a magazine. Anyway, I don't imagine we'd find any cards here.

ROSEMARY. I always bring a deck with me for solitaire.

LOUISE. Well, you'd probably rather play your solitaire then. Thank you, but I think I'll just read this magazine.

ROSEMARY. Suit yourself. (*Rosemary settles down to a game of solitaire. Louise gets up and fiddles with radio trying to change station. She has difficulty finding the right buttons, turns volume all the way up, turns it off, eventually gets nothing but static. Rosemary gets up and adjusts radio*) You want to drive me crazy?

LOUISE. I'm sorry. I couldn't figure out ...

ROSEMARY. What is it you were trying to do, anyway?

LOUISE. I was just trying to change the station.

ROSEMARY. Not a country fan, huh?

LOUISE. Well, no ...

ROSEMARY. Well, I am. Listen to it, you might learn something. About real people. (*Radio is back on country station. Loud*)

LOUISE. Could you at least turn it down? (*Rosemary gives Louise a look, then turns radio down. Louise goes back to her magazine. Tries another magazine, looks at her watch. After a bit, she gets up and looks over Rosemary's shoulder while she's playing solitaire*) I think you can put the red jack on the black queen.

ROSEMARY. I know.

LOUISE. And if you move the three over here it will open up the four of diamonds.

ROSEMARY. Right.

LOUISE. But you certainly want to put the ace up here. (*She reaches to move card*)

ROSEMARY. You know why they call it solitaire? Because you're supposed to play it alone. Solitaire, solitary, get it?

LOUISE. I'm sorry, it's just that —

ROSEMARY. I hear something. I better go check. (*Exits*)

LOUISE. (*After Rosemary has left the room the phone rings. Louise goes toward it, remembers Rosemary's admonition, goes to the door and yells after Rosemary*). Guard, guard! The phone! (*The phone stops ringing. We hear a tape with a woman's voice saying: "You have reached the office of Dr. Elaine Severt, oncologist and hematologist. Our office hours are nine a.m. to six p.m., Monday through Friday. Please call back during those hours to make an appointment." There is a click, then: "This is Dr. Severt. Is there a problem there? I'm about to catch the Trump Shuttle to Washington." Louise has gone for the phone, has lifted the receiver and is saying "Hello, hello. Dr. Severt? It's me, Louise Penniman!" to no response. She is madly pushing buttons on the machine, trying to break into the call. The tape continues with: "There's some interference on this line. I'll call in the morning." We hear a dial tone. Rosemary enters*)

122
▼

LOUISE. Dr. Severt just called and I missed her.

ROSEMARY. Well, call her back.

LOUISE. I can't. She called from the airport. She's on a plane now.

ROSEMARY. You said you didn't talk to her.

LOUISE. I could hear her voice on the machine but I couldn't get her to hear me and she hung up.

ROSEMARY. All you do is push this button here. (*She demonstrates*)

LOUISE. That doesn't help me now! She's gone.

ROSEMARY. You're not very good with machines, are you? Well, it's not a big deal. One of your friends will call.

LOUISE. You're blaming it on me! You told me not to answer the phone and then you left.

ROSEMARY. There's nothing I can do about it now.

LOUISE. I've got to get out of here. Can't you break down the door?

ROSEMARY. Absolutely not.

LOUISE. It doesn't look that solid.

ROSEMARY. You think I'm going to destroy the property in a place I'm paid to protect? No way.

LOUISE. Well, what am I going to do? I can't just stay here.

ROSEMARY. Why are you asking me? I didn't get you into this situation. It's not my job to get you out. Can't you do anything for yourself?

LOUISE. If you hadn't told me not to answer the phone I'd be on my way out of here by now.

ROSEMARY. And if you hadn't waited quietly in that room like a good little girl you wouldn't be stuck here in the first place.

LOUISE. Don't you think I know that?

ROSEMARY. O.K., I suppose there's one thing I could do.

LOUISE. To get me out of here?

ROSEMARY. Well, what I could do is . . . I guess I could call Gina, my . . . roommate, ask her to bring some clothes for you.

LOUISE. Would she do that?

ROSEMARY. If I ask her.

LOUISE. She doesn't even know me. But if she would bring me some clothes, I'd be happy to pay her for her time and trouble.

ROSEMARY. Get this straight. I'm not for sale. Neither is Gina. You got a problem, it's partly my fault, so we'll help you out. That's it. (*She picks up phone and dials*)

LOUISE. I'm sorry ... I was just trying. ... I'd appreciate it if your ... friend brought me some clothes.

ROSEMARY. (*Puts down phone*) She's not home.

LOUISE. You don't have a machine?

ROSEMARY. Why would we have one of those things? We're home, we're home. We're not, we're not.

LOUISE. I never quite thought of it that way. Well, thank you for trying.

ROSEMARY. Maybe I dialed a wrong number. (*She dials again, waits for more than five rings, hangs up*) Goddammit! Why isn't she home?

LOUISE. Perhaps she had a date tonight.

ROSEMARY. A date?

LOUISE. Well, yes, perhaps she and her boyfriend. ... People do go out at night.

ROSEMARY. Her boyfriend? I can't believe this.

LOUISE. What?

ROSEMARY. You mean you couldn't tell?

LOUISE. Tell what?

ROSEMARY. That I'm a dyke?

LOUISE. Well, I try not to notice ... I mean ... and I never would have used that word. ... Oh, I see, your roommate is ... yes, I see. So she wouldn't be on a date with a boyfriend. I see.

ROSEMARY. You got it all figured out now?

LOUISE. Yes. You don't have to explain anymore.

ROSEMARY. You don't even want me to describe what we do together? Most straight people are curious about that.

LOUISE. No, that's all right, I ... you don't have to ... I'd rather you didn't.

ROSEMARY. I was just kidding.

LOUISE. Oh.

ROSEMARY. Anyway, that's why I didn't want you to answer the phone. In case she called back. She was already pissed off at me and if she'd called and another woman had answered the phone. . . .

LOUISE. But, surely she wouldn't have thought that I was a . . . you mean she might have thought that you and I were. . . . But I'm not . . .

ROSEMARY. Why not? You can't tell over the phone. (*Dials*) C'mon, answer! (*Hangs up*) Shit! I don't know what to do. You don't think she'd walk out on me just because I forgot our anniversary, do you?

LOUISE. Your anniversary? But, you can't get married, can you? How can you have an anniversary? An anniversary of what? (*Rosemary gives her a look*) Oh.

ROSEMARY. I forgot our damned anniversary and Gina's angry and now she's not home and I don't know where she's gone.

LOUISE. I don't think I'm the person with whom you should be discussing this.

ROSEMARY. Why not?

LOUISE. I just can't identify with your problems. I don't understand.

ROSEMARY. You can't understand what? That I'd be enough of a jerk to forget our anniversary?

LOUISE. Well, no, it's not that, it. . . . I'm not used to talking about private matters with strangers and your problems are so different from mine. I mean I've never even known any . . .

ROSEMARY. Dykes? Its O.K., you can use the word. I give you permission.

LOUISE. I always thought that word was insulting, not polite. I thought lesbian was the polite word.

ROSEMARY. Lesbian always sounds to me like you gotta go to college to become one. You know, I got my lesbian degree at Harvard.

LOUISE. (*Pause*) Oh, you're kidding again.

ROSEMARY. I guess I'm just one for telling it like it is. I'm a dyke. You're missing a tit. Those are the facts. No reason to dance around them.

LOUISE. Look, you can talk the way you want about yourself, use words like that, but I'm not accustomed to that kind of language. I don't appreciate what you said about me. And I don't think that being . . . homosexual and having a . . . mastectomy are in the same category.

125

▼

ROSEMARY. I'm sorry. I didn't mean to offend you.

LOUISE. And frankly, I don't like it that you even noticed that about me, about my ... surgery. I'm very uncomfortable about your looking at me that way, especially since you admit you're a ... well, since you like women.

ROSEMARY. Don't worry. I'm not coming on to you. You're not my type anyway.

LOUISE. Well, how am I supposed to know? Its confusing. You tell me you're a ... lesbian. You make comments about my looks, my body. How am I supposed to know what that means?

ROSEMARY. I said I was sorry. Get over it.

LOUISE. Just so you understand I'm not ... like you.

ROSEMARY. Yeah. I got that. (*She goes to phone and starts dialing*)

LOUISE. What do you mean I'm not your type?

ROSEMARY. I didn't mean anything by that, really. You're an attractive woman. Or aren't I supposed to notice that?

LOUISE. I don't know. I just don't know how to act around you.

ROSEMARY. I can see that. (*Dials again. Waits. Hangs up*) Shit!

LOUISE. You're really worried, aren't you?

ROSEMARY. I thought you couldn't identify.

LOUISE. I'm just sorry you're upset.

ROSEMARY. Thank you for your concern. (*A silence. Rosemary dials again. Hangs up. Louise pages through a magazine. Louise starts to say something a few times and stops herself. Rosemary deals out a game of solitaire*)

LOUISE. Would you still like to play some cards? To pass the time. While we're waiting.

ROSEMARY. I guess. What can you play? I pretty much know them all.

LOUISE. I haven't played anything but bridge for years.

ROSEMARY. Bridge. It figures.

LOUISE. I used to play gin rummy with Daddy when I was a child.

ROSEMARY. Gin? That's more like it. Do you remember how to play?

LOUISE. I think so. ... I'd better warn you, though, I'm not very good at cards. My husband, ex-husband says ... well, that I'm not very good. Actually I used to be pretty good, when I played gin with Daddy. Maybe I'm just not very good at bridge.

ROSEMARY. You want to play or don't you?

LOUISE. Sure, sure, let's play.

ROSEMARY. (*Finds paper and pencil. Starts shuffling cards. Louise sits opposite her*) The way we play we deal seven cards each and flip one up. If you don't want it the dealer gets a chance at it. You ever score Hollywood? (*Louise shakes her head no*) O.K., what we do is we have three columns. The first hand goes in the first column, the second in the first and second, and the third in all three and so on. That way we play three games at one time. Cut for deal. High card deals. (*They cut. Louise wins deal, shuffles a bit and begins dealing. As soon as the hand is dealt they begin to play. For the rest of the card game the winner of the hand will shuffle and deal the next hand*) So what's your name?

LOUISE. Louise Penniman, Penny with an "i", man. What's yours?

ROSEMARY. Rosemary Gertz. Rhymes with Hertz.

LOUISE. (*Pause*) You know, I just realized, even if I get some clothes I can't go home. My keys are locked up. And my money. And my cigarettes.

ROSEMARY. But you were smoking.

LOUISE. Well, I, while I was looking for some keys I —

ROSEMARY. Stop! Don't tell me. I don't want to know. So if you do get some clothes, where will you go?

LOUISE. I suppose I could go to the Plaza.

ROSEMARY. Without money?

LOUISE. They know me. They'd check me into a room without money or credit cards. I'd tell them I'd been mugged.

ROSEMARY. Must be nice.

LOUISE. Being mugged?

ROSEMARY. Being known at the Plaza. They probably wouldn't let me in even with money.

LOUISE. You've never stayed there?

ROSEMARY. Are you kidding? I've never been inside even. It's a little intimidating. All those women in mink coats going in and out, limousines driving up.

LOUISE. The staff there is really very nice.

ROSEMARY. I'm sure they are. To you. The main thing I know about the Plaza is when I was a kid I used to read that book about the girl who lived there. Whatshername.

LOUISE. Eloise. I read those books too. Gin!

ROSEMARY. Yeah, Eloise. You caught me with fifty. That's seventy-five for you with the gin. Only on one game though. I always thought I'd just like to go into the Plaza and look around, you know?

LOUISE. I'm sure no one would object to your going in and looking around the lobby.

ROSEMARY. I'd feel out of place. I'd look out of place. So I guess you have pretty much money, huh?

LOUISE. Well, yes, I inherited from my father.

ROSEMARY. I inherited from my dad too. A taste for booze and a lot of gambling debts.

LOUISE. I was luckier. I inherited money. I never really think about it. I guess that's what's good about having it. You don't have to think about it.

ROSEMARY. Yeah, well, take it from me, you don't have money, you think about it a lot. (*Louise looks at card on facedown pile, puts it back down and takes Rosemary's discard*) What the hell do you think you're doing?

LOUISE. I was just looking at the card.

ROSEMARY. That's cheating! You can't look at it and then change your mind.

LOUISE. Daddy always used to let me —

ROSEMARY. Yeah, well, I'm not your daddy. You wanna play with me, we play by the rules.

LOUISE. All right. I just didn't know your rules. I won't do it again.

ROSEMARY. Damned right you won't.

LOUISE. There's no need to be so unpleasant. Perhaps we won't be friends, but we could at least be civilized. (*Pause*) Do you live nearby? Close to the clinic?

ROSEMARY. Nope. Brooklyn.

LOUISE. Brooklyn!

ROSEMARY. Yeah, you cross the East River —

LOUISE. I know where it is. But it's so far. You mean your . . .

128
▼

your roommate would come all the way in from Brooklyn to do a favor for someone she doesn't even know?

ROSEMARY. Oh sure. That's how she is. She'd give you the shirt off her back. Which I guess is what you need. Always going out of her way for people. Until she gets mad. Then watch out.

LOUISE. She won't be angrier at you, will she? About bringing in the clothes?

ROSEMARY. She couldn't be any angrier at me than she already is.

LOUISE. It's just that I don't want to put any additional pressures on your ... relationship. I'm sure you have enough as it is. I'll go down with three.

ROSEMARY. Already? I've got twenty. That's seventeen for you on the first two games. What do you mean, pressures?

LOUISE. Well, you know ... society ... I mean it can't be easy ...

ROSEMARY. Society? Society's the least of my worries. Biggest pressure in our relationship is Gina getting all bent out of shape about little things, like me forgetting our anniversary.

LOUISE. Little things! Of course she's upset. You forgot an important occasion.

ROSEMARY. I don't see what's the big deal. It's just a day. She knows I love her, so I forget our anniversary, so what?

LOUISE. How does she know that you love her?

ROSEMARY. Well, I'm with her, aren't I? We just bought a co-op together for god's sake!

LOUISE. Maybe she'd like a little romance. And maybe she doesn't know you love her. Do you tell her?

ROSEMARY. What are you, some kind of expert on relationships?

LOUISE. Hardly. I'm more of an expert on breakups. I'm just thinking how I felt in Gina's situation.

ROSEMARY. Are you on her side or something? You don't even know her.

LOUISE. Just because I haven't met her doesn't mean I can't understand how she feels about some things.

ROSEMARY. I thought you couldn't identify with dykes, excuse me, lesbians. Now all of a sudden you're an expert on how Gina feels. Gin! Got you this time!

LOUISE. I've got ten. I never said I was an expert on Gina. And I certainly don't understand about a relationship between two women. But I'm trying. You brought up the subject.

ROSEMARY. And now I want to drop it.

LOUISE. That's fine with me. (*Rosemary dials again. Waits for several rings. Slams phone down*) No answer?

ROSEMARY. Yeah, she answered. I just decided not to talk with her.

LOUISE. Why would you ...? Oh. (*Rosemary gives her a look*)

ROSEMARY. (*Louise picks up a card that Rosemary has discarded*) You just discarded a six!

LOUISE. And now I want one.

ROSEMARY. (*Pause*) You think maybe I should take Gina out to dinner? If I ever get a hold of her?

LOUISE. I thought you didn't want my opinion.

ROSEMARY. Well, I changed my mind. So what do you think?

LOUISE. I think it would be a good idea to take Gina out to dinner.

ROSEMARY. I suppose it would have to be some fancy place with tablecloths and candles and a wine list, huh?

LOUISE. I don't think going to McDonalds would qualify as a special evening.

ROSEMARY. I hate going to fancy restaurants. I feel out of place. I go crazy trying to figure out what to wear.

LOUISE. I'm sure there are evening clothes that would be becoming to you.

ROSEMARY. Yeah, right. I get dressed up I look like a suma wrestler with ruffles and bows.

LOUISE. I don't think you're the type for ruffles and bows.

ROSEMARY. No kidding.

LOUISE. What you need are good fabrics, tailored. (*Louise studies Rosemary*)

ROSEMARY. What are you staring at me for?

LOUISE. I'm trying to decide if you're a fall or a winter.

ROSEMARY. What do you mean fall or winter?

LOUISE. I'm sure you're not spring or summer.

ROSEMARY. What is this spring, summer, fall, winter stuff? Is it like astrology or something?

LOUISE. No, it has nothing to do with astrology.

ROSEMARY. Good, because I don't go for that astrology shit.

LOUISE. I think you're a winter. Black, bright colors, does that sound right?

ROSEMARY. This is about colors?

LOUISE. Yes, what colors look best on you. They're in groupings of seasons.

ROSEMARY. How the hell would I know what colors look best on me?

LOUISE. Well, I think you're a winter. Purple, fuscia, black ...

ROSEMARY. Whatever. You know, you remind me of my mother. "It wouldn't hurt you to dress up every once in a while, Rosemary. Maybe if you paid a little attention to your appearance you'd meet a nice man."

LOUISE. I didn't mean ...

ROSEMARY. I really don't give a crap whether I'm a winter or a May or a Scorpio or whatever.

LOUISE. Sorry, I was just trying to be helpful.

ROSEMARY. I just don't like it when people try to make me over. Pretty soon you'll be whipping out your Mary Kay cosmetics.

LOUISE. I don't use Mary Kay. I use Lancome. (*Rosemary gives her a look*) Apparently I can't say anything right. Perhaps we should just play cards and not talk.

ROSEMARY. Fine by me.

LOUISE. One.

ROSEMARY. Thirty.

LOUISE. Am I out in the first game yet?

ROSEMARY. Not quite. Where did you ever get the idea that you couldn't play cards?

LOUISE. I wasn't at all good when I played bridge with Harold. (*Rosemary gives her a questioning look*) My ex-husband.

ROSEMARY. He was probably the one who wasn't any good and he blamed it on you.

LOUISE. You think so?

ROSEMARY. Definitely.

LOUISE. He is like that.

ROSEMARY. A lot of them are.

LOUISE. How do you know that, about men? I mean ...

ROSEMARY. I was married before I met Gina.

LOUISE. To a man?

131

▼

ROSEMARY. Uh–huh. He was all right. But Gina, she's special.

LOUISE. She sounds it.

ROSEMARY. I just hope I haven't really screwed things up.

LOUISE. I'm sure it will be all right. (*Pause*) I've been thinking . . . and I don't want you to think this is about buying Gina's help but if Gina does come into the city to bring me clothes what if I put the two of you up at the Plaza for the night? Then you could have something special for your anniversary. And you wouldn't have to get dressed up.

ROSEMARY. We couldn't accept that. Anyway, I don't know when she'll get home. If she gets home. You should probably try your friends again or you could be stuck here all night. (*Dials*)

LOUISE. Why is it all right for Gina to go out of her way to bring me clothes and it's not all right for me to get you a room at the Plaza?

ROSEMARY. (*Hangs up*) It's just different, doing things for people and giving them money. Besides I'd be uncomfortable there. All those women in their sable stoles.

LOUISE. You really have a problem with fur coats, don't you? Are you one of those animal rights activists?

ROSEMARY. No. I just hate rich people.

LOUISE. Oh. (*Pause*) Gin!

ROSEMARY. That puts you out on the first game.

LOUISE. Look, I've got to have a cigarette. I can't sit here all night without —

ROSEMARY. This is a doctor's office!

LOUISE. I don't care! I'm going to have a cigarette whether you like it or not.

ROSEMARY. All right, go ahead, just don't blow it at me.

LOUISE. You mean you're not going to shoot me? (*Lights cigarette*)

ROSEMARY. Why waste a good bullet? You're killing yourself anyway. You don't need my help.

LOUISE. Maybe so. But what a way to go. (*She blows a smoke ring*) Why do you hate rich people?

ROSEMARY. I just do. They seem to think they're better than ordinary people. I always imagine they're looking down their nice straight noses at me.

LOUISE. I'm surprised that would bother you. You seem so self–confident.

ROSEMARY. I'm not really. Just tough.

LOUISE. I don't look down my nose at you.

ROSEMARY. You took that personally didn't you? What I said about rich people?

LOUISE. Of course I did. Why wouldn't I?

ROSEMARY. Well, I didn't mean it personally. I was talking about rich people in general.

LOUISE. So you don't hate me because I'm rich?

ROSEMARY. No. Anyway, I hardly know you.

LOUISE. Gin! Does that put me out on the last two games?

ROSEMARY. It sure does.

LOUISE. Not bad for a woman with one tit, huh? (*She laughs*) I can't believe I actually said that.

ROSEMARY. I can't either.

LOUISE. You're either a very good or a very bad influence on me.

ROSEMARY. Me? Influence you?

LOUISE. Sure. Why not?

ROSEMARY. I'm just surprised is all. You won in all three games. Skunked me in the last two. I want you to know that is a very unusual occurrence. Anyone beating me in gin. Want to play another?

LOUISE. Absolutely. I haven't had this much fun in . . . I don't know. Since I was a child, I think.

ROSEMARY. Glad you're having such a good time, but I gotta warn you I'm about to get serious about this game. The next game won't be as much fun for you because I'm gonna win. (*They cut for deal. Rosemary wins deal*)

LOUISE. Promises, promises. We'll see about that. So, deal dyke!

ROSEMARY. Well, well, well. . . . Get ready for some serious competition, One Tit. (*She deals*)

LOUISE. (*Picks up the cards as they are dealt*) I'm waiting. Well, these go together nicely! Keep 'em coming!

ROSEMARY. You're not supposed to pick those up until I've finished dealing!

LOUISE. (*She puts down the cards*) Why not?

ROSEMARY. That's just the way it's done. When grown-ups play. (*She picks her hand, Louise picks up hers*)

LOUISE. Oh. I see. (*Pause. Studies hand*) I have a confession to make to you.

ROSEMARY. You've been cheating?

LOUISE. Don't you wish? No, it's about my friends. I . . . Uh . . . I didn't leave any messages with friends. I lied about that.

ROSEMARY. What do you mean you didn't leave any messages? Why not? That doesn't make sense.

LOUISE. I did call Dr. Severt. And I called Bergdorf's to try to get some clothes delivered but . . . well, it's a long story. But my friends, well, no one knew about my surgery, you see, and without my bra it's pretty obvious.

ROSEMARY. No one knew?

LOUISE. No.

ROSEMARY. But how could your friends not know, you go into the hospital for surgery?

LOUISE. I just didn't tell anyone. (*She counts her cards*) I think I have only six cards.

ROSEMARY. What do you mean you only got six? Did you discard one and not pick up another?

LOUISE. I don't think so.

ROSEMARY. Damn! I'll have to deal over. And I had a good hand. (*She shuffles and redeals*) So why didn't you tell anyone? About your surgery? I don't get it.

LOUISE. I'm a very private person. I don't confide in people.

ROSEMARY. Sounds awfully lonely to me. So you don't have any close friends, huh?

LOUISE. Well, I did, once . . .

ROSEMARY. What happened?

LOUISE. My friends, well, you see, uh . . . they pretty much deserted me when I married Harold.

ROSEMARY. What kind of friends were they that they deserted you? What's wrong with Harold? Is he a mass murderer or something?

LOUISE. No, nothing like that. There's nothing wrong with Harold.

ROSEMARY. He can't be perfect. You got a divorce, didn't you?

LOUISE. Well, he . . . Harold is . . . a philanderer —

ROSEMARY. A what?

LOUISE. I mean he fooled —

ROSEMARY. Oh, yeah, he cheated on you.

LOUISE. Well, yes, but that wasn't why, not exactly.

ROSEMARY. Well, then, what was their problem? Your friends?

LOUISE. Uh . . . Harold was my best friend's husband. Until he ran off with me.

ROSEMARY. Oh.

LOUISE. You're shocked, aren't you?

ROSEMARY. It's none of my business.

LOUISE. I'm not proud of what I did.

ROSEMARY. Like I said, it's none of my business.

LOUISE. But you think what I did was really terrible, don't you?

ROSEMARY. Look, you did a crummy thing. What do you want me to say? Congratulations? I don't get you people anyway, so I really shouldn't say anything. I don't understand your lifestyle, O.K.?

LOUISE. What do you mean?

ROSEMARY. We're two totally different people. You're rich, I'm poor. You're straight, I'm gay. The only thing we have in common is playing gin rummy. As soon as you get out of here, we'll never see each other again. So why do you want my opinion?

LOUISE. I thought you were enjoying playing cards with me.

ROSEMARY. I never said I wasn't. Actually, I haven't had such a good game of gin in a long time.

LOUISE. Really? I assumed you played all the time.

ROSEMARY. Gina and I play sometimes. But . . . well . . . I love Gina to death but she has no card sense. No competition. I can beat her with my eyes closed. I'll go down with one.

LOUISE. You got me this time. I've got thirty-six. You think I have card sense?

ROSEMARY. Are you really asking that question? You go to Vegas, they'll ban you from the blackjack table.

LOUISE. (*Louise smiles. Pause*) So you don't think we'll see each other after tonight?

ROSEMARY. No, why would we? We have completely different lives. I can't see you coming out to Brooklyn on the subway

135
▼

and I can't see me going to, where is it you live when you're not at the Plaza? Park Avenue?

LOUISE. Uh, no ... Sutton Place.

ROSEMARY. Right.

LOUISE. We could get together to play cards.

ROSEMARY. We could, I guess, but we won't. It's like meeting someone on a plane or a bus, you know? Give me one of those cigarettes, would you?

LOUISE. Why? So you can tear it up?

ROSEMARY. Tear up a good cigarette? You think I'm crazy? I'm going to smoke it.

LOUISE. But you don't smoke. You were lecturing me.

ROSEMARY. Yeah, well, I quit. But, now, I'm going to have one.

LOUISE. If you quit you really shouldn't start again. You know they say ...

ROSEMARY. I know what they say! Just give me a damned cigarette.

LOUISE. But this is a doctor's office! (*Hands Rosemary a cigarette and matches*)

ROSEMARY. Yeah, yeah, yeah. (*Lights cigarette*) God, that tastes good!

LOUISE. (*Gets out cigarette. Rosemary lights it for her*) Now we have two things in common. Gin rummy and cigarettes. You know, cigarettes taste even better in a doctor's office. Maybe I'll get one of those "No Smoking" signs for my house. Just to enhance my smoking pleasure.

ROSEMARY. We have one at home.

LOUISE. A "No Smoking" sign?

ROSEMARY. Uh-huh. Actually, we have one on the door of our apartment and one in every room. Gina really hates smoking. Watch out! This hand is coming together faster than two horny teenagers.

LOUISE. You quit because of Gina?

ROSEMARY. She wouldn't even go out with me unless I quit. It wasn't enough I promised not to smoke around her. She kept complaining of how I smelled of smoke and I was ruining my health. So I quit.

LOUISE. Now I believe you really love her. I admire you for quitting. I know it's hard. I've tried.

ROSEMARY. It's hard all right. The worst thing was I gained about a ton. I have to hand it to Gina there. She's never complained about all the weight I put on. Says she'd rather have me alive with a few extra pounds than giving myself cancer. God, I hope I can find some breath mints. She finds out I've been smoking, I won't live long enough to worry about cancer.

LOUISE. I'll go down with six.

ROSEMARY. I thought I might have a chance at this hand. Twenty-two. (*A banging is heard offstage*) What the hell's that? I'll be right back. Don't mark the cards. (*Exits. From offstage*) Oh shit!

GINA. (*From offstage*) Happy Anniversary, honey! What's wrong? Aren't you happy to see me? Look, I brought everything we need for a party! Champagne, whipped cream, and me! C'mon Rosemary we can't party out here! (*Enters carrying bottle of champagne, two champagne glasses, and a can of whipped cream*)

ROSEMARY. (*Entering behind Gina*) Gina, there's something I should explain ... (*Gina sees Louise, stops short*) Uh, Gina this is ... uh I forgot your name ...

LOUISE. Louise. Louise Penniman. Penny with an "i", man —

GINA. You forgot her name! She's half naked and you forgot her name!

ROSEMARY. Gina, it's not how it looks. Louise ...

GINA. So this is why you couldn't leave work tonight! It's our anniversary! I can't believe you did this to me!

ROSEMARY. Gina, I can explain —

LOUISE. (*With Rosemary*) Gina, I can explain. I was trapped here and Rosemary discovered me when she was on her rounds.

GINA. Which doesn't explain why you're half naked. Do I smell smoke?

LOUISE. Well, yes, I did have a cigarette ...

GINA. In a doctor's office! Rosemary, I can't believe you let her do that! All those poor sick people getting even sicker from her secondhand smoke!

ROSEMARY. I couldn't stop her Gina!

LOUISE. She tried! She even threatened me with her gun ...

ROSEMARY. (*Comes very close to Gina*) Look, Gina, I'm really glad you came. I've been worried. I've been trying to call.

GINA. Let me smell your breath. (*Rosemary tries to back away*) Oh my god! I can't believe it! You've been smoking! It isn't enough that you have a date with another woman on our anniversary! No! You have to turn the knife by smoking a cigarette.

ROSEMARY. But, Gina . . .

GINA. Don't "But Gina" me. You're killing yourself. You promised me!

ROSEMARY. Gina, I was upset. I thought you'd left me.

GINA. Why would you think that?

ROSEMARY. You were so angry. That I forgot our anniversary.

GINA. Sure I was angry, but I wouldn't leave you for that. Yell at you, yes. Leave you, no. My promises mean something. But you, you were consoling yourself with a cigarette and another woman!

ROSEMARY. Louise isn't another woman.

GINA. She looks like one to me!

LOUISE. Gina, I'd like to explain. In the first place I'm not —

GINA. You! You're the one who got her to smoke a cigarette. I have nothing to say to you. If you had any sense of decency you'd just take your cigarettes and go.

ROSEMARY. She can't leave.

GINA. You're choosing her over me! After all the years we've spent together! Then I'm leaving! You can have your cigarettes and your new girlfriend. (*Starts for the door*)

LOUISE. No, I'll go.

ROSEMARY. But you can't . . .

LOUISE. Gina, if I could just borrow your jacket, I'll leave.

GINA. First you borrow my girlfriend! Now you want to borrow my jacket.

ROSEMARY. Wait a minute. Gina, please listen for a minute. (*Gina stands in doorway*) Louise was left in here in the doctor's office without her clothes. She can't leave because she doesn't have anything to wear. (*Louise takes off sheet she's been wearing as a shawl and begins folding it*)

GINA. You mean the doctor went home and left you here? But where are your clothes?

LOUISE. Locked up in that room over there.

138
▼

GINA. (*Goes to Louise*) You poor thing! They left you here with your clothes locked up! Rosemary, why didn't you break the door down? You're strong enough.

ROSEMARY. Of course I'm strong enough. But, I'm paid to protect this property, not destroy it.

GINA. Well, you could have lent her your jacket, Rosemary.

ROSEMARY. It's much too big for her.

GINA. To be so selfish, Rosemary. I can't believe it. I'm sure she wouldn't have cared if your jacket was too big. She just wanted to get out of here.

ROSEMARY. But, Gina, you gave me that jacket.

GINA. So?

ROSEMARY. It's ... I just didn't want anyone else —

LOUISE. Gina, Rosemary was really very nice to me. She kept me company.

GINA. You mean she got you to play cards with her.

LOUISE. And she kept trying to call you to ask you to bring some clothes for me. She was so worried when you didn't answer the phone.

GINA. (*To Rosemary*) You were?

ROSEMARY. Yeah, I was. I thought. ... Hey, Gina? (*Goes to Gina*) Forgive me? For forgetting our anniversary?

GINA. No kisses until you brush your teeth! You stink of smoke!

ROSEMARY. But I don't have a toothbrush with me!

GINA. Then you'll have to keep your distance until we get home. Serves you right for smoking.

ROSEMARY. Maybe I could go out and get a toothbrush.

LOUISE. I really should leave the two of you alone. Could I borrow your jacket, Gina? If you're going to be here in the morning when they come in you could wear my coat home.

GINA. Of course you can borrow my jacket. But you don't have to leave. I brought champagne for a party. Why don't you join us? As long as you agree not to smoke.

LOUISE. Well, thank you, but I don't want to intrude. And I've never had a drink without a cigarette. I don't know —

GINA. Well, you certainly can't smoke in a doctor's office. Not while I'm here! Rosemary, see if you can find another champagne glass.

ROSEMARY. Another champagne glass!

GINA. Well, honey, I'm sure you can find something.

ROSEMARY. All right, I'll try. (*Exits*)

LOUISE. I'm sorry to have caused trouble between you and Rosemary.

GINA. It wasn't you that caused the trouble.

LOUISE. Rosemary was so upset about forgetting your anniversary.

GINA. She told you it was our anniversary? Wow! I always told her she was too big to fit in that closet.

LOUISE. She said she wants to do something special with you. To make it up to you.

GINA. That's sweet, but I'm not going to hold my breath. Rosemary isn't too great about occasions.

LOUISE. I got that idea. I did offer to treat the two of you to a night at the Plaza. I'm staying there tonight because I don't have the keys to my apartment. But she said that she couldn't accept.

GINA. That was very nice of you. But she's right. We couldn't do that.

LOUISE. But I thought if you let me borrow your jacket and I put you two up in a room then you could bring my clothes there after the office opens. I'd just be repaying a favor with a favor.

GINA. You can have my jacket. That's O.K. It's not that cold out. And I have a shirt and sweater. You need something. You don't have to do anything for us. Really. (*A knocking sound is heard offstage*)

LOUISE. What's that?

GINA. Rosemary makes a lot of noise whenever she's looking for something.

LOUISE. When I mentioned the Plaza to Rosemary she said that she'd always wanted to go there.

GINA. She did?

LOUISE. She read the Eloise books when she was younger and she always wanted to see a room there.

GINA. I didn't know that.

LOUISE. So, if you want to reconsider. I'm sure you could talk her into it.

GINA. Well . . .

LOUISE. It would be my pleasure to be able to do something for the two of you. And I'd enjoy your company.

GINA. You're sure? (*Louise nods*) Then, we'll accept. It'll be fun.

MISS TATE. (*From offstage*) Is she here?

ROSEMARY. (*Offstage*) Well . . . yes . . . but, uh, she's with the doctor right now. Can I help you?

MISS TATE. (*Offstage*) She asked me to have some clothes delivered to her from Bergdorf's. Would you please —

LOUISE. (*Overlapping Miss Tate, to Gina*) Oh my God! It's Miss Tate. (*Takes a deep breath, decides, calls out to the hall*) It's all right, Rosemary, Miss Tate can come in.

GINA. Who's Miss Tate?

LOUISE. A saleslady from Bergdorf's (*Rosemary enters, Miss Tate behind*) Miss Tate, I can't tell you how much I appreciate you going to this trouble.

MISS TATE. Hello, Mrs. Penniman, it's good to see you. I selected some evening clothes for you. I hope you approve of my choice.

LOUISE. I'm sure I'll like the clothes you picked. You have such perfect taste.

MISS TATE. Thank you.

LOUISE. Thank you.

MISS TATE. It's quite all right.

LOUISE. As you can see I need them rather badly. I wasn't quite truthful over the phone.

MISS TATE. It's not necessary to explain.

LOUISE. I'm afraid I was forgotten by the doctor and her staff. Wearing only this gown. And my clothes are locked up. They're right in that closet over there, but I can't get at them.

MISS TATE. How dreadful for you.

LOUISE. At first it was, but . . . you know, it's been fun, actually. (*Pause*) How did you convince Bergdorf's to let me use my charge?

MISS TATE. Unfortunately, I wasn't able to do that.

LOUISE. Then how did you . . .

MISS TATE. I was so angry at them — I charged the clothes to my own account. You can repay me at your convenience.

LOUISE. I'm overwhelmed! Miss Tate, it was so kind of you to do that.

MISS TATE. It's my pleasure. You've always been very kind to me. But I didn't bring you a coat and it's quite chilly out.

LOUISE. I'll be fine, Miss Tate. (*Looks at clothes*) The clothes you picked out for me are beautiful, as always. And the top is nice and loose.

MISS TATE. Yes, well, I thought ...

LOUISE. You knew.

MISS TATE. Well, yes, in the dressing room you see ...

LOUISE. And you never said anything.

MISS TATE. I didn't like to intrude. (*Pause*) But I have been concerned. Are you all right? I mean, your visit to the doctor ...

LOUISE. My visit was routine. A checkup. Oh dear, I'm being awfully rude. Miss Tate this is Rosemary and this is Gina. Miss Tate I don't know your first name and I don't know Rosemary and Gina's last name.

GINA. Rosemary and I don't have the same last name, although I wouldn't mind.

ROSEMARY. Gina!

GINA. But it couldn't be Rosemary's. I'd rather not have the last name Gertz.

ROSEMARY. Gina!

MISS TATE. Rosemary, Gina, my name is Elvira. (*Rosemary and Gina shake hands, say "Glad to meet you," etc.*) Are you two young ladies special friends? A couple?

ROSEMARY. Well ...

GINA. Yes, and it's our anniversary. We've been together ten years.

ROSEMARY. Gina, I'm sure Miss Tate wouldn't understand ...

MISS TATE. Of course I do. Congratulations, Gina, Rosemary!

GINA. Thank you.

ROSEMARY. You're not shocked?

MISS TATE. Oh goodness, no. Two young ladies loving each other. Why should I be?

ROSEMARY. Well, um ... my parents would be.

MISS TATE. Well, they're very silly, then. I think you two are very sweet together.

GINA. Miss Tate is a modern woman.

MISS TATE. Oh dear me, no. But my special friend and I celebrated thirty-eight anniversaries together before she passed.

ROSEMARY. She?

MISS TATE. Yes, she. Oh dear, it seems so odd to say it finally. I must confess we weren't as brave as you young people. We never celebrated publicly. We never ... well, I'm afraid we let ourselves be viewed as "old maids."

ROSEMARY. But you're ... I mean you look just like my Aunt Sally ...

MISS TATE. My dear, your generation didn't invent love between women. You're just more open about it.

GINA. (*Looking at Rosemary*) Some of us are. (*To Miss Tate*) Thirty-eight years! You must miss her.

MISS TATE. I do. Very much. But, life goes on. Oh dear, that sounds so trite. But it is true.

LOUISE. Yes, it is.

MISS TATE. Cecile would have been so delighted to see you youngsters enjoying life together.

LOUISE. All these years I've known you and I never knew.

MISS TATE. No one did. We were very private.

LOUISE. I'm sorry you lost your ... you lost Cecile. She was very lucky to have spent her life with you.

MISS TATE. Thank you.

GINA. Miss Tate, Elvira, would you do us the honor of joining our party? I brought champagne so we could celebrate. Louise is going to stay until Rosemary gets off work. Then we're going with Louise to the Plaza.

ROSEMARY. We're what?

GINA. Louise is treating us to a night at the Plaza.

ROSEMARY. But we can't possibly —

GINA. Louise and I have discussed it. We're going.

MISS TATE. (*To Rosemary*) If I were you, young lady, I'd just accept the inevitability of going to the Plaza and enjoy it.

LOUISE. Miss Tate ...

143
▼

MISS TATE. Please call me Elvira.

LOUISE. Only if you'll call me Louise. (*Miss Tate nods*) Elvira, I'm going to try on these lovely clothes. You'll stay to tell me how I look in them, won't you?

MISS TATE. Of course. I wouldn't miss it.

GINA. And you'll have some champagne, won't you?

MISS TATE. Well, just a taste. To help you celebrate. (*Louise exits to bathroom. Miss Tate goes to closet and digs in her purse*)

GINA. Rosemary, did you find a champagne glass?

ROSEMARY. No, I didn't find a champagne glass. I didn't find anything.

GINA. Did you really look?

ROSEMARY. Yes, I really looked.

GINA. (*Yells offstage*) Louise, are there any glasses or cups in there?

LOUISE. (*From offstage*) I don't see any. Come in and look. (*Gina enters bathroom*)

MISS TATE. I believe that I've managed to open the door. Now Louise will have her coat. It's so chilly out. (*She opens the door to the closet*)

ROSEMARY. How did you do that? It was locked. I tried it. Louise tried it.

MISS TATE. I just slid in a credit card.

ROSEMARY. Where did you learn that?

MISS TATE. I'm always forgetting my keys. My nephew Randolph taught me how to do it. The skill has been very helpful. (*Notices cards*) Did I interrupt a card game?

ROSEMARY. Louise and I were playing gin rummy before Gina got here.

MISS TATE. I do enjoy a good game of gin, but I must confess that my favorite game is poker. Lately it's become so difficult to find other serious poker players.

ROSEMARY. You play poker?

MISS TATE. Not as much as I'd like to. Unfortunately most ladies of my generation are bridge and canasta players. Such slow fussy games, don't you think?

ROSEMARY. I hate bridge! So you're a poker player. Do you play those games with all the wild cards like Woolworth and so on?

MISS TATE. Absolutely not! Five-card stud, five-card draw, real poker.

ROSEMARY. Miss Tate, Elvira, you are my kind of woman! What do you say we talk those two into a couple of hands? I was losing that damned gin game to Louise anyway.

MISS TATE. I will play poker with you only if you agree to watch your language.

ROSEMARY. You mean I can't swear during a poker game?

MISS TATE. It will be an excellent discipline for you.

ROSEMARY. All right, all right.

GINA. (*Enters with two urine sample cups*) These were all I could find. I promise they're never been used. See, plastic wrappers. (*Rosemary is shuffling cards*) What are you doing?

ROSEMARY. Elvira here is a poker player. We're going to play a few hands.

GINA. I thought we were going to celebrate our anniversary.

ROSEMARY. We'll all play.

GINA. But you always get mad at me and call me stupid when we play together.

ROSEMARY. That's just when we play gin. Please, honey, just a couple of hands?

MISS TATE. We won't play if Gina would rather not. After all it is your anniversary.

GINA. I don't mind as long as Rosemary doesn't yell at me.

ROSEMARY. (*To Miss Tate*) You know what she does in gin? She saves all the face cards.

GINA. They're prettier. The number cards are boring.

LOUISE. (*Entering in new outfit*) Ta-da!

ROSEMARY. Holy shit! You look fantastic!

MISS TATE. Watch your language, young lady! You do look lovely Louise.

GINA. Wow! It's a shame you're a breeder. A beautiful woman like you.

LOUISE. A breeder?

ROSEMARY. She means that you're a hopeless heterosexual. It's not a very nice word though.

GINA. I didn't mean it like that.

LOUISE. I know you didn't.

MISS TATE. Breeder. I've never heard that term. I rather like it.

LOUISE. I feel a little left out. Being the only ...

GINA. That's all right, Louise, some of my best friends are breeders. I just wouldn't want my daughter to marry one. Anyway, you can explain to us about what it is men and women do together. I've never been able to figure it out.

MISS TATE. That really won't be necessary, Louise.

LOUISE. (*Notices the open closet door*) The closet door's open!

MISS TATE. Yes, I opened it for you.

LOUISE. How in the world did you manage?

MISS TATE. I wanted you to have your coat.

ROSEMARY. She used a credit card, can you believe it?

LOUISE. What?

ROSEMARY. Yeah, she just slid in a credit card.

LOUISE. (*Goes to closet. Brings out coat and purse*) Miss Tate, you are a woman of many talents.

GINA. Don't even think of getting out your cigarettes! (*Approaches Louise*) Louise, what a beautiful coat!

LOUISE. Thank you. (*Gina is stroking the coat*) Would you like to try it on?

GINA. I couldn't. I'd be afraid ...

LOUISE. I'd love to see how you look in it.

GINA. Well, if you don't mind ...

LOUISE. Not at all.

GINA. (*Puts on the coat, twirls around in it*) What do you think?

MISS TATE. You look lovely, my dear.

GINA. I feel so elegant. Can I just wear it for a while? If I'm very careful? Do you mind?

LOUISE. Please do.

ROSEMARY. So are we going to play cards or not? (*She holds up a bottle of aspirin*) We can use these for chips.

MISS TATE. Oh, I have several rolls of pennies in my purse.

ROSEMARY. Always ready for a poker game?

MISS TATE. No, I learned that trick in my self-defense course. With a few rolls of pennies at the bottom my purse makes a nice cosh. (*She gets out the pennies. Rosemary digs in her pocket for money and buys two rolls from Miss Tate, hands one to Gina*)

ROSEMARY. Elvira, you're full of surprises.

GINA. Louise, we're going to play some poker. Do you play?

LOUISE. Not really. I've played blackjack. (*Louise goes in her purse for money to buy a roll of pennies*)

ROSEMARY. Don't worry, you'll pick it up. (*To Miss Tate*) This woman is the best card player I've ever met. She was beating me in gin. O.K., let's cut for deal.

GINA. (*Passing around champagne*) First let's have a toast.

MISS TATE. To Gina and Rosemary on their anniversary. May they have many more.

GINA. To Miss Tate, a grand old dyke.

ROSEMARY. To Louise, the best card player east of the Mississippi!

LOUISE. To friends.

ROSEMARY. (*Looking at Louise*) To many more card games. (*Louise looks at Rosemary acknowledging the promise of continuing friendship*) So let's play. Cut for deal. (*They cut. Show cards*) It's Gina's deal.

GINA. (*Picks up deck of cards and shuffles inexpertly*) O.K., I made up a new game. It's called Honeymoon. Sixes and nines are both wild, but only if they're together in your hand. And, let's see, we have to have at least one more wild card ... I know, queens. Oh, and a pair of queens beats a straight. (*Rosemary starts to comment, then closes her mouth*)

A Quiet End

■

BY

ROBIN SWADOS

▼

For Earl Graham, with infinite gratitude,
and in memory of Roger (1944–1983);
Randy (1947–1985); and David (1952–1987)

A Quiet End

I began to write *A Quiet End* just after I turned thirty. In spite of an inert acting career — one I had trained for and pursued professionally for nearly fifteen years — I harbored no particular aspirations as a writer, a career move I viewed as somewhat akin to leaping from the frying pan into the fire, financially if not artistically.

And yet something compelled me to write. My play began less as a deliberate decision on my part to veer from one career into another than as an attempt to give voice, in some fashion, to early warning signals that a number of things were seriously amiss in the world, not in the easily recognizable sense of war or famine or impending ecological disaster, but in a far more insidious and personally devastating way: my friends began to die. They died not in the way one might expect, either naturally (my grandfather, for example, at age ninety-one) or not (my father, for another, of a brain aneurysm, at age fifty-two). However traumatic my father's death may have proved to me (I still attempt, some twenty years later, to comprehend why, at the age of nineteen, I was robbed of a parent) it nevertheless seemed, at least on a purely intellectual level, more "comprehensible" to me than the innumerable ones that succeeded it barely a decade later: robust, vital contemporaries of mine, rapidly and inexplicably disintegrating into hollow shells of their former selves, valiantly waging personal war after personal war against nausea, diarrhea, incredible weight loss, painful body sores, even dementia. The AIDS crisis had begun.

Though over the course of the ensuing decade it would balloon into an international issue of staggering social and political significance, for me it had its earliest and most profound effect on an almost purely personal level. I was living in Los Angeles in the summer of 1983 when two events occurred that were, in many ways, to change my life forever. First, I was approached by the AIDS Project L.A., one of the earliest organizations dedicated to bettering the lives of people with the disease, and asked to contribute any clothing or other items I might have in an attempt to set up and support three men in a Hollywood apartment. They were all young; they had all been abandoned by their families; and they all had AIDS. For all I knew they may have had nothing more in common than this — their own suddenly immediate mortality. At the same time, I learned that my closest friend, a New York actor, had contracted the virus and was in rapidly deteriorating physical condition. I discovered this on a visit home to my family in Manhattan on the occasion of my thirtieth birthday. It had been less than six months since I had last seen Roger. The previous Christmas he had appeared to be in perfect health — the same handsome, dashing figure I had known since our college days. Now, however, his voice was reduced to a whisper, and his body had withered to rail-thin. We spent that week together, he and I, walking to the nearest bench, then resting; walking to another bench, sitting under another tree, talking, resting, then talking some more. Typically, his concerns focused less on himself than on the lives of those around him. "Who will take care of my dogs?" he asked me. "Is there someone to whom I might give my collection of plays?"

It was these things — the bits and pieces of which any one life is composed — that most concerned Roger; and it was these things, in turn, that eventually formed the basis of my play.

Those two events, thousands of miles apart geographically, served as the initial inspiration for *A Quiet End*. I never met the three men in that Hollywood apartment, and when six months later Roger finally succumbed to AIDS-related pneumonia, I put the play away, too pained by the immediacy of the situation to continue it. One year later, my acting career finally behind me, back in my native New York, and urged by a friend to pick up where I had left off, I resumed writing *A Quiet End* in earnest, basing each of the roles on memories I had of people I had known at various points in my life. Over the course of the play's gestation, one of them — and in certain ways, all of them — turned out to be me. Unlike Roger, I had somehow managed to avoid ever waiting on tables throughout my acting career, just as he had managed to escape the drudgery *I* endured supporting myself as a typist in one anonymous office after another. I was deeply frustrated and angry at my lack of success as an actor, a frustration I shared with Roger over the course of many evenings of conversation and games of Scrabble. And though I had spent the better part of my childhood and adolescence training to be a pianist, I had never really found what I considered to be a suitable outlet for my favorite avocation — composing — until the character of Billy walked on stage in my play, heard the same piano across the hall I'd heard in my *own* apartment, and thus began to come to life for me, sometimes through words, sometimes through music, even as I struggled to create him.

My final year in Los Angeles, which I spent working in television production, only served to solidify earlier impressions I'd had that Hollywood was, arguably, the most homophobic place in America in which to pursue a career in show business, whichever side of the camera one happened to work on. These fears, nearly always repressed by virtue of sheer necessity, served in turn as the source of inspiration for the character of Jason, a man trapped in both his public *and* private life. And though many of the character traits that formed his psychological makeup stemmed from my own experience, from a purely physical standpoint I had always envisioned the role being played by an actor whose looks bordered on a kind of "heroic beauty," for lack of a better phrase. This was a self-image I most assuredly did not possess myself; on the contrary, I had written the role specifically for a neighbor of mine in Santa Monica, an actor whose work I knew and admired. One year later, as casting was about to begin for the play's premiere in Long Beach, California, I asked him to read the script. He confessed that he was suffering, ironically, not from AIDS, but rather from aplastic anemia, a rare and fatal disease that robs the body of its bone marrow and subsequently its ability to ward off infection. David died in 1987, shortly after his thirty-fifth birthday.

As for Max, there is little to say but that he very early on became the "conscience" of the play, though whether by accident or design I am not certain I will ever know.

And so it was that the men of *A Quiet End* began to crystallize in my mind. Since its premiere in January 1986, the play has undergone many changes, as has the nature of the AIDS epidemic itself. Its basic premise, however, remains intact. I consider it now, as I did at the outset, when Billy, Tony, and Max first sat down together to play a game of Scrabble, to be essentially a story of love and commitment; of learning to care more about others than we do about ourselves; and of suddenly finding courage in times of trouble.

Since the play's completion, thousands more have died of AIDS — men and women; children and infants; the rich and famous; the poor and forgotten. Of the quartet of real-life counterparts I attempted to bring to theatrical life in *A Quiet End*, I remain, now, the sole survivor.

Robin Swados

A Quiet End opened off Broadway at Theatre Off Park on May 29, 1990. It was produced by Albert Harris, by arrangement with Richard Norton and Ted Snowdon. It was directed by Tony Giordano; the scenery was by Philipp Jung; the costumes were by David Murin; the lighting was by Dennis Parichy; the sound was by Tony Meola; and the original piano music was composed and performed by Mr. Swados. The cast, in order of appearance, was as follows:

MAX .... Lonny Price

TONY .... Philip Coccioletti

BILLY .... Jordan Mott

DOCTOR .... Paul Milikin

JASON .... Rob Gomes

The production history of the play is as follows: It was first presented by Shashin Desai as the inaugural production of the International City Theatre in Long Beach, California, on January

17, 1986. It was directed by Jules Aaron; the scenery was by J. L. White; the costumes were by Cathy A. Crane; and the lighting and sound was by Mario Mariotta. The cast, in order of appearance, was as follows:

MAX .... Fred Bishop

TONY .... Randolph Powell

BILLY .... Bruce Wieland

DOCTOR .... David Herman

JASON .... Thomas Jackson

The British premiere of the play was presented by Buddy Dalton at the Offstage Theatre, London, on February 4, 1986. It was directed by Noel Greig; the scenery and costumes were by Caroline Burgess; and the lighting was by Bob Lyons. The cast, in order of appearance, was as follows:

MAX .... Peter Whitman

TONY .... Thom Booker

BILLY .... Zane Stanley

DOCTOR .... Bob Lyons

JASON .... Erick-Ray Evans

The play was subsequently presented by Raphael Brandow at the American Repertory Theatre, Amsterdam, Holland, on September 17, 1986. It was directed by Mr. Swados; the scenery and costumes were by Ries Fess; and the lighting was by Nick Snaas. The cast, in order of appearance, was as follows:

MAX .... David Swatling

TONY .... Tony Edridge

BILLY .... Steve Thomas

DOCTOR .... John Kingsbury

JASON .... Michael Krass

Steven Woolf next presented the play at the Repertory Theatre of St. Louis on October 30, 1987. It was directed by Sam Blackwell; the scenery was by Mel Dickerson; the costumes were by Jim Buff; and the lighting was by Mark Wilson. The cast, in order of appearance, was as follows:

MAX .... Jack Kenny

TONY .... Tony Hoylen

BILLY .... Bruce Wieland

DOCTOR .... Joe Proctor

JASON .... Jack Koenig

CHARACTERS

MAX . . . . early 30s

TONY . . . . late 30s

BILLY . . . . late 20s

JASON . . . . early 30s

DOCTOR . . . . mid 50s (voice only)

PLACE

The action takes place in an apartment on Manhattan's Upper West Side.

TIME

Act 1: Early winter, a few years ago. Evening.

Act 2, scene 1: Two months later. Middle of the night.

Act 2, scene 2: Three days later. Early afternoon.

Act 2, scene 3: A day shortly thereafter. Late morning.

Act 2, scene 4: Several months later.

ACT I

COMPLETE darkness. Then we hear the opening strains of Billy's music playing. At the conclusion of the music, the lights come up on the stage to reveal the living room of a run-down apartment on one of the worst streets in Manhattan's otherwise rapidly gentrifying Upper West Side. It has been furnished with a collection of things donated from various sources, and if anything matches, it is purely by accident. The furniture has the look of "Salvation Army" written all over it — stuff that no one wanted any more. In spite of this, the place has been put together with a certain care and is neat and clean, if not exactly cheery.

Upstage, one can see part of the kitchen which extends into the living room: a long counter, somewhat resembling a bar, in front of which one can sit on tall stools. Placed atop the counter are a few things: an old toaster, circa 1958; a small electric clock; a plug-in radio.

Two doors, side by side, lead to two bedrooms. An upstage center door is the entrance to the apartment; another opens into a bathroom, in which a toilet can be seen. A window looks out onto the street.

Tony is seated on the sofa, staring down at a Scrabble board set up for three players, trying to think of a word. It is clear that he has been having no luck. Max stands upstage, staring out of the living room window onto the street.

MAX. Suddenly I get this image in my head. It all begins here, in a very small way, in this apartment, on this night, where I stand patiently waiting. (*He turns to face Tony, who responds with a glare when appropriate, which is most of the time*) Billy's gone for groceries. Shortly thereafter I leave the apartment and go shopping at Bloomingdale's, since they're open late. I look around — I find nothing I like — I return to the apartment. More time passes. (*A killer look from Tony*) The neighborhood improves. Once-shabby entryways are replaced with elegant facades. Uniformed doormen politely tip their hats as we come and go. (*Pause*) Miracles are accomplished in the fields of science and medicine. (*Pause*) Peace comes to the Middle East. (*Pause*) The world becomes a better, more complex and frightening place. It's a panoramic vista of an entire generation in transition and flux, and it all happens in the time it takes you to make one word. (*Pause. Tony almost places a tile on the board, then rethinks his move yet again*) And that's being optimistic. (*Max exits to the upstage bedroom. From the bedroom*) Where did you say they were?

TONY. Above the dresser. On top.

MAX. (*Offstage; much effort in his voice*) Christ — what am I — a gazelle? God — I mean — I can barely reach —

TONY. You want me to get them? (*There's a small crash offstage*)

MAX. (*Offstage*) No — it's O.K. — I got it. (*Max enters from one of the bedrooms with a couple of blankets, some sheets, and a pillow, and places them out of the way on a table behind the couch. He looks back toward the bedroom*) Wow, is that ugly.

TONY. Hmmmn?

MAX. That lamp. I still can't get over it. It's hideous. I didn't expect high tech, but I mean, *look* at it. Those big, purple grapes at the base — and those breasts at the top — my God! Someone actually designed that! (*Pause. He keeps looking at it*) You know ... if you turned it upside down, you might have something. (*Pause*) Did you do your word yet?

TONY. I'm working on it, professor. Did you take your medicine?

MAX. I was just about to — doctor. You seem to know my schedule better than I do. (*He exits to the bathroom for a moment, then returns with a prescription bottle of liquid. He's studying the label and stops in his tracks*) Wait a minute, this isn't mine. (*He exits again to the bathroom and returns almost immediately with another bottle, nearly identical to the previous one*) This is mine. (*Holding up the bottle*) This stuff is positively evil.

TONY. What is it? (*Max tosses the bottle to Tony*) Oh yeah. This really is awful. Like being on the down part of a roller coaster. (*He tosses the bottle back to Max*)

MAX. Four times a day. Why can't they make it stronger, so you only have to take it twice? Or *really* strong, so you could just take one slug in the morning and be done with it?

TONY. Because as soon as you woke up you'd pass out.

MAX. I do anyway. (*He goes and gets a spoon from behind the counter*) I never liked roller coasters. Not even when I was a kid. (*He takes a spoonful of medicine, grimacing*) They made me sick then and they make me sick now. (*The front door opens, and Billy enters, wearing a winter coat and scarf and carrying a grocery bag with a quart of milk in it. As he closes the door behind him, he leans forward with his head against the door, breathing heavily and looking utterly exhausted*) Did you get it? (*Billy nods*) Is it fresh? (*Billy nods again*) Are you O.K.? (*Billy shakes his head no, still catching his breath, and holds the bag out for Max to take, which he does, taking the milk out of the bag*)

TONY. How is it out?

BILLY. (*Deliberately*) Very cold. (*Removing his coat, still very much out of breath*) Look at me. (*Referring to the stairs he has just climbed*) One flight. You're looking at a runner, can you believe that?

TONY. (*Delighted to have found an ally*) I didn't know. D'ja do a lot?

BILLY. Three, maybe four miles a day.

MAX. God. I don't walk that much.

TONY. I did about ten. Twelve on the weekends.

MAX. Two runners?

TONY. It was kind of a religious thing with me.

MAX. Don't you get those pains — you know, where you have to squeeze your side?

TONY. That goes away. It's in your head.

MAX. It seems to me I always felt it in my waist. Anyway, when did you have the time?

TONY. I'm an actor, remember?

MAX. Oh, well, that explains it.

TONY. I like to run before an audition. It revs me up and calms me down at the same time — you know what I mean?

MAX. No.   (*Together*)   BILLY. Yeah.

BILLY. You ever run, Max? (*Max laughs*) Did you?

MAX. Never. In high school, maybe — when forced. (*Pause*) I don't remember.

BILLY. What do you do for exercise?

MAX. I do nothing. Never been sick a day in my life. (*Referring to the milk*) You want this now?

BILLY. Thanks. (*Max exits into the kitchen with the milk. Billy goes to the radio and turns it on. Jazz music can be heard. He goes to the window, right of kitchen*) You know, I kind of like this place. The view's not bad. If you look out here and turn your head a little you can almost see — (*Max returns with a glass of milk, which he hands to Billy*)

MAX. (*Interrupting him*) Here.

BILLY. Thanks. (*He sits on a stool in front of the counter and starts to gulp the milk down*)

MAX. (*Coddling*) Slowly. Slowly.

BILLY. Sorry. (*He puts the milk down*) It's dumb. I should have bought it this morning, instead of running out in the dark. I'm frozen. (*He looks over at Tony. To Max*) Did he go yet? (*Exasperated, Max gestures toward Tony with his arm, wordlessly: "As you see — no"*) Oh boy. It's gonna be a long night.

MAX. (*Referring to the radio*) Would you mind terribly if I turned it down — or off — just for a while?

BILLY. No. Sure. (*Max quickly and with great relief turns off the radio*) Go ahead. Just a little something to make me feel at home.

MAX. I didn't know they played jazz in Idaho.

BILLY. (*After a beat*) I'm from Iowa.

MAX. Sorry. (*Pause*) Middle America!

BILLY. That's me. Smack dab in the center.

MAX. Is jazz very popular there?

BILLY. Everywhere!

MAX. I'm referring to Iowa in particular. (*The next three speeches overlap as closely as possible*)

BILLY. Oh, sure. There really is no "Iowa music" —

MAX. No, I wouldn't imagine so —

BILLY. — so we have to look elsewhere for cultural fulfillment. (*Pause*) You like jazz?

MAX. (*Avoiding the issue*) I'm sorry — you were saying something before — I interrupted you —

BILLY. What?

MAX. Just now. By the window. You were saying something.

BILLY. Oh, I said the view isn't bad.

MAX. (*Goes to the window, looking out. Shrugging*) It's a view.

BILLY. It's not Central Park.

MAX. It certainly isn't.

BILLY. But it's not a brick wall, either.

MAX. No, it's many brick walls. At a distance. That's how you'd describe it anywhere else. In New York, it's called a view.

BILLY. You don't like the city?

MAX. I didn't mean it to sound like that. Actually, if you really want to know, I wouldn't live anywhere else. I came here a long time ago. I discovered everything here. I'll die here. (*Points to window*) But this is not the greatest view I've ever seen. (*Looking around him*) Neither is this apartment. (*Before Billy can protest*) I know. The project more than makes up for its lack of taste with its boundless displays of generosity.

BILLY. (*Defensive*) I, for one, am happy to be here.

MAX. As an alternative to the street, it's magnificent. (*Looking around him*) All these beautiful things! (*Pause*) Sorry. After food, shelter, and clothing, I wouldn't imagine interior design is high on the project's list of priorities.

BILLY. (*Mocking Max's earlier words*) No, I wouldn't imagine so —

MAX. (*Responding in kind*) — so I'll just have to look elsewhere for cultural fulfillment. I suppose they did what they could. I've no right to kvetch.

BILLY. (*Pronounces "kvetch" badly*) It's O.K. You can k-vetch if you want to.

MAX. (*Laughing*) God, you're such a WASP!

BILLY. I'm not, actually.

MAX. Oh no?

BILLY. No. I was born Catholic.

TONY. (*Still hard at work*) Me too.

MAX. Two Catholics?

BILLY. But I'm not really much of anything now.

MAX. Do you go to church?

BILLY. No.

MAX. Do you believe in God?

BILLY. Uh ... yeah. Kind of.

MAX. What do you mean, "kind of"? Either you do or you don't.

BILLY. I do sometimes.

MAX. Even now?

BILLY. Especially now.

MAX. Well ... hallelujah. That's all I have to say. Hallelujah, brother.

BILLY. (*Straightforward*) I take it you don't believe in God.

MAX. I believe in nothing. Except myself. I believe in my power to survive. That's all.

BILLY. Even now? (*Silence. Billy goes and sits down on the couch, joining Tony. He resumes looking at his letters for the game*)

MAX. Who gets the couch tonight?

TONY. My aching back tells me it's you. (*To Billy*) Or you?

BILLY. (*Shaking his head*) Right the first time.

MAX. That's what I was afraid of. I knew there had to be some reason I felt compelled to go mountain-climbing in the bedroom. A mystic search for sheets!

BILLY. It's only fair.

MAX. There is no fair. Just as there is no God.

BILLY. (*Bristling*) If you can think of a more suitable arrangement, I'm certainly open to discussion.

MAX. No, no, no. If there's one thing I hate, it's open discussion. You're right. This is what we agreed upon. (*Pause. Now Max joins Tony and Billy in the chair by the couch*) You see? I can be a very good person.

BILLY. Yes, I can see that. This is not freshman year at the dorm, in case you hadn't noticed.

MAX. I didn't know you went to college.

BILLY. I didn't. But I've heard about it, and I gather it is nothing like this. We really have to live here.

MAX. I know. (*Almost under his breath*) Shit. (*He picks up his letters and studies them, then turns to Tony, pleading with him to move*)

Tony — please?

TONY. (*Defensively*) All right, all right!

BILLY. It doesn't have to be brilliant. It doesn't even have to be good. Just put *some*thing down.

TONY. (*Pressured*) Gimme a second, wouldja?

MAX. (*Totally out of patience*) Oh God. (*To Billy*) Look, next time, ask me to play when he's out somewhere.

BILLY. He's never out.

TONY. Screw you guys! I'm new to this.

MAX. Obviously.

TONY. (*Mad now*) Fuck. O.K. (*Putting four letters down on the board*) Here. You want me to put *some*thing down? I'm putting *some*thing down. (*Billy and Max "leap into action," studying the new word like true veterans of the game*)

BILLY. That's not something. That's just any old thing.

MAX. (*Quoting Tony's word*) "Punt." (*Silence. They all look at each other*)

TONY. What's wrong with that?

MAX. "Punt"? For this I waited forty-five minutes?

TONY. Gimme a break, wouldja? It's a good word.

BILLY. Well, I wouldn't go so far as to call it *good* —

MAX. "Mediocre," maybe, but not "good." Try "pathetic."

TONY. Snobs — you're just total snobs —

BILLY. I am not.

MAX. *I* am.

TONY. Yeah — you are. (*To Billy*) How many points did I get? (*To Max*) You're just pissed 'cause you never would have thought of "punt" yourself.

MAX. You're right. I wouldn't have. How ever did it come to mind? Your old football days?

TONY. Maybe. Probably. Yeah. How does anything come to mind? From your past experience.

BILLY. (*Keeping score*) Fourteen. (*He writes it down on a pad*) My turn.

MAX. (*To Tony*) Your past experience is very weird, anyway.

TONY. Yeah? How?

MAX. (*With great disdain*) Football?

TONY. What about it?

MAX. How could you have played *football*, for God's sake?

TONY. What the hell did you want me to play in high school? Backgammon?

MAX. No, but I mean, come *on*. It's so — base.

TONY. You don't know the first thing about it.

BILLY. (*Hard at work; to both*) Hey — please? I can't think. (*They ignore him completely*)

MAX. (*Ongoing*) So animalistic!

TONY. Yeah, like a leopard. Graceful.

MAX. Graceful, yet! I think I'm going to throw up.

BILLY. Just don't do it here.

TONY. (*To Max*) You don't like football because you don't understand it, that's all.

MAX. I understand it perfectly well.

TONY. Did you ever play it?

MAX. (*Incredulously*) Me?

TONY. You see?

MAX. You don't have to play a game to understand it.

TONY. Why don't you explain it to me then. Gimme all the fine points.

MAX. (*Shrugging*) There aren't any. (*Pause*) All right. There are a bunch of guys — one team and another team — and they all stand in two lines — sorry, *squat* in two lines — *glaring* at each other while one guy on one of the teams calls out a bunch of things.

TONY. "Things"?

MAX. Secret things, like "hut" and "forty-nine" and "Marjorie."

TONY. (*Cringing*) Jesus.

MAX. Then, on one of those secret words, one team lunges into the other team and all these men push and shove each other and fall into a big pile. (*Tony's head is in his hands*) Now, let me backtrack.

BILLY. Must you?

MAX. You just do your word. (*Resuming*) The man who calls out all the secret words has his hands between another man's legs —

BILLY. I always liked that part.

MAX. — and the man whose legs the other man's hands are between passes the ball to him — an obviously Freudian gesture — and while all the other men are pushing and shoving each other, the man with the ball throws it to *another* man — which I find really dumb —

TONY. Why?

MAX. What do you mean, "why"? It's unnecessary. (*Tony gives a flabbergasted laugh*) I mean, why doesn't he just take the ball to the other end of the field himself?

BILLY. (*Puts down a word; counting his score*) Thirty-two, thirty-three, thirty-four —

TONY. Thirty-four?

BILLY. — times two ... sixty-eight.

TONY. Oh man, I don't stand a chance with you guys. What'd you do?

BILLY. "Quirk."

MAX. (*Nonchalant*) Nice word.

TONY. "Nice"!

MAX. Anyway, when one of the men finally gets the ball to the other end of the field, they score points, and whoever scores more points wins the game. It's really quite simple. (*He begins studying his letters*)

BILLY. Actually, I have to confess I kind of like football.

MAX. Shame on you.

BILLY. Not because I understand it —

TONY. Unlike some people we know.

BILLY. No, I just think it's kind of sexy.

TONY. It is sexy.

MAX. The truth comes out — so to speak.

TONY. I don't even want to talk to you!

BILLY. I mean, football players are so *big*. They're like cartoons. Huge shoulders, enormous chests, great big thighs ... (*To Tony*) You're right, by the way. It is graceful.

MAX. Disgraceful, you mean. Although I suppose in slow motion just about anything can look good. Even praying. (*He goes into extreme slow motion, vocally and physically, looking upward toward God*) We are grateful, dear Father — (*Back to normal. Acidly*) — for *nothing*. (*To Tony*) Really graceful.

TONY. You're a jerk. Also disrespectful.

MAX. Oh, I'm so sorry! For some ungodly reason, I'm always

166
▼

forgetting there's a Good Lord hovering above us somewhere in the heavens. Now there's a mystery I'd like to see solved ... how someone purported to be so magnanimous in his beatitude can be so completely unavailable for even a simple chat. I mean, *where is this man?*

TONY. (*Simply*) He can't be seen. (*Max is about to renew his argument*)

BILLY. (*Leaping in*) I like to fantasize about football players. All those clothes to take off ... all that padding ... all those strings to untie ... and just when you think you've gotten down to nothing, there's still more to go. (*Dreamily*) Some piece of plastic, or a strap.

MAX. (*Putting down a word; grudgingly*) Twenty.

BILLY. (*Looking*) That's all?

MAX. I know it's shit, but there's nothing to do. (*Referring to Tony*) It's all *his* fault. (*To Tony*) You put "punt" there ... you closed off the whole upper right hand side of the board!

TONY. (*Delighted*) Gosh, I'm really sorry!

MAX. And you wanted to be an actor? Funny, I don't believe a thing you say.

TONY. Want to be an actor.

MAX. That's what I said.

TONY. No you didn't. You said "wanted." (*Pause*) The word is "want."

MAX. (*Completely ashamed*) All right. You *want* to be an actor. (*To Billy*) Touchy, isn't he? (*Silence. Really dead silence. None of them moves. Finally this is broken by the faint sounds of notes being struck randomly on the upper sections of a piano keyboard, as made by a child. This comes from an apartment across the hall. Finally Tony gets up, holding his stomach*)

TONY. God, I feel awful. (*He goes to get a prescription bottle of liquid from the counter. From across the hall, the piano plunking continues for a second; then a woman's voice: "Brian, honey, don't!" Silence, followed by a baby's crying*)

BILLY. (*To Tony*) Are you O.K.?

TONY. (*Pouring medicine into a spoon, swallowing it*) I'll survive.

BILLY. (*Almost to himself*) Did you hear that piano?

MAX. (*To Tony; genuinely*) What can I do?

TONY. (*Not an attack; matter-of-factly*) You can shut up, Max. You can just shut the fuck up. (*To Billy*) Mind if I lie down on your bed?

BILLY. No — sure — go ahead. (*Tony exits*) Call if you need anything.

TONY. (*Offstage*) Yeah. (*Silence. The baby's crying can still be heard but is subsiding rapidly. Billy gets up, goes to the front door and listens*)

BILLY. Did you hear that? There's a piano in the apartment across the hall.

MAX. There's also a baby in the apartment across the hall. (*He crosses to Tony's bedroom door. Billy opens the front door a few inches, looking out*)

BILLY. The door's open.

MAX. (*At the bedroom door*) What's the matter with the bed *I* slept on?

BILLY. When's the last time you made it? (*He turns back to his view of the hall and makes faces at the baby*) Hi — hello — hi there —

MAX. Probably doesn't want to catch anything he couldn't shake off . . . like a severe case of prolixity.

BILLY. Prolixity?

MAX. (*Coming back to the center of the room*) Words. Too many words. I was stricken with it in my youth and suffer chronic attacks from time to time.

BILLY. (*To the baby's mother, who is taking it back inside*) Good evening, how are you? (*To the baby, waving*) Bye — see ya — (*He closes the door and rejoins Max*) Are you feeling sorry for yourself? (*Max takes a deep breath, sighs*) Come on, Max . . . he's upset.

MAX. I'm allowed, once in a while. Am I really such a rotten person?

BILLY. What do you want, Max? A list of your "Positive Qualities"? He's not angry at you. He's just angry.

MAX. I hate football, I really do!

BILLY. Football's got nothing to do with it, Max.

MAX. (*Oblivious again*) What? (*Then continuing*) No, but he really has no idea. Do you know why I never learned to play baseball?

BILLY. I give up. Anyway, I thought it was football we were —

MAX. Wait. I hate baseball too. Do you remember how they would stand you all up in a line, side by side, at the beginning of class, like some sort of army boot camp?

BILLY. (*Wearily hearing him out*) I remember.

MAX. Well, then they'd choose two captains — talk about big men! These guys looked like they belonged in a zoo somewhere, with the brains to match. Then came the "Assignment of Positions" — first to their friends; then to *their* friends; and finally to the few bits of detritus dangling at the end of the line — and I was always the last to be chosen. But always! Bottom of the barrel — the dregs! And whichever team had to take me would let out this unanimous groan of — what? — disapproval — disappointment — *despair* — at the *tragedy* they'd been subjected to: "Schechter's on our team!" Which was totally ironic, of course, because all I ever did was stand in outfield right —

BILLY. (*Correcting him*) Right field.

MAX. (*Flustered*) — right field — wrong field — whatever — reading a book. Nancy Drew, or the Hardy Boys. And I never made it to bat, since I was always number three hundred and twelve in line.

BILLY. Is there a point to this little tale of woe?

MAX. Yes, there is. Tony has no idea of what I went through — that's the point —

BILLY. You know what your problem is? You don't listen. You don't listen to *any*one. Did it ever occur to you what *he* might have gone through? You were already out in high school.

MAX. I was already out in nursery school.

BILLY. All right. You've got a good twenty-five years on him.

MAX. And I'm younger than he is! Figure that one out.

BILLY. No, you figure it out. You could use the practice. (*Makes as if to put the board away*) Shall I?

MAX. We're not done yet!

BILLY. You won, Max. You always win.

MAX. Even with your sixty-four?

BILLY. (*Smiling, pointed*) Even with my sixty-*eight*. That was a fluke.

MAX. I'm not so sure about that. You're getting really good.

BILLY. Thanks.

MAX. One of these days you're going to beat the pants off me, and I'll be so devastated I won't know what to say.

BILLY. What a relief *that*'ll be.

MAX. Thank you very much. (*Pause. Tony can be heard coughing a little in the bedroom. Billy and Max both look in his direction*) Is he all right?

BILLY. Why don't you talk to him and find out?

MAX. Will *he* talk to *me* — that's the question. (*Billy gives him a look: "Go." Max gets up, stands for a moment, then shakes one leg*)

BILLY. (*Quietly exasperated*) What are you doing?

MAX. My foot's asleep.

BILLY. (*Quietly*) Go, Max.

MAX. All right, all right. (*He goes to the door of Tony's room. Very softly*) Tony? (*He immediately turns to Billy; whispering*) He's asleep.

BILLY. (*Smiling*) He didn't hear you.

MAX. (*Back to the door; a little louder*) Tony?

TONY. (*Offstage; almost unintelligible*) Yeah?

MAX. Can I come in? (*Very quickly, so as to keep the flow of action continuous, lights black out on the apartment and come up in a single spot on Max, whose question, above, becomes directed at a psychiatrist, unseen throughout the duration of the play, but whose voice is heard live, and whose first line is spoken simultaneously with Tony's last*)

TONY. Yeah, sure, if you (*Together*) DOCTOR. Of course. Make want.   yourself comfortable. So where were you?

(*The doctor's voice does not have a "larger than life" quality to it. His voice sounds no different to the audience than the voices of the men in the apartment*)

MAX. When we left off?

DOCTOR. That's right. (*Pause*)

MAX. (*Remembering*) On a boat.

DOCTOR. Where?

MAX. I don't know ... Greece — Portugal — someplace sunny. Who cares where the boat is?

DOCTOR. And you're with this guy.

MAX. Yeah.

DOCTOR. Is it Jason?

MAX. No, it isn't Jason. Whatever gave you that idea? (*Pause*) Do *you* fantasize about *your* lover . . . in *your* spare time?

DOCTOR. Occasionally.

MAX. (*After a beat*) Don't you get bored?

DOCTOR. No.

MAX. Bully for you. It sounds like a good life.

DOCTOR. So who is he?

MAX. Who?

DOCTOR. Your friend on the boat.

MAX. First of all, he's no friend of mine, and second of all, he's not a "who," he's an "it."

DOCTOR. How do you mean?

MAX. I mean he doesn't exist. He's just an image in my mind. A fantasy. Fantasies aren't people, they're just — fantasies. Dreams. Desires. Impossibilities.

DOCTOR. Impossibilities?

MAX. Yes. If they weren't, they wouldn't be fantasies. They go hand in hand.

DOCTOR. O.K. So you're with this guy. Let's pretend for a moment that he *is* someone — even if you don't know who. What are you doing with him?

MAX. Having sex.

DOCTOR. Like what?

MAX. Just stuff. It's all pretty standard, and I'm not going to get into it because it's not important. Anyway, I'm not paying you so you can get off. Oh, right. Sorry. I'm not paying you. I'm still not answering the question.

DOCTOR. (*No anger at all; calmly*) All right. Without getting into it, can you tell me if you're enjoying yourself?

MAX. Sure I'm enjoying myself. It's a pipe dream, for Christ's sake. When you fantasize —

DOCTOR. When *who* fantasizes?

MAX. — when *I* fantasize, O.K.? — Christ, this crap about "taking responsibility for what I say" — I mean, it's completely irrelevant now since I can't *do* anything anyway. It's all hypothesis.

171
▼

DOCTOR. Why?

MAX. What?

DOCTOR. Why can't you do anything? (*Pause*) Are you dysfunctional?

MAX. (*A mixture of derision and fear, both*) No, I am not "dysfunctional" — at least, not in the way I think you mean. (*Pause*) I would simply rather . . . *look* at the way of the world than be a *part* of it. I mean, it's a nice place to visit, but I wouldn't want to live here.

DOCTOR. Why such a telescopic view? What does it get you?

MAX. (*After a beat*) Distance. (*Pause*) I determine the parameters of who I am in relation to the rest of the world. I want to feel a little — that's my prerogative. I want to feel a lot — that's my prerogative too. Distance.

DOCTOR. You mean, how close you allow yourself to get to someone. Or them to you.

MAX. Or not.

DOCTOR. Right. Or not. Go on.

MAX. When I choose to really feel, I'm not exactly thinking about grading papers, or standing on line in the cafeteria. I'm thinking about sex, and perfection, and . . . (*Pause*)

DOCTOR. Yes?

MAX. . . . I don't know.

DOCTOR. What were you going to say?

MAX. I wasn't going to say anything. I ran out of ideas. (*Pause*) Pleasure. I guess I was going to say pleasure.

DOCTOR. Why do you think you find "pleasure" so difficult a feeling to articulate?

MAX. I don't find it difficult. I told you — I drew a blank. It happens.

DOCTOR. I think this is important. Is pleasure something you find unobtainable, and therefore perhaps difficult to articulate?

MAX. (*After a beat*) You have the screwiest syntax sometimes, do you know that? How am I supposed to "articulate" pleasure? By emitting small, animallike grunts and groans? I told you, I don't find it difficult. People have accused me of being a lot of things — stupid, maybe — insensitive — but not inarticulate.

DOCTOR. (*Fast*) When's the last time you felt pleasure? (*Silence*)

Hmmnn?

MAX. God. I don't know.

DOCTOR. Try and think.

MAX. I am. I can't remember.

DOCTOR. This year?

MAX. (*Fast*) No.

DOCTOR. Last year.

MAX. I don't know. Yes, of course, I'm sure there was *some*thing —

DOCTOR. Can you recall what it was?

MAX. (*Struggling; after a beat*) It's like ... trying to remember someone's face you saw at a party for twenty seconds.

DOCTOR. As quick as that?

MAX. All right, look. I enjoyed being with friends. I enjoyed sex. I enjoyed — (*Pause*) — food. I enjoyed my *life*, I really did. There were a lot of things that left me unsatisfied — unfulfilled — but my God! I'm only human. I'll tell you what I *did* enjoy: my students.

DOCTOR. And now you don't have them.

MAX. No.

DOCTOR. How did this happen? Why? (*Max shrugs a little*) Can you talk about it? (*Silence*)

MAX. (*Slowly, the following*) There was a boy.

DOCTOR. (*Prompting, a little*) A boy —

MAX. A young man. Just a kid, really. Sixteen, seventeen. His name was Carlos.

DOCTOR. A student? (*Max nods yes. Pause*)

MAX. He found out I was sick.

DOCTOR. You told him?

MAX. (*Smiling a little, shaking his head no*) It wasn't necessary. Everybody assumes these kids are stupid — they can't read, they can't write — but they're not. They figure stuff out — the dizzy spells in the middle of class, the frantic trips to the bathroom —

DOCTOR. Yours?

MAX. If there was time. Otherwise theirs. They're shooting up in one stall, I'm throwing up in another. (*Silence*) He came to me after school one day. He told me he thought he was sick too: What should he do? Who should he see? I said I'd see what I could do. (*Pause*) I brought him some material.

DOCTOR. What kind of material?

MAX. Brochures. Leaflets. Safeguards. Answers to his questions. (*Pause*) His friends found out. *Their* friends found out. His parents found out. Everybody found out. It was like some . . . chain letter gone haywire.

DOCTOR. What did they accuse you of?

MAX. (*A little dully*) Proselytizing. Pamphleteering. Dissemination.

DOCTOR. In other words, telling the truth.

MAX. My truth, definitely. Yours, probably. Maybe even Carlos's. But not theirs.

DOCTOR. Are you saying what you did was wrong?

MAX. It wasn't wrong. (*Pause*) It was . . . ill timed. It was destructive.

DOCTOR. Not to Carlos, surely —

MAX. To me! It was destructive to me! They took away my students. (*Pause*) Even at their worst, they gave me a kick. They were so alive. I would come into class in the morning feeling like shit, half-dead from fatigue, or boredom, and they would shoot me full of energy. They demanded it. And they got it back about eighty percent of the time.

DOCTOR. So that gave you pleasure.

MAX. Yeah. A lot. (*Silence*) Why are you staring at me like that? Why don't you say something? (*Simultaneously, the spot fades on Max and lights come up on the living room to reveal Billy as before, now responding to the above question*)

BILLY. (*Referring to Tony's room*) Because I'm waiting for you to go in that room. (*Begrudgingly, Max finally gives a soft knock on the bedroom door and exits into it. Billy is in the kitchen now, getting medicine. There is a knock at the entrance door. Billy goes over to it*) Who is it?

JASON. (*Offstage*) It's Jason. (*Billy opens the door to reveal Jason, who carries a small plant as a gift. The two men eye each other with a certain wariness*)

BILLY. I'm Billy Jones. You're Max's friend.

JASON. Yes. Nice to meet you.

BILLY. Nice to meet you too. Come on in.

JASON. Thanks. I'm sorry I didn't call — I just got out of work.

BILLY. Max tells me you work in television.

JASON. That's right.

BILLY. Tony — our other roommate — he's an actor.

JASON. (*A little smile*) I work in production. (*Pause*) Are you also in the theatre?

BILLY. (*Shaking his head no*) I play piano. Sort of pop–jazz. My own compositions.

JASON. So you perform on your own?

BILLY. I did, for a while, in a bar in the East Village. I filled in for the regular guy a couple of nights a week.

JASON. Not any more?

BILLY. He didn't want to use the same piano. He was a little obsessive. First he started washing the keys down with ammonia. Then he refused to touch them at all. So they fired me.

JASON. (*Struck dumb. Silence. Then*) Is Max around?

BILLY. He is — but he's actually sort of engaged at the moment.

JASON. Oh. Is he out?

BILLY. No, he's in the bedroom with Tony.

JASON. (*Misunderstanding*) I'll come back some other time. If you could just tell him that I stopped by — (*Re: the plant*) I just wanted to drop off —

BILLY. (*Grinning, taking the plant from him*) Holding hands is just about our biggest thrill these days. (*Pause*) They're just talking.

JASON. I don't want to interrupt anything.

BILLY. It's all right, really. Tony's not feeling well anyway.

JASON. Nothing serious, I hope — (*Quickly realizing his gaffe*) — I mean, today.

BILLY. It's always serious. Just more or less so, that's all.

JASON. How are you all . . . doing?

BILLY. Every morning we wake up. Every night we check our vital signs. Or vice versa. (*Pause*) Tony's pretty bad.

JASON. I'm sorry to hear that. (*Silence*)

BILLY. I'll get Max. (*He goes to the bedroom, knocks softly, and exits into it, leaving Jason to survey the room. Despite his best efforts to the contrary, he can't help but overhear snippets of dialogue — muffled but unmistakably frantic — emanating from the bedroom, approximating the following*) Max?

175
▼

MAX. Yes?

BILLY. Guess who's here — Jason.

MAX. (*Panicked*) Jason!?

BILLY. Yes. He's here to see you.

MAX. I don't want to see him.

BILLY. Come on, Max —

MAX. Tell him I'm out.

BILLY. No.

MAX. Yes.

BILLY. (*Firmly*) No! (*Billy returns from the bedroom smiling: the very picture of composure. Extremely pleasantly*) He'll be out in a minute. Just give him a chance to mop the smelling salts off the floor. (*He moves toward the front door, opening it*) It was nice to meet you.

JASON. (*Not really anxious for him to leave*) You're going out — ?

BILLY. Just across the hall. I think I found a piano. 'Bye. (*He exits, closing the front door behind him. Jason goes over and picks up the plant from where Billy left it on the counter, looking around for a suitable place to put it. Not succeeding, he takes it over to the kitchen sink to give it some water. His back is to us as Max enters from the bedroom, nervously running his hands through his hair and closing the bedroom door behind him. He stops and stares for a moment at Jason, who turns around, plant in hand*)

MAX. Hi.

JASON. (*Putting the plant down*) Hi.

MAX. How are you?

JASON. O.K., I guess. How are you?

MAX. Not so hot. (*Pause*) Christ! You'd think we were at summer camp, writing our first letters home.

JASON. Sorry. I'm not comfortable being uncomfortable with you. (*Pause. Max stares at Jason for a beat, then laughs a little*) Was it something I said?

MAX. (*A little flustered*) No, I — just got this flash of the first time we met. (*Pause, Jason begins taking off his coat and scarf. Pointedly*) Let me take your coat. (*He does so, pausing for a second when he touches Jason. Indicating the apartment*) Well. What do you think? Homey, huh?

JASON. It's all right.

MAX. I'm glad you approve. We who live here call it "Good Will Chic."

JASON. (*Genuinely*) It's not that bad.

MAX. Good old Will. We certainly are grateful to him. (*Pause*) Well. You don't mind if I sit down. (*He does so*) I get kind of tired standing up. Actually, I get kind of tired sitting down. That's life. What are you going to do?

JASON. (*Plowing through; extremely concerned*) How are you feeling? (*Max shrugs helplessly*) Tell me.

MAX. (*Simply*) Awful. I wake up, I throw up, I go back to sleep, I take a walk, I take a pill, I get a checkup, I get better, I get worse. (*Pause*) But enough about me. You, on the other hand, look good. Something about the burnished glow in your cheeks. Aladdin, Aladdin, will you rub your lamp and grant me three wishes? (*Jason says nothing, smiling*) Two wishes? (*Jason as above*) One wish. I really only need one —

JASON. (*Sitting down*) I'm glad to see you've lost none of your bite.

MAX. Not yet. Some hair, maybe, a few pounds here and there — (*Looking at himself*) — and there and here — but my bite survives. Like the cockroach after the bomb. I was, in fact, trying to extricate my foot from my mouth not more than two minutes ago in the bedroom there. (*Pause*) How's Ralph?

JASON. He's all right. Lies around a lot.

MAX. I miss him.

JASON. He misses you too. He knows something is wrong.

MAX. How about Piccolo?

JASON. (*Matter-of-fact*) Piccolo bit me again.

MAX. (*Smiling*) Again?

JASON. (*Holding up his hand*) Again. Not a major bloodletter, but I'm getting really tired of just recuperating from one wound when he takes it upon himself to give me another.

MAX. He was never especially bright — biting the hand that feeds him.

JASON. It's his way of letting me know he doesn't like sharing a studio. (*Pause*) I . . . think I've found someone to take him.

MAX. (*Deeply upset*) Piccolo?

JASON. I can't take care of them both.

MAX. I did.

177
▼

JASON. They're your dogs, Max — they always will be. When you got really sick you asked me to take them in and I did. They were happy in your apartment. Mine is the size of this room. It's hard enough to take care of one. I just don't have the time —

MAX. But Piccolo —

JASON. — and I'm hardly ever home. It's not fair to them, being cooped up like that all day long.

MAX. (*Sadly*) I just hate the thought of his going to some strange place —

JASON. He won't be.

MAX. Who is it?

JASON. (*Having gotten over the hurdle; warming up now*) Her name's Shelley. I met her in the park a few times when we were both walking the dogs.

MAX. She already has a dog?

JASON. Yes. Really huge. A wolfhound — Irish, or Russian, or something. Piccolo bit him.

MAX. And she wants to take him in?

JASON. Yeah. I don't think her dog's going to be too thrilled, but she seems pretty happy about it. She really likes Piccolo. She thinks he's "spunky."

MAX. (*Shaking his head*) Poor Piccolo.

JASON. He'll be fine. It's the wolfhound I feel sorry for.

MAX. What about Ralph — you're not going to give *him* away, are you?

JASON. (*Hedging*) I'll do my best to keep him, but I can't —

MAX. Promise me.

JASON. (*Protesting, but weakly*) Max —

MAX. Promise. (*Pause. Quietly*) Please.

JASON. (*Sighing*) All right. (*Max stares at him demandingly*) I promise.

MAX. Thank you. (*Pause. Brightly*) You always said you wanted a kid.

JASON. A child, Max. Not a dog.

MAX. You're close. Very close. (*He gets up, with a good deal of effort*) I'm totally parched, for a change.

JASON. Does that happen often?

MAX. (*Heading for the kitchen*) It's the drugs. (*He goes to the kitchen, pours some cider in a glass, takes a sip for himself, then brings it to*

Jason) Here.

JASON. What is it?

MAX. Apple cider.

JASON. (*Shaking his head*) No thanks.

MAX. You love cider.

JASON. Really, I'm not thirsty. You go ahead.

MAX. Come on. How often do you get the real thing — from
New England? A friend of Tony's brought it.

JASON. I don't *want* any — please *and* thank you!

MAX. (*Retreating*) All right, all right. You don't have to get
snippy. (*He takes the glass back to the kitchen*)

JASON. I'm sorry. I'm tired — I haven't had anything to eat —

MAX. Why didn't you say so? I'll fix you something.

JASON. I don't want you fix me anything.

MAX. (*Bristling*) *Fine*! (*Silence. He stares at Jason for a moment.
Bluntly*) Why are you here? (*Pause. Jason is about to respond
directly, then rethinks it*)

JASON. Do you have anything to *drink* —

MAX. (*Not quite getting it*) Drink — ?

JASON. (*Elaborating*) — you know, alcohol?

MAX. You?

JASON. Me.

MAX. You're always so temperate.

JASON. (*Mustering a smile*) Yeah, well, I'm off tonight.

MAX. (*Mulling it over*) Let's see. We have ... (*He picks up a plastic
bottle of rubbing alcohol on the counter*) ... this!

JASON. Not quite what I had in mind.

MAX. They say that after two it tastes just like Stoli.

JASON. I'll take your word for it. That's it, huh?

MAX. House brand. I wasn't expecting company.

JASON. I'm sorry I didn't call.

MAX. For two months?

JASON. I'm sorry about that too.

MAX. (*Deliberately*) Eight weeks.

JASON. I said I was sorry.

MAX. I kept thinking you were on vacation. (*He goes to the kitchen
counter and finds a postcard there. Bright and bitter*) I loved your
card. (*Holding up the card: nothing but solid black, with four words*

printed in yellow, which Max reads) "New York at night."
(*Reading from the back of the card*) "Thinking about you" —

JASON. I was.

MAX. (*Reading*) — "Hope you feel well" —

JASON. I do. Why can't you believe that?

MAX. (*Reading*) "XXX Jason." What does that stand for — errors in judgment?

JASON. Mine — or yours? Is that what three X's on a postcard mean to you? It's pathetic the things you choose to see! You wouldn't recognize an intimate gesture if it crawled into your bed at night!

MAX. Do you speak from experience, or is this just hearsay?

JASON. (*Struggling to control himself*) Don't. Don't do that. I phoned the apartment. You didn't answer. I wrote — (*Max waves the postcard*) — you didn't reply. I called the center. They told me you'd moved.

MAX. Been moved.

JASON. *Been* moved. Right. How could you keep such a thing from me?

MAX. How could I not?

JASON. Not to even let me know where you were — *how* you were — or *are* —

MAX. — or *expect* to be. Look at me. Look at this place!

JASON. I told you — it's not that bad.

MAX. It's not mine. Other people live here.

JASON. It's not theirs, either.

MAX. There's no place for me to escape to here. When things got strange, or difficult, I could always come home —

JASON. (*Finishing his sentence*) — and isolate yourself, right?

MAX. (*Ignoring the remark; backtracking slightly*) — I could always come home and just be by myself, alone and away from everything and everyone. Even you.

JASON. Especially me.

MAX. I didn't say that.

JASON. You didn't have to. What's really bugging you, Max — aside from the obvious? The fact that I didn't show up until now — or the fact that I did?

MAX. I'm not sure. You still haven't told me why you're here.

JASON. I was on the street. I wanted to see you.

MAX. What made you so sure I wanted to see *you*?

JASON. I wasn't. Would you like me to leave?

MAX. No. (*Pause*) North of Ninety-sixth Street — I'm flattered. Lucky thing they didn't move me to Riverdale — I might not have seen you for a year. Where *were* you coming from — work? (*Jason nods his head yes*) This is awfully late, even for you.

JASON. I had a doctor's appointment. I went back to the studio.

MAX. When?

JASON. What — the doctor's appointment?

MAX. Yes.

JASON. This afternoon.

MAX. Are you sick?

JASON. No.

MAX. Why'd you go, then?

JASON. No particular reason — just a checkup.

MAX. And?

JASON. (*Overly bright*) Nothing!

MAX. Good. (*Casually*) Everything O.K.?

JASON. (*None too strongly*) I guess so. Who the hell knows any more?

MAX. Did he tell you something was wrong?

JASON. No.

MAX. Then nothing's wrong.

JASON. It's not that simple. You know it, and I know it.

MAX. Did you go to him with a specific problem?

JASON. Not exactly.

MAX. Did you feel ill?

JASON. I told you. No.

MAX. Then what's the problem?

JASON. (*Blurting it out*) I'm scared! (*Pause*) Every little ... blemish. Every shaving nick. Sometimes, in the middle of the night, I can't sleep. I'll get up — bump into a chair, maybe. The next morning — a little bruise — I'll stare at it for an hour. Was it there yesterday? Or a sore throat — just a dumb sore throat, because I didn't wear a scarf and it's cold outside — or a stomachache — everything turns into some — major — (*He*

181
▼

breaks off. Pause) What's going to happen to me?

MAX. I don't know.

JASON. That's not good enough! (*Pause*) I need to know. (*He sits down. Silence. Then*) I decided to get tested today. (*Silence. Max goes over to him and places his hands on Jason's head, running them through his hair affectionately — an old and familiar gesture that Jason responds to with minimal effort*)

MAX. That must have been very hard.

JASON. Not once I'd made up my mind. It's having blood drawn I hate.

MAX. Did it hurt?

JASON. It never hurts. It just terrifies me. I have to lie down and look the other way. Stupid, huh? Childish.

MAX. Which arm was it? (*Jason shows him. Max comes around and sits again, taking Jason's arm*) Let me see. (*Jason takes his jacket off and rolls up his sleeve. There's a Band-Aid in the crook of his elbow*) You're not supposed to leave the Band-Aid on.

JASON. I know.

MAX. They give you an alcohol swab to hold on it for a second and then that's it.

JASON. I wanted a Band-Aid.

MAX. Well, you're supposed to take it off.

JASON. (*Pause. He extends his arm, looking away*) You do it. (*Max gently pulls the Band-Aid off. Jason is still looking away, his arm extended*)

MAX. It's O.K. You can look now.

JASON. (*Rolls down his sleeve and puts his jacket back on. With great relief*) Thanks.

MAX. You're welcome. When will you know?

JASON. Soon enough.

MAX. It's hard, sitting around and waiting.

JASON. And for what? Maybe it's a "false positive" — maybe I don't have it. Maybe it's a "false negative" — maybe I do. Maybe this, maybe that — I'm drowning in a flood of useless knowledge! What good is it? What's it doing for *you*? (*Pause*) You know what it boils down to? A bunch of desperate scientists shaking their heads each night, staring at each other and saying, "I don't know."

MAX. If they did, don't you think they'd tell you?

JASON. I'm not so sure. Sometimes I think they deliberately with-
hold information from me — from anyone who really needs
to know — as if —

MAX. What?

JASON. — as if they were punishing me, or something.

MAX. You don't think you might be punishing yourself, maybe?
In your head?

JASON. For what — because *you* slept around? (*Silence*)

MAX. (*Really stung*) I suppose I deserved that.

JASON. All that . . . *bilge* about holding on to your personal freedom,
about having an "open relationship," about how it would
keep things from going stale! How angry it made me, how
profoundly I disagreed with it, how you somehow twisted
everything around and made *me* out to be stuffy and repressed
about the whole thing. The times when I was desperately
lonely for you at three o'clock in the morning and you weren't
there, and then I'd call your place and you weren't there either —
how humiliated I felt every time you rubbed it in my face.
And now this talk about me "punishing myself" — try ex-
tricating your foot from that one! What exactly were you
trying to accomplish?

MAX. (*Simply*) Making myself feel a little bit better each night —
more wanted.

JASON. So you could feel ten times worse the next day, when you
came running to me — I, who *really* wanted you? *I* was the
one who made you feel valuable in the end — not them!
(*Pause. Quietly*) It was never enough, was it? (*Pause*) I just
wish you'd lay off the therapy talk for once. All those thousands
of dollars you spent — the hundreds of hours regurgitating
the same old crap, over and over again. Where did it get you?

MAX. (*Treading a fine line between defense and anger*) First of all, it
wasn't "the same old crap." (*Pointedly*) Every *week* there was
something new. (*A beat*) Secondly — it happened to have
been very important to me at the time.

JASON. "At the time." Oh, that's just terrific. Really swell. It's me
you're talking to, Max, not your little Thursday night therapy
group. Where are all your bosom buddies now, when you

really need them? I don't notice any of them coming around with bouquets of flowers or bowls of chicken soup!

MAX. Two of them are dead.

JASON. (*Frustration, not anger*) Oh, Christ — !

MAX. As for the others, you might recall that I left them all behind, "regurgitating" their problems, as you so condescendingly put it, shortly after we met — at your request. This I did for you. I abandoned them; you abandoned me. Perfect. I see no need to sit around now, defending —

JASON. Nobody's asking you to defend anything. It wouldn't kill you to think about it, though.

MAX. Then again, it might.

JASON. I'm not laughing, Max. I don't think it's funny that you look back on those days so fondly. And while we're at it, if memory serves me correctly, I suggested — not requested, but *suggested* — that you part company with your weekly dose of psychobabble because I genuinely felt it was doing you ill. Such a wonderfully supportive group — so nurturing, so kind!

MAX. They were.

JASON. Hack analysts! There wasn't a single notion they proposed that was worth a dime, and nothing you couldn't have seen through in five minutes if you'd taken one deep breath and exhaled slowly. Instead you kept running from one dumb idea to the next, constantly searching for some miracle cure for your loneliness. The baths went out of business, and what did they suggest? Go back to the bars. The bars grew stale — *again* — and what did they suggest? Pick up the phone and call your local stranger. You got tired of talking dirty, and what did they suggest? Forego conversation altogether and join the ranks of the video voyeurs. Brilliant advice!

MAX. I never especially felt the people *you* hung around with were a dazzling bunch either, if the truth be known.

JASON. Why? Because they talk about poetry and art, instead of the bars and the baths?

MAX. Poetry and art be damned! Since when do Betty Grable and Judy Garland qualify as either? I always found it kind of spooky that they were always the only two women ever

184
▼

invited to those chic little parties — two ghosts in a bathing suit and tails. And all the rest — eight or ten or twelve neatly paired-off men in polo shirts and khaki slacks, babbling incessantly about The MGM Musical, 1940 to the present.

JASON. I can't understand why you're filled with such incredible contempt for them —

MAX. Why? Because they're "my kind?"

JASON. Not necessarily, no —

MAX. Bet your ass, "not necessarily." Not only are they not my kind, I don't believe they're yours, either. They're only *their* kind. And as such, yes, I suppose I do hold them in contempt — but only a little. It's all I can muster — the same contempt I feel for anyone who's boring, and petty, and predictable. You never really picked up on this, did you — you who've always been so desperate to blend in. You want to blend? Then stop using separate standards of judgment — one for your gay friends and another for the rest of the world. It doesn't work for me.

JASON. Say what you like. Somehow I don't think I'm ever going to go to bed at night wondering if my attendance at one of those parties was responsible for the loss of my job, the loss of my apartment, *or* the loss of my life.

MAX. Only the loss of your mind.

JASON. And I'll take the advice of my friends over yours any day.

MAX. They didn't know any better, and neither did I. Maybe a lot of the stuff we said *was* stupid. Maybe a lot of the advice *was* foolish. But not intentionally, God knows! What do you think — I had E.S.P. or something — some prescient gift? Well, I didn't. They certainly didn't. And I can assure you, if I *were* to go back there now, they'd do anything in their power to see to it that my — suffering — would be kept to a minimum. At least they would do that. At least.

JASON. *My* suffering, I suppose, wouldn't have *mattered* to them — *or* to you.

MAX. You know that's not true.

JASON. No matter what the situation, you have the most manipulative habit of making other people feel guilty for stating their point of view.

MAX. Only when I disagree with them. It's an inherited trait.

JASON. You're really something, you know that? Nothing, but nothing is good enough for you. Just tell me: how in God's name did I ever fit in?

MAX. (*Simply*) I've had a bit of a problem, you see. From my somewhat bewildered perspective, no one was ever good enough, and everyone was better than I. (*Pause*) You looked beautiful when you woke up; you looked beautiful when you ran. You looked beautiful in a tuxedo, you looked beautiful in dirty laundry. In forty-five minutes of attempting to improve my self-esteem each morning, I still couldn't hold a candle to the way you looked tumbling out of bed.

JASON. And that was it — that was all you saw?

MAX. No — but it was a good start. You filled me with envy and you filled me with contempt. It was everything I could do to stop myself from crawling into your skin, I wanted so badly to be who you were. I looked at you and tried to see me, but I never did.

JASON. How could you think —

MAX. I just did, Jason. It's got nothing to do with smart or dumb. I just did. I kept looking. And somewhere in the middle of those worlds — those ... muddled galaxies swirling around in my head — I kept coming back to you. And maybe it's just another point of confusion — one more thing for me not to understand — but I happen to adore everything about you.

JASON. I'm not that good.

MAX. You're better. And the thought of losing you drives me out of my mind.

JASON. *I'm* losing *you*. I'm the one who's going to be walking the streets, shaking my head with rage and still asking questions, questions, questions.

MAX. Question: are you seeing anyone?

JASON. (*Incredulous*) What??

MAX. (*Repeating himself*) Are you seeing —

JASON. I heard you the first time. (*Answering the question*) No.

MAX. Why not?   (*Together*)   JASON. (*Livid*) Surprised?

JASON. How could you ask such a stupid, insulting — I don't *understand* you!

MAX. What are you doing these days for pleasure?

JASON. Pleasure? What are you talking about — "pleasure?"

MAX. Just what I said. Pleasure. Gratification.

JASON. (*Angrier still*) I haven't given it much thought lately!

MAX. I think you should.

JASON. Why?

MAX. Why not?

JASON. I've got better things to think about!

MAX. Such as?

JASON. Such as you! — though God knows, you certainly don't deserve it — not at times like this —

MAX. You still haven't answered my question.

JASON. (*Incredulous, still, but anxious, also, to pursue the issue*) Sorry — I forgot what it was —

MAX. (*Measured, deliberately*) What do you do for pleasure?

JASON. That wasn't your first question —

MAX. Not my first question —

JASON. — something about "who was I seeing?"

MAX. That was my first question. Forget that — I know the answer. How about the second question?

JASON. You mean about pleasure?

MAX. Yeah. (*Dead silence*)

JASON. I masturbate. (*Pause*) I mean . . . what do you *think* I do? (*Silence. Calmer now*) How about you? That's why you asked, isn't it?

MAX. You shouldn't be alone.

JASON. I'm not alone. I'm here — with you.

MAX. For how long? An hour? And then next week, another hour? It's not enough. Not for me. (*Silence. Then, faintly from across the hall, Billy is heard at the piano, playing a different tune than was heard before*) You should go.

JASON. (*More a plea than a statement*) I'm not ready to go.

MAX. Neither am I. There's a street just outside that window with people on it — and beyond that another street, and another and another, with hundreds of thousands of people. Go. *Be* with them. I'm stuck here. You're not. You should leave.

JASON. I don't know how.

MAX. Turn around, put one foot in front of the other, and walk out the door.

JASON. That's not what I meant.

MAX. I know it's not, but it's what I mean.

JASON. I hate sleeping without you. I'm not used to all the space on the bed. I miss holding you.

MAX. You can't hold me.

JASON. I miss touching you.

MAX. You can't.

JASON. You think I can't, but I can!

MAX. No.

JASON. I want you inside of me!

MAX. No! (*Pointing to the window*) That's where you'll find what you're looking for.

JASON. (*Heartbroken*) There's nothing out there! I don't know where to go — I don't know who to see ... (*Silence. He goes and puts on his coat, then turns to face Max again*) So what do I do? Shake your hand? Billy says that holding hands is just about the biggest thrill you guys get these days.

MAX. Is that what he said?

JASON. Yes.

MAX. (*Extending his hand*) Go ahead. (*They stand facing each other. Pause*) Go ahead, Jason. Thrill me. (*Jason, too, extends his hand and takes Max's, holding it for a moment, then moving closer to him until their faces touch. Tentatively, almost as if for the first time, they embrace; then, in all-encompassing gesture, they kiss full on the lips, very passionately, then separate: two broken hearts pulling apart. Jason moves away, pauses ever so briefly at the front door, then walks out of the apartment, closing the door behind him. Max stands alone for a brief moment, then goes and sits on one of the stools by the counter, looking completely lost. The only sound comes from the piano across the hall. Almost as an afterthought, he runs to the front door, peering through the peephole to the hallway beyond; but Jason is gone. Max returns to the couch and sits down, staring around him — a lonely, solitary figure in the middle of an empty room*)

ACT 2

Two months later. Middle of the night. The stage is empty. The couch has been made up as a bed, and the bedclothes lie all over it in disarray. A lamp by the couch is on, giving the room a warm glow, and a shaft of light also streams in from the bathroom, the door of which is ajar. The sounds of Tony being sick can be heard: coughing; running water; the toilet being flushed.

Billy enters from the upstage bedroom, obviously having just woken up. He crosses toward the bathroom.

BILLY. (*Calling softly*) Tony? (*Lights out on the apartment. A spot comes up on Billy's face. He is talking to the psychiatrist we met earlier in the play*)

DOCTOR. When did he die?

BILLY. (*Confused, a little*) What? — Who?

DOCTOR. Your father.

BILLY. When I was nineteen.

DOCTOR. Were you close to him?

BILLY. (*A quiet laugh*) Jeez.

DOCTOR. What?

BILLY. This is funny.

DOCTOR. What?

BILLY. Max said you would do this, eventually.

DOCTOR. What's that?

BILLY. He said you would ask me about my father.

DOCTOR. I'd like to know.

BILLY. I don't mind. I just think it's kind of funny. He said, "You can talk all you want about anything else — but sooner or later they all get down to Daddy." He's had a lot of experience with therapy.

DOCTOR. Evidently. I'd still like to know. It helps me to understand you better, do you see that?

BILLY. (*Genuinely, but still amused*) Oh sure, sure! It's just that I was under the impression I was the one who was supposed to be doing the understanding. (*Pause*) I don't think he was wild about the idea of starting again.

DOCTOR. I beg your pardon?

BILLY. Max. (*The doctor's following three speeches run smoothly and professionally into one another, barely allowing Billy the opportunity to respond*)

DOCTOR. Oh. Yes. Well, as you know, this is a purely voluntary program. Nobody's forcing him to attend. Or you.

BILLY. I know.

DOCTOR. It was suggested as a means of providing the three of you with an emotional outlet you might not otherwise have —

BILLY. I know.

DOCTOR. — and also as a means of minimizing any feelings of loneliness or isolation resulting from your move into the apartment.

BILLY. (*Not hostile*) Okay, okay! (*Pause*) For your information, I've never been *less* lonely in my life. (*Pause*) Boy oh boy. You have this way of saying things —

DOCTOR. Hmmmn?

BILLY. You kind of remind me of Max. (*Pause. Imitating the doctor*) "I think you might possibly, under certain circumstances, consider eradicating any irreversible evidence of tangible . . ." And on and on. (*Pause*) You know what your problem is? Prolixity. Acute. (*He's pleased with himself. Silence*) Sorry.

DOCTOR. Perfectly all right. (*Pause. Gravely*) So.

BILLY. (*Mocking him yet again*) So. (*Back to normal*) What were we . . .

DOCTOR. Your father.

BILLY. Right. We didn't talk much. I liked him, though.

DOCTOR. What did he die of?

BILLY. Heart. On his mail route one morning.

DOCTOR. So it was sudden.

BILLY. Yes.

DOCTOR. Where were you at the time?

BILLY. Living in an apartment about twenty miles away. He was dead when I got to the hospital.

DOCTOR. That must have been very painful.

BILLY. Yeah. My mother was there, and my kid brothers, and my little sister. They were all crying.

DOCTOR. What about you? (*Pause. Billy stares straight ahead*) Did you cry?

BILLY. Not right there. Later.

DOCTOR. What happened?

BILLY. (*Uncomfortable*) Well, my father was dead. It was only a couple of hours later. It was winter. (*Silence*) This weird thing happened that night when we left the hospital. I'm driving along, and there are no lights or anything, and it's really hard to see — it was the middle of nowhere — and all of a sudden I see these two eyes staring at me right in the middle of the road. It was a dog. Crazy, wild eyes. I killed him. (*Silence*) It was so weird. I was completely freaked out. My mother and sister were totally out of it to begin with. My father wasn't even dead an hour and there I go killing this dog. (*Silence*) A couple of hours later, I went out to the garage and looked at the front fender. It had a big dent in it, and there were spots of blood. The snow had washed most of it away. That's when I started to cry. I just kind of broke down. I'm glad my mother and sister didn't see me.

DOCTOR. Why?

BILLY. I don't know. I'm just glad. I was supposed to be strong. They needed me to be strong.

DOCTOR. How about now?

BILLY. What about it?

DOCTOR. You need them.

BILLY. Like a hole in the head!

DOCTOR. Let them be strong for you.

BILLY. Oh, they'll be strong all right. You have no idea! (*Pause*) They know nothing about me. That's all they need, to have me march on home, totally unannounced, with my exciting news from the big city. "Everybody — sit down now. There's something we all need to talk about."

DOCTOR. What do you think they'd do?

BILLY. They'd freak right out, that's what they'd do. They'd die. First I'd die, then they'd die. I can see it now — a great big old house in Mason City filled with dead people.

DOCTOR. They don't know you're gay?

BILLY. No.

DOCTOR. Are you sure?

BILLY. Oh, I am sure. *Very* sure.

DOCTOR. Are you planning on keeping it from them forever?

BILLY. Most likely, and then some. (*Silence*) I know you think I'm doing some terrible ... *injustice* to myself, to say nothing of them, by keeping it all hush-hush. You're wrong. Certain things are better left unsaid. (*Pause*) My mother gets up every Sunday morning and goes to church. When they sit down to dinner, someone *always* says grace. I'll bet you thought no one said grace any more. I can't just walk in there and wipe all that out.

DOCTOR. Do you think —

BILLY. I really don't wish to discuss it. Believe me, I know what it would do. It's not worth it. At some point they're going to know what happened — when I'm not around — and that'll be bad enough.

DOCTOR. Did you ever stop to think it might be worse that way?

BILLY. For them or for me?

DOCTOR. For them.

BILLY. Right. Of *course* for them. *I* won't *be* here. (*Pause. Firm*) It's as if you're asking me to go in and have this really complex discussion about — well, like I was to go in there and speak fluent French or something, and they don't even know how to say "bonjour." You see what I mean?

DOCTOR. Language can be taught, Billy. It can also be learned.

BILLY. (*After a beat*) Well, now that is truly profound, do you know that? (*Pause*) This is not the School of Foreign Studies we are discussing here. I'm talking about my family! I will not destroy the life they have. It's bad enough I've wrecked my own.

DOCTOR. Is that how you feel?

BILLY. Who else is to blame? The one wrong choice I made? He's got his own set of circumstances to sort through.

DOCTOR. If you found yourself face to face with him at this moment —

BILLY. (*Suddenly a little terrified*) I'm not.

192
▼

DOCTOR. But if you did —

BILLY. But I'm not! (*Silence*)

DOCTOR. What would you say?

BILLY. (*Sighing*) I would say ... (*Pause*) I would say ... I forgive you. (*Silence*) I forgive you, and I love you.

DOCTOR. (*Very, very quietly*) You sound as if you have a very clear picture in your head of who it is you're talking to.

BILLY. I do. (*Silence*) I can count the number of men I slept with on one hand. (*The spot fades on Billy. Lights up very dimly on the living room, as before. Once again we hear Tony being sick. Billy sits on the couch, neither asleep nor awake. Finally Tony enters from the bathroom in his pajamas, very ill, and looking terrible. He heads for the couch*)

TONY. (*In great discomfort*) Hello sleepyhead. How ya doin'?

BILLY. I haven't decided yet. How about you? (*Tony shakes his head "no good" and sits on the couch. Billy gets up and exits to the bathroom. Running water can be heard for a moment. Tony bends forward, letting his head fall between his legs, then comes up again, falling back against the couch. Billy returns with a damp washcloth, sits down next to Tony and puts his arms around him, propping him up and cradling him, wiping his forehead with the cloth*) There.

TONY. God.

BILLY. Breathe. (*Billy continues to wipe Tony's forehead*)

TONY. (*Breathing deeply*) Oh boy.

BILLY. Do you want some water?

TONY. (*Shaking his head*) I don't think I could keep it down. What time is it?

BILLY. I don't know. Middle of nowhere.

TONY. Sorry I woke you.

BILLY. You're forgiven. What happened? You've been pretty good the past couple of days.

TONY. I don't know.

BILLY. You said you were feeling better.

TONY. I was.

BILLY. What's going on?

TONY. I don't know. I had the worst dream. It started out O.K. I was sitting in a glassed–in porch somewhere. Everything's very pretty. Lots of plants, nice furniture. White wicker. The sun is shining. Some country house or something. Anyway, I'm sitting in my bathrobe, reading the paper, and I see my obituary. It was about an inch long, all the way down at the bottom of the page. No picture even! It depressed the hell out of me. I woke up and started to puke. (*Looking toward Max's room*) I can't believe he's not up.

BILLY. I finally talked him into taking a sleeping pill. I don't think he's closed his eyes since Tuesday.

TONY. I never even knew what insomnia meant until I met him. He must have some weird mind, I gotta tell you. I mean, can you imagine? — lying there, four, five years old, staring up at the ceiling all night long, waiting for sleep to come? What kind of a childhood was that?

BILLY. So how about you?

TONY. What about me?

BILLY. Why are you depressed?

TONY. I need a reason?

BILLY. (*Mock hostile*) Yeah. (*He sees some scraps of paper on the floor by the couch and picks several of them up, looking at them*) What's this?

TONY. (*Leaning over, looking*) That's my chin.

BILLY. (*Looking at another piece*) This — ?

TONY. My left ear. Tony van Gogh! (*He laughs, and goes into pain as a result, bending over double, then relaxing a bit*) Can't even laugh anymore. (*Billy picks up several more pieces of the photograph from the floor, then sees a small wastebasket by the couch and pulls it over, looking inside. He reaches in and pulls out a pile of similar, torn up fragments in his hand*)

BILLY. What are you doing, Tony?

TONY. I don't think I'm going to be needing them.

BILLY. You don't know that.

TONY. Always the optimist, huh? I like that about you.

BILLY. (*Defensively*) I get down, too.

TONY. Hey, you don't have to defend yourself to *me*. You wanna smile through all this, that's your privilege. (*Back to the photographs*) They're just a bunch of pictures. There's hundreds of them floating around the city. Anyway, didn't you know? You're supposed to get new ones every couple of years. And boy, do I need new ones. (*He picks up a scrap of photograph and goes to a mirror on the imaginary fourth wall, staring directly at us and holding the piece of paper to his face. The brilliant, youthful smile in the photograph stands in jagged contrast to the rest of his face*) A miracle of science: a thirty-eight-year-old chin on a fifty-year-old face. (*He returns to the couch, sitting again*) I think I have a problem.

BILLY. You don't just take your dreams and tear them up like this into little pieces —

TONY. Hey — I'm finished tearing them up. (*He sits down on the floor in front of the torn pieces of photographs, staring at them helplessly*) Come here. C'mon. Sit with me. (*Billy joins Tony on the floor. Tony's loneliness and pain take hold of him at this moment and he holds Billy tightly against him in an embrace. Finally he pulls away from Billy*)

BILLY. Tony — what do you want me to do?

TONY. The puzzle of my life. (*Pause*) Listen to me. I didn't give up on show business. I really gave it a shot. Sometime — I don't know when, exactly — I started to feel it slipping away from me. Like climbing the greasy pole at camp — remember? The way people's eyes would glaze over before I'd even answered their questions: "What have you done recently." "Be sure to let me know the next time you're in something." (*Pause*) You know what my problem was? I couldn't handle the matinees. At the evening performances I was brilliant. I walked into the bars and I *had* those guys. I exploded in the dark. I could really turn it on, you know what I mean? If I was blind, it didn't matter. I had the lights to see for me. And if I was dead, I didn't know it. Nobody knew. Outside, where there's sun, and air, and people just living their lives, disco music's come and gone. But it's still there in the bars, beating away like an extra heart in case your own breaks down. And I never went home empty-handed. Ever. (*Pause*) Fuckin' show business. Fifteen years ago they said, "You're too young." I said, "O.K., I've got time," and took another all-night tour of the bars. They *like* 'em young in the bars, I thought. And I was right. I felt like a failure if I went to bed before five. Three, four, five years go by . . . I'm pounding

away, doing my little thing, you know ... another hundred
and fifty photographs hot off the press. Now they're saying
I'm at a "funny age." What the hell does that mean? There's
nothing funny about being twenty-eight. They tell me I'm
going to be really hot when I get into my thirties. I say,
"O.K. — fine. I'm a patient guy." More bars, more baths.
Nobody's telling me to wait until my face fills in *there*. Who
gives a fuck about a face when all that matters is two hands
and a crotch? I survived worse things than impatience anyway.
I was my father's son and I survived. I served in Nam and I
survived. I came out and I survived.

BILLY. You were in Viet Nam?

TONY. (*Matter-of-fact*) Yeah.

BILLY. Really?

TONY. Yeah.

BILLY. That's amazing. (*Tony stares at him for a second, unable —
and unwilling — to believe that Billy could possibly have the
slightest interest in digressing from the topic at hand*)

TONY. (*Resuming; deliberately*) Anyway, I wait another couple of
years. I'm making good money as a waiter, I'm working in
good places.

BILLY. Were you in combat and everything?

TONY. Yes. You're not listening to what I'm saying!

BILLY. I am — I just ...

TONY. What?

BILLY. I don't know ... I never met a real veteran.

TONY. (*Extending his hand*) My pleasure.

BILLY. (*Shaking his hand*) Did you kill people?

TONY. What kind of question is that? I'm trying to talk to you.

BILLY. Sorry. I just want to know this one thing.

TONY. Why?

BILLY. I want to know. (*Pause*) Did you?

TONY. Yeah. (*Silence*) What, do you find this exciting or something?
(*Silence*) What was I talking about? (*Lights black out on the
living room and come up on a single spot on Tony, whose question,
above, becomes simultaneously directed to — and answered by — the
same doctor as in the previous scenes*)

DOCTOR. (*Offstage*) Killing people.

TONY. (*Tentatively*) No, that isn't it. (*Pause*) He keeps interrupting me.

DOCTOR. You're talking to me now.

TONY. What about?

DOCTOR. Killing people.

TONY. In the war?

DOCTOR. Not in the war. Here, Tony. Here at home.

TONY. (*Confused*) These drugs . . .

DOCTOR. They're not easy.

TONY. They make me forget things. Right in the middle of a sentence, I can't remember what I'm saying. I wake up in the middle of the night and I don't know where I am. My mouth is all dried out. I can't pee.

DOCTOR. Why does Billy's question upset you so much?

TONY. Because sometimes . . . when I think about the men I slept with . . . I feel like a murderer or something.

DOCTOR. What happened to them has also happened to you. You have to know it wasn't the result of anything deliberate on your part. Or theirs.

TONY. Then it was manslaughter.

DOCTOR. Just like that? No trial? No jury?

TONY. Mea culpa, O.K.? I don't need a jury.

DOCTOR. Why are you doing this to yourself?

TONY. I don't know. Just looking back over my shoulder, I guess.

DOCTOR. What do you see?

TONY. A lot of waste. A lot of love lost. Dumb decisions. Compromises. Loving people I never slept with. Sleeping with people I never loved.

DOCTOR. No exceptions?

TONY. No exceptions.

DOCTOR. How does that make you feel? Angry? (*Tony shakes his head*) Disappointed?

TONY. (*Nods. Pause*) Just once. Just once, I would have liked . . . (*Pause*) Never mind. (*Pause*) What was I talking about? (*A quick reversal: as the spot dies quickly on Tony's face, the lights come up on the apartment as before, picking up where we left off, with Tony facing Billy once again*)

BILLY. (*Prompting*) Your acting.

TONY. Right. (*Pause*) Blah, blah, blah. What the hell do you want to hear about that for? (*Silence*) I never wanted to wind up like one of those middle-aged guys running around from one agent's office to the next, peddling these things (*Picking up a pile of scraps from the wastebasket*) day in and day out. (*Pause*) You know what I was thinking? This is something I was considering a long time ago. You know all those tables I waited on? I got to know a lot about the restaurant business in the past ten years or so. You ever seen a Chinese restaurant go out of business?

BILLY. You want to open a Chinese restaurant?

TONY. Not just any Chinese restaurant. A Chinese-*Italian* restaurant.

BILLY. You're joking.

TONY. No. Great idea, huh?

BILLY. What are you going to call it — "Via della Shanghai" or something?

TONY. That's not bad, but it's not good enough.

BILLY. It's kind of late. Forgive me if I left my mind back there in the bedroom —

TONY. Listen. I have three possibilities, and they're all brilliant.

BILLY. (*Yawning, genuinely tired*) Uh-huh. (*Silence*)

TONY. "Spaghetti Eastern." (*Billy stares at him. Absolute zero reaction*) Don't you get it? Two cultures — both say they invented spaghetti —

BILLY. I can see them now, the Imperial Dragons versus the Colombo Clan, shrieking at each other from across the room. The first spaghetti gang war.

TONY. You think so? No.

BILLY. What's the next one?

TONY. (*Pause*) "The Peking Order."

BILLY. God. That's awful.

TONY. All right. This one you're really going to like. (*Pause*) "Taiwan On." (*Silence. Then they both begin to laugh, more from relief stemming from the momentary cessation of Tony's pain than because of the jokes*)

BILLY. (*Laughing*) That's completely horrible —

TONY. Come on — it's brilliant!

BILLY. — the worst idea I've ever heard in my life. (*They trail off. Tony begins having spasms of pain again. Billy tries to stave them off*) Tony — what are you going to have on the menu?

TONY. "Drunk chicken, lovingly hacked." (*They crack up again. Tony gets up and starts walking around the room, holding his gut in pain*) Jesus — oh Jesus Christ —

BILLY. What is it?

TONY. (*Having trouble breathing; garbled*) My —

BILLY. What.

TONY. (*Struggling*) My —

BILLY. What? Try and tell me. Is it your chest again? (*Tony nods*) Do you want me to call the hospital? (*Tony shakes his head no*) I think I should.

TONY. (*Definitely*) Don't.

BILLY. You don't look so hot.

TONY. I don't look so hot because I'm dying, that's why I don't look so hot.

BILLY. (*Cajoling and pleading both*) Come on, come on.

TONY. I just want this to be over.

BILLY. Tony, don't.

TONY. (*Pacing around the room*) Don't what? Talk about the truth? What the fuck am I doing, telling jokes at four o'clock in the morning? I've got nothing going on. What the hell do you think would happen if all of a sudden I got better? You think everything would just fall into place?

BILLY. (*Getting up, with Tony now*) Maybe. Maybe it would do exactly that.

TONY. Bullshit. I fucked up. You fucked up.

BILLY. Speak for yourself. Don't do this. Don't give out on me, and don't tell me I fucked up. I don't believe it, and I don't need to hear it.

TONY. You look like an angel. Big deal! Doesn't make you a saint! Doesn't even make you an angel.

BILLY. (*Goes to the counter, looking for medicine. Frantically searching*) Where's your inhaler? Huh? Help me out. Where is it?

TONY. I can't.

BILLY. When's the last time you took it?

TONY. Before. In the bathroom.

BILLY. (*Rummages through the bottles of pills at the counter, finally pulling one out*) Then take one of these, would you please? It'll make you feel better.

TONY. I *want* this pain. I *like* it. I *deserve* it.

BILLY. (*Handing him the pill*) Here. (*He goes to get some water for the pill*)

TONY. Never knew I was into S&M, did you?

BILLY. (*Comes back with the water*) The only problem is there's no "S" to go with your "M." Take the pill or I'll be happy to remedy the situation and shove it down your throat. (*Tony takes the water, washing down the pill with it. As he hands the water back to Billy, he is seized by a new spasm of pain. The glass of water flies out of Billy's hand into the kitchen. Tony grabs Billy by the collar*)

TONY. Oh Billy, Billy, I hurt so bad —

BILLY. Why won't you let me call the doctor? What's the matter with you? (*Max enters, heavily drugged from the sleeping pill, to find Tony and Billy ostensibly locked in combat*)

MAX. I think I'm hallucinating. What time is it? Why are you fighting?

BILLY. We are not fighting, and you are not hallucinating. Would you pick up the phone and call the doctor, please? (*Max heads for the phone, picking it up. Tony tries to take the phone from him*)

TONY. Don't. I can't go back there. I can't face it. I don't want more tubes shoved up my arm, up my nose, up my ass — (*Billy and Max pry the phone from Tony's hand. Max dials. Billy takes hold of Tony*)

BILLY. (*To Tony*) They're ready for you. They've got stuff to keep you going.

TONY. I DON'T WANT TO KEEP GOING! Don't you understand?

BILLY. (*To Max*) What's happening?

MAX. I'm calling, I'm calling. Shit. I got his answering machine.

BILLY. Call the hospital.

TONY. (*Falls to his knees in pain. To Billy*) Come here.

BILLY. (*Joins Tony on the floor*) What are you doing?

TONY. Pray with me.

BILLY. You don't need prayer — you need medical attention.

TONY. I'm not praying to get well.

BILLY. (*Pulling Tony up with him*) Then I will certainly not join you.

MAX. (*Into phone*) Yes, hello, this is Max Schecter. I'm Dr. Kellman's patient — (*Billy drags Tony to the couch*)

BILLY. Come on. You've got to lie down. Maybe you'll fall asleep.

MAX. (*Into phone*) Yes, that's right. I'm with the project. Yes. No, I'm O.K. It's Tony Venniero. My roommate. He's really sick. (*Billy is cradling Tony in his arms now, as at the opening of the scene. Max's dialogue into the phone runs over and through the remainder of the scene*) I don't know exactly. But he's in a lot of pain, and whatever he's taking doesn't seem to be doing a thing.

BILLY. (*To Max*) And he's having trouble breathing.

MAX. (*Into phone*) And he's having trouble breathing. (*To Billy*) He is?

BILLY. Just tell them to send an ambulance!

MAX. (*Into phone*) We really need an ambulance. I've never seen him this bad.

BILLY. (*To Tony*) Talk to me. (*Tony is nearly incoherent now. He groans*) C'mon. Say something. Say anything.

MAX. (*Into phone*) Two-oh-five West One-hundred-and-first Street. Two B.

TONY. (*Giggling; to Billy*) To be or not to be ...

MAX. (*Into phone*) Between Broadway and Amsterdam.

TONY. Bill had a billboard. Bill also had a board bill. The board bill bored Bill so Bill sold the billboard to pay for the board bill.

MAX. (*Into phone*) I don't know what kind of insurance he's got.

BILLY. (*To Max*) Jesus!

TONY. Then the board bill no longer bored Bill.

MAX. (*Into phone*) You have him on file. You've treated him before. Look at his records. What did you do the *last* time he was there?

BILLY. (*Looking down at Tony*) Tony? (*No response*) Tony?

201
▼

MAX. (*Into phone*) Well it's about fucking time. Yes. Venniero. Yes. That's him. Yes. All right. So stop asking questions and get over here.

BILLY. (*To Tony*) Tony? (*No response. Billy shakes Tony*) Oh no, come on. (*He cries out*) TONY!! (*Max hangs up the telephone. Billy holds Tony on the couch, rocking him gently back and forth*) Shit ... (*He continues to rock Tony in his arms. Max moves toward the couch a couple of steps*)

MAX. (*Almost a whisper*) Is this how it happens? (*The lights fade slowly on the three men. Billy's music is heard playing, then fades*)

Three days later. Early afternoon. Lights up on the apartment. It is empty. The curtains on the window are drawn shut. The couch has been restored to its original "sit-upon" state. The front door opens and Billy and Max enter, wearing coats, scarves, etc. Billy sits on the couch, staring ahead. Max goes over to the curtains and opens them, letting in the pale, washed-out light of the winter sun. He removes his coat, then goes over to Billy, gently patting him on the shoulders and wordlessly helping him out of his coat.

MAX. Are you all right?

BILLY. (*Nodding*) You O.K.?

MAX. I'm all right.

BILLY. All those people. I never knew he had so many friends.

MAX. He would have loved it — the whole lot of them, overladen with everything — flowers, lasagne, cheesecake, chocolate-covered cherries ... bundles and packages and pounds of stuff, as if the excess weight of it all could bring him back to life, or something. (*Pause*) You know, I really *hate* cemeteries. There's something so ... *final* about them. They're not going to put *me* in one of those endless rows, I can tell you that.

BILLY. What do you mean?

MAX. Just what I said. I don't want it. I want to be cremated. I just feel, when you're gone, you're gone. That's it. Nothing left.

BILLY. There'll be ashes.

MAX. Yeah, well they can scatter them all over the Brooklyn—
Queens Expressway, as far as I'm concerned, just so long as I
don't have to lie there permanently, rotting away under the
offramp.

BILLY. What about some nice place — in the country somewhere?

MAX. (*Definitively; no anger*) I don't want to lie in the *ground*.
*Any*where. (*Pause*) Well, here we are. Just you and me. It feels
weird not to have him here.

BILLY. Uh-huh.

MAX. I don't think I could have gotten through the whole thing
on my own.

BILLY. Me neither.

MAX. Your piano playing was beautiful, Billy.

BILLY. Thanks.

MAX. Really beautiful. Everybody thought so. It was the nicest
thing you could have done.

BILLY. Thank you.

MAX. I'm glad you're here.

BILLY. Thanks.

MAX. Are you all right?

BILLY. I'm fine.

MAX. How about some tea to warm us up?

BILLY. No thanks.

MAX. Nice and weak — the way you like it. I'll barely touch the
water to the leaves.

BILLY. (*Shaking his head*) No. Really. (*He gets up. Max senses he
wants to say something*)

MAX. Billy? What is it? (*Billy is struggling*) Talk to me.

BILLY. I don't know how to tell you.

MAX. Whatever it is, it can't be so terrible —

BILLY. It's not terrible. It's just hard. (*Silence. Max waits*) I'm
leaving, Max. (*He waits for Max's reaction*) Did you hear me?

MAX. (*Denying the inevitable*) Yes, of course I heard you. Where
are you going? (*Together: a jumble of sound*)

MAX. It's freezing out.   BILLY. I'm going home. (*Pause*)

MAX. What?

BILLY. I'm going home.

MAX. To your mother?

BILLY. Uh-huh.

MAX. Your brothers and sisters?

BILLY. Yes.

MAX. But ... you can't do that.

BILLY. Why?

MAX. They won't take you back.

BILLY. I disagree.

MAX. They won't even let you in the house.

BILLY. What makes you so sure?

MAX. (*Confidently*) I know them.

BILLY. (*Contradicting him*) *I* know them.

MAX. (*Retreating*) People like them.

BILLY. (*Impassioned*) You don't know them or anyone like them, you don't understand them, you don't even know what they look like.

MAX. Billy, you're courting disaster!

BILLY. Nothing to lose the second time around.

MAX. Why are you doing this?

BILLY. I used to think it was wrong to cry — not because I was ashamed, but because it showed people who I was, or who I thought I was and didn't want to be. Tony wasn't ashamed to cry. He wasn't ashamed to tell me he was in pain. He wasn't ashamed to ask me to hold him. He just grabbed me and I knew. He refused to hide from anyone. All I've *done* is hide.

MAX. You didn't hide from Tony. You didn't hide from me.

BILLY. I didn't need to. Now comes the hard part.

MAX. What — what are you —

BILLY. I don't want to die alone.

MAX. You won't. You'll be here — with me —

BILLY. I want to go home, Max. I want to see my mother.

MAX. You said you couldn't live with her.

BILLY. (*A tiny beat*) I've lived with you.

MAX. Yes — all right, look — I know I'm difficult — obnoxious — a bore —

BILLY. (*Smiling*) All of the above, and I wouldn't want you to change any of it.

MAX. I don't understand.

BILLY. You know what you make me think of?

MAX. I'm not sure I want to know.

BILLY. The books you've told me about. The ones I never read myself. "Difficult but rewarding." That's you.

MAX. That's all well and good, but I am not a book. I am a person. I am your friend. (*Pause*) I am, aren't I?

BILLY. (*Genuinely*) The best *and* the brightest.

MAX. I'm not fishing for compliments. Goddamit, you're leaving me!

BILLY. Yes.

MAX. You can't do that! I'm going to be completely alone!

BILLY. You won't be.

MAX. What do you mean, I won't be? I don't see anyone else here!

BILLY. I called Jason. (*Max is stunned into silence. Pause*) I called him.

MAX. (*A slow burn*) *When*?

BILLY. Yesterday.

MAX. Is that when you'd made up your mind? You had no right!

BILLY. Sorry, Max. I wasn't about to walk out on you.

MAX. But you were kind enough to arrange for my care after your departure. Jesus!

BILLY. He's crazy about you, Max. You're crazy about him. But you're so damned proud, anything more permanent than a glance in the mirror terrifies you!

MAX. That's not true.

BILLY. It is. You look upon relationships like you do lying in the cemetery there by the Queens—Bronx Expressway, or whatever you call it —

MAX. Brooklyn—Queens.

BILLY. — as if it'd kill you to spend more than five minutes with one person at a time. (*Silence*)

MAX. That is a very bizarre and morbid analogy.

BILLY. Let him in, Max.

MAX. I can take care of myself!

BILLY. (*Simply, not argumentative*) You can't, Max. Neither can I. That's why I'm going home.

MAX. Is it me? Is that it? I'm impossible, aren't I?

BILLY. You're a fine person. Very smart, very caring, very alive.

And yes, you *are* impossible. I don't envy Jason. I know you. You'll fight him till the end.

MAX. (*Referring to Billy's home*) What are you going to *do* there?

BILLY. Talk to them. Get to know them. I left a long time ago.

MAX. They're going to be devastated.

BILLY. Probably. But so will I. There are a lot of things I left behind. There's a piano. It belonged to my grandmother.

MAX. The piano across the hall —

BILLY. I can't do that anymore. It's not right for me, any of it. I thought I could hide there too, but I was wrong. (*Pause*) Every time I play, that little boy reaches out for me. He goes like this with his hands. (*He mimes the gesture of a child saying with his hands "Give me — I want"*) I've wanted to hold him, but I never did, because I thought his mother would never forgive me if she found out. Last week he crawled into my arms, and do you know what she said? "Go ahead — touch him. I don't mind."

MAX. She knew?

BILLY. For weeks.

MAX. How?

BILLY. Does it matter? That's when I made up my mind — when I knew I had to go. Remember what you said about Jason the night he left? — if you couldn't have him all the time, you didn't want him at all? That's the way I feel about my music. (*Pause. More gently now*) Do you have any idea what it's like — sitting in a room with all the windows open, the sky so blue it hurts to look, the air so clean you can almost taste it?

MAX. (*Simply and utterly bereft*) No, I don't.

BILLY. You should find out.

MAX. Yeah? What do you suggest?

BILLY. Come visit. My family would like you.

MAX. (*With the purest irony*) Oh, *sure*! (*Silence*) When are you leaving?

BILLY. Thursday morning.

MAX. So soon! How do you propose to get there?

BILLY. Bus. I want to see things too. It's a beautiful ride. (*Pause*)

Isn't it funny? For the first time, I think I feel happy.

MAX. I'm glad for you.

BILLY. No you're not. You're mad at me.

MAX. No I'm not.

BILLY. Yes you are.

MAX. Yes, I am.

BILLY. It's all right.

MAX. No, it is *not* all right. Christ, you're always so fucking *unflappable*. Don't you ever get *ruffled*?

BILLY. I get ruffled. Inside. I'm not an outside person, like you. I'm not Jewish.

MAX. It's got nothing to do with being Jewish. Don't you ever just blow up and lash out at people for no particular reason? (*Billy just stands there. Max trembles with rage and hurt*) Oooh God! You piss me off! (*Billy comes over to him and puts his arms around him*) Goddamit. Shit. (*Billy continues to hold him*) I just thought —

BILLY. What?

MAX. I just thought — you'd *be* here.

BILLY. (*Pulling away now*) Spring's coming, Max.

MAX. What's that got to do with it?

BILLY. It's a nice time. Let's try to make it through.

MAX. But not together. (*Billy shakes his head ruefully, standing apart from Max now*) Call me when you get there. (*Billy nods, turns around, and exits into a bedroom. He is gone. Max, softly, to himself*) Otherwise I'll worry. (*Music, briefly. Lights cross-fade into the glow of evening, then cross-fade again into another day shortly thereafter. Late morning. Max lies on the couch asleep, or perhaps merely withdrawn. The front door opens gently and softly: it's Jason. He walks on stage, sees Max on the couch, and quietly begins to gather his things. Max turns on the couch to see him. He now manifests a terrible weariness, both from physical illness and psychological fatigue. Jason, on the other hand, displays a newfound confidence — maturity, perhaps. It is not jaunty, just strong*) Did you forget something?

JASON. Please. No jokes. (*He exits into the bedroom*)

MAX. It was a perfectly serious question. I can't imagine why else you'd be here. Anyway, if you won't allow me to die wittily, you can leave. (*Pause*) What *are* you doing here, as if I didn't know?

JASON. (*Reenters with a small suitcase*) I've come to get you.

MAX. (*No anger here; weariness is the prevailing tone*) That's presumptuous of you. Did you ever think to ask permission — how I might feel about it?

JASON. I don't particularly care how you feel about it. I'm taking you home.

MAX. (*Pondering*) Gee. (*Pause. Sarcastic and grateful both*) Thanks!

JASON. You need me, Max.

MAX. I do?

JASON. I know you don't think so — and I came here knowing it was unlikely you'd be willing to perceive that fact —

MAX. (*Mocking, but weakly*) "Perceive the fact"? —

JASON. (*Struggling to get through*) It's not part of the world as you see it. And don't start pulling apart my every word, either. Now is not the time. Later it'll be all right.

MAX. Why — because you know it's not for very long?

JASON. Partly that, yes —

MAX. Screw you, Jason!

JASON. (*Exploding*) Why don't you shut up for once! Why don't you just — (*He tries to pull himself together*) — shut up. (*Silence. The following word is shot out like an arrow*) Selfish! (*A bit calmer now*) What do you think — I derive some secret satisfaction in knowing you're going to die? Pulling away as I did probably wasn't the most loving or maybe even sophisticated reaction to the situation. I was frightened. I was angry. I just want — I'm just beginning to realize that none of it is ever going to be enough. Not for me, anyway. If you last six months, that won't be enough. Six *years* won't be enough. Please — oh please, stop being angry for two minutes. Take my sentences — every word I say — and pick them to the bone, if you want. Think of it as your legacy to me. Maybe I can teach you a thing or two about me. About changes I've been through.

MAX. These changes —

JASON. Wanting to make what's left of your life meaningful.

Filling it with some warmth — some kindness.

MAX. Treacle!

JASON. (*Undeterred*) Getting you to believe that you're valuable. To yourself, and to me. I don't think I knew how to let you know before. Not the way I was. I'm not even sure I know now. (*Pause*) There's some — reason we fell apart. I could never quite figure it out. There was a kind of — distance in what I thought was the act of giving to you.

MAX. A kind of what?

JASON. (*Unaware of the echo*) Distance. I thought about things — I stopped — I examined them — I weighed the pros and cons — and then I safely proceeded to do what I felt would please you the most. Blending. Remember? I don't want to blend any more.

MAX. Let me tell you something, Jason — this is hardly the most opportune moment for me to be discovering things.

JASON. It's the best moment, don't you see? Not because it's easy but because there *is* nothing else.

MAX. And you're going to teach me.

JASON. Allow me the luxury of making your life something more than this emptiness. Like I felt last night. (*Pause*) A friend from the office came up to me after work. "Why so blue?" he said. When I told him you weren't well, he said, "That's too bad, but we won't talk about it any more." (*Pause*) I *wanted* to talk about it. Maybe not right there, O.K. But to have had the discussion summarily dismissed like that, as if the problem didn't even exist —

MAX. It doesn't exist for *him*.

JASON. It exists for *every*one, doesn't he realize that?

MAX. So now your eyes are open. You might say he did you a favor.

JASON. I might say that, yes. And it made coming here today just a little bit easier.

MAX. Look, I'm here, living my life — just taking it day by day — and what I really want to do is tie up the loose ends, you know? *Quietly*.

JASON. Is that all you aspire to — a quiet end?

MAX. It's a little late for me to be "aspiring" to anything. What gives you the right to march in here all hot and bothered and mess up my little corner of the world?

JASON. Because for one thing — (*He hesitates here*) I really don't enjoy feeding your dog. He's a nice animal, but what the hell am *I* doing taking care of him? It's *your* job.

MAX. I go to the hospital every day and get zapped with radiation. I can't walk him.

JASON. I don't mind the walking so much. I hate feeding him.

MAX. I can't feed him. I can barely feed myself, are you aware of that?

JASON. I hate the cans — that revolting smell — washing the food out of his dish. You do it. You *like* doing it.

MAX. Did you hear what I said?

JASON. You're wasting time! If you want to wither away by yourself, that's one thing.

MAX. Jason —

JASON. But it's not going to happen with me. There are exercises —

MAX. You must be joking. I never did them when I was healthy!

JASON. They're not hard. I'll help you.

MAX. You're asking something very major here, and you'd better know I'm not talking about the dog. (*Pause*) You're asking me to open up my heart all over again. I closed it a long time ago. Even before I stopped seeing you. There's been great comfort — great safety in my isolation. (*Pause*) I'm very used to my life now. Everything's come tumbling down on my head in the past few months, like an avalanche. A huge, incredible noise, and then silence. Silence and sickness. At night, steam blasts out of the radiator and I shiver in a cold sweat. During the day I feel like I'm burning up even as the ice forms on the inside of the window. I lie here staring up at the ceiling, soaking the sheets in the sweat of my past mistakes, choking back the bile that seems continually to rise in my throat. Is it anger that makes it rise, or just another nameless malady? Is it even my bile — my sweat — or someone else's mixed with mine, someone whose arms and legs I tangled with some night years ago? And him — the other guy — the one who casually chatted me up in some noisy, smoke–filled room somewhere — or maybe he didn't even bother to chat me up. Maybe he just felt me up instead. What about him? You think he's lying somewhere too, desperately wondering, and knowing he'll never know, who was responsible for his imminent demise? Which one was it? Which one? (*Silence*)

JASON. (*Softly*) Are you O.K.?

MAX. Right now I can't seem to feel anything.

JASON. Yes you can ... (*Pause. He comes over to Max and touches him lightly on the head, stroking his hair — a tiny, affectionate gesture. Whispering*) Can you feel that? (*Max nods almost imperceptibly. Jason brings both hands down to Max's shoulders, touching him even more warmly*) That? (*Max nods a little more. Jason bends down now, slipping his arms around Max's torso, burying his face in Max's neck and embracing him with the deepest and gentlest affection*) That? (*Again Max responds, but just a little*) You're shivering. I'll get you a blanket.

MAX. I don't need a blanket. I'm nervous. (*Pause*) Is that all right? I'm uncomfortable. I'm scared. I'm not used to any of this. (*Pause. Still Max doesn't look at Jason*) Help me. (*Silence*)

JASON. I will. (*Taking the suitcase in hand, he exits once again into the bedroom. Max sits alone for a moment, then has a sudden thought. He gets up and calls to Jason*)

MAX. Jason ... (*He's at the bedroom door now*) I want that lamp. (*As he exits into the bedroom, the lights fade on the scene. Music briefly. A spotlight comes up on Jason alone*)

JASON. It took weeks to take care of everything. I'd never been to a funeral, much less arranged one. I didn't know who to call. It's just not the kind of thing I'd ever thought about. I never knew anyone who died. I always figured it was something I'd have to deal with when I was sixty. (*Pause. Reconsidering*) Fifty. (*Pause*) Three new people moved into the apartment after he left. I was thinking of visiting them. Do you think I should? I don't even know them. (*Pause*) When I was going through his things, I found a journal he'd been keeping. He told me, before he died, that he wanted me to read it. I wouldn't have, when he was alive — I didn't need to. If there was something on his mind, he told me. Anyway, one thing I didn't know was that he was seeing you. I knew he'd been in a group a few years ago, and we argued about it — the stuff he talked about, whether it was good for him or not — but he never mentioned anything about you. It must have been something very private to him. Special, I guess. He respected you a lot. I just wanted to meet you once. I've never been to a psychiatrist. I don't know why. I guess I always thought you had to be crazy or something. (*Pause*) I'm O.K. now, I really am. I don't get out much. I just don't feel like it. I'm very involved in my work. (*Pause. Very softly, we hear the opening notes of the music we heard at the beginning of the play: an echo of another place and time*) I saved a few things which are important to me. A couple of books. A photograph I took of him in Vermont one weekend, a couple of winters ago. He hated having his picture taken. I think he was embarrassed that he was having such a good time. It's a nice picture. He looks very healthy. Very happy. (*Pause. We hear another few notes of the music. Jason glances down at his arm*) This is his shirt. (*We hear one last chord from the music. Fade-out*)

Tell

■

A PLAY FOR VOICES

BY

VICTOR BUMBALO

▼

Tell

Tell is a play of storytelling, not unlike the ancient tribal rites that kept myths and histories alive through times of trial. The stories in *Tell* try to keep sexuality alive. For the patient in a hospital, the spirit becomes mute as the procedures surrounding AIDS strip and rob the body of its purpose. If health is a balance between body and mind, then when the body is being attacked it is almost an obligation of the mind to try to restore the balance. It is an obligation to remember and imagine and tell.

Victor Bumbalo

CHARACTERS

Visitor . . . . a male voice

Man . . . . another male voice

Nurse . . . . a female voice

PLACE

A stage. Two men and a woman, in casual dress, sit on stools and face the audience. The woman sits apart from the men. There is a floor lamp near the woman's stool. The lamp is out. The lighting is unsettling. There is an absence of color.

TIME

Evening.

THE PLAY

VISITOR. Are you sure we're going to be alone?

MAN. The door is closed.

VISITOR. But she'll be back.

MAN. She's finished for a while.

VISITOR. I don't want to be interrupted.

MAN. You won't be.

VISITOR. But won't she be suspicious?

MAN. Of what?

VISITOR. The door being closed.

MAN. She knows I like it that way. Begin. Please. I've waited all day.

VISITOR. Did you?

MAN. Yes. Come on, tell me.

VISITOR. I didn't plan on it.

MAN. That's how it usually begins.

VISITOR. But I couldn't sleep.

MAN. It's the heat out there. They tell me it's unbearable.

VISITOR. Are you sure she's not coming back?

MAN. Christ! I told you she's finished for a while.

VISITOR. I don't want her barging in.

MAN. She won't. So ... you couldn't sleep.

VISITOR. My room was hot and silent.

MAN. So you went out.

VISITOR. Not so fast. I had to get dressed.

MAN. Of course. What were you wearing?

VISITOR. When I went out?

MAN. Before you got dressed?

VISITOR. What do you think you wear before you get dressed?

MAN. You could wear a lot of things.

VISITOR. Like what?

MAN. Like underwear. You could have been wearing underwear.
VISITOR. Well, I wasn't.
MAN. Then maybe you were wearing . . .
VISITOR. What?
MAN. Nothing.
VISITOR. So, you see, I had to get dressed. I was warm and the sweat . . .
MAN. I remember. I remember that smell . . .
VISITOR. I was going to take a shower, but . . .
MAN. Why bother? In a few minutes . . .
VISITOR. That's right. The sweat would begin again.
MAN. So you got dressed.
VISITOR. Quickly. I needed air.
MAN. So you put on your socks . . .
VISITOR. No. I just slipped into my boots, put on a shirt. But I made a mistake. My underwear . . .
MAN. What I thought you were wearing while you were asleep.
VISITOR. The underwear I had worn all day. I put those shorts back on.
MAN. It was a mistake, was it?
VISITOR. They made me sweat more. Making my jeans feel as if they were perspiring on their own.
MAN. But the air. I bet the air was a relief.
VISITOR. There was a whisper of a breeze. It had a smell.
MAN. I remember. Like you were walking near an ocean.
VISITOR. People were sitting on stoops. Drinking liquids from bottles in paper bags.
MAN. And there was music playing.
VISITOR. No. Not last night. I didn't hear any music. But some people were yelling . . .
MAN. In a different language.
VISITOR. In many different languages. They were hot too. Like me, they didn't have an air-conditioner. And their fans were making way too much noise. So like me, they couldn't sleep.
MAN. So they were yelling.
VISITOR. And I was walking.
MAN. Where to?
VISITOR. I didn't know. I didn't want a drink.

MAN. A bar would have been crowded. Filled with smoke.

VISITOR. And I needed air.

MAN. Those tiny breezes. I can remember their smell.

VISITOR. So I walked.

MAN. Farther than you wanted.

VISITOR. No. Not for very long.

MAN. It was that easy to find what you wanted?

VISITOR. I wasn't looking for anything. I swear. And all I wanted was air. I was taking in full breaths. Breathing deeply. I wasn't thinking about anything in particular. I really wasn't. But then . . .

MAN. You saw him.

VISITOR. Coming out of a grocery store. An all-nighter.

MAN. With his beer.

VISITOR. No. With a quart of milk. Maybe some cookies. It was a midnight-snack bag he was carrying. The late-night bag filled with treats. Filled with comforts. Maybe he was lonesome.

MAN. I know about that. Tell me what I want to remember.

VISITOR. His skin was like a magnet. Made you want to touch it, lick it, devour it. His skin created a hunger.

MAN. Young. I bet he was young.

VISITOR. And naive. That was my suspicion. He looked at me.

MAN. And you knew he was interested.

VISITOR. No. It was just a glance. A quick glimpse across my face. He was probably thinking about what was in the bag. The milk, the cookies. His mind wasn't on the street. His mind wasn't on me. I was jealous of a brown paper bag. I wanted to be held by those hands.

MAN. So you caught his eye.

VISITOR. No. I had to follow him. Walking behind him. Watching him claim the street. I didn't know what I should do. How should I let him know I was interested.

MAN. In the old days you knew. In the old days you knew what to do, what to say. In the old days you would have passed him. And as you did, you would have given him a short smile. Somewhere ahead of him you would have stopped. Hoping when he neared you, he would do the same.

VISITOR. The old signals seemed tired, worn out. There's no time anymore for "can you guess what I'm after?" So I caught up with him.

MAN. And you said . . .

VISITOR. "I'm following you."

MAN. Was he frightened? Did he think you wanted his wallet?

VISITOR. He told me he had never been followed.

MAN. He was that young.

VISITOR. He said people didn't do that anymore. People met through friends, through ads in the paper. People didn't walk the streets. I told him I came from the old school. Walked the streets in the old style. He had full, fleshy lips. The kind that always look like they are pouting. But at that moment they parted and made a smile. I moved closer to him. He had no idea that I was breathing in his skin, his breath.

MAN. So you just stood there.

VISITOR. Only for a moment. I had to start walking. If I stood there another fraction of a second, I would have touched him.

MAN. But you walked with him?

VISITOR. I walked with him.

MAN. In silence?

VISITOR. We talked.

MAN. Telling the stories of your life?

VISITOR. No. Making nervous talk. Weather talk. How-ya-doin' talk. Aren't-these-days-awful talk.

MAN. But you climbed his stairs?

VISITOR. I climbed his stairs. (*There is a brief pause. The woman switches on the floor lamp. All lights brighten*)

NURSE. (*Looks at the men and begins to speak*) Oh, you have company. It's so dark in here. I thought you were alone.

MAN. We like it that way.

NURSE. Feels a bit gloomy to me. Well anyway, I need light. I've got to take some blood.

MAN. Again?

NURSE. Again. It will only take a second. Something is wrong with your air-conditioner. It's too warm in here.

MAN. I don't mind.

NURSE. Maybe your friend does.

VISITOR. No, I'm fine.

NURSE. You sure you don't want me to send somebody up to look at it?

MAN. No, please.

NURSE. There. That wasn't bad, was it? It always amazes me. I'm so good at taking blood. It's a talent. Maybe I should leave the door open.

MAN. No. Don't.

NURSE. You want this light back off?

MAN. Yes, please.

NURSE. You're the boss. (*The woman switches off the floor lamp. All lights dim*)

MAN. Thank you. (*After a moment*) So you climbed the stairs.

VISITOR. Wait.

MAN. She's gone. Go on. When you walked into his apartment, what did you do?

VISITOR. Looked around. Sat on his couch. I didn't lean back. I leaned forward. I sat in a temporary way.

MAN. What did he do?

VISITOR. Acted the host. Asked me if I wanted anything to drink.

MAN. And did you?

VISITOR. No. I didn't want to waste our time with unnecessary decisions. I didn't want to waste the time with — is it a beer or seltzer? I didn't want to waste those moments with him out of the room, finding the right glass, getting the ice if it were to be seltzer. I didn't want him thinking about me in another room.

MAN. You wanted him there with you. Sitting on the couch.

VISITOR. I wanted him at an easy arm's reach. I wanted to trace those lips with my finger. (*The woman switches on the floor lamp. All lights brighten*)

NURSE. (*Trying to be cheerful*) Excuse me. I had to turn those awful lights on again. Your temperature. I forgot to take it. I don't know what's happening to me.

MAN. I don't have a fever.

NURSE. Well, I'll have to see.

MAN. Take it later.

NURSE. I'm here now. I'm making my rounds. I have to take temperatures when I make my rounds. It will only take a second. Now, open up.

MAN. Jesus.

NURSE. Don't talk with that in your mouth. (*To the visitor*) How long do you think this weather's going to last?

VISITOR. They say for a while.

NURSE. I hate going home late at night in this kind of weather. It takes forever. I have to take two subways and a bus.

VISITOR. Where do you live?

NURSE. The Bronx. Way up in The Bronx. How about you?

VISITOR. The Village.

NURSE. Well, you don't have far to go. But me, God, I hate going home in this kind of weather. Too many unhappy people out on the streets. (*Referring to the man*) He's looking better today. He has more color.

MAN. Don't talk about me in the third person.

NURSE. And don't talk with that in your mouth. I'm sorry. I know you don't like that. Don't *you* look better today. *You* have more color.

MAN. Thank you.

NURSE. Don't talk. (*To the visitor*) Do you have to stand up on your job?

VISITOR. No.

NURSE. That's nice. Do you sit behind a desk?

VISITOR. Most of the day.

NURSE. Someday, I would like a desk job. I've had enough of the walking–up–and–down–the–halls–standing–on–your–feet jobs. They never mention in school this is a standing–on–your–feet job. I mean, I never thought that I would go from room to room by means of a golf cart, but they should have mentioned what happens to your feet, your legs, your body when you have a job like this. They should have been more honest. I thought this was a profession where you were liked, respected. Nobody ever told me once this uniform goes on, nobody likes you. When you're in school there's so much they don't tell you. Well, let me take a look. God, I can hardly see this. My eyes are going too. I think you've got a slight fever.

MAN. I don't feel it.

NURSE. Nothing to worry about. Just a little one. Well, I'm off.

Are you boys going to miss me? Just kidding. I know, I'll turn off the lights. Have a good evening. (*The woman switches off the floor lamp. All lights dim*)

MAN. Close the door.

VISITOR. She'll only open it again.

MAN. (*Irritated*) It's not her door. Close it!

VISITOR. (*Equally irritated*) All right.

MAN. (*After a moment*) Thank you. Where were you?

VISITOR. Climbing his stairs.

MAN. No, no. You were beyond that. You were on the couch.

VISITOR. In his arms . . .

MAN. No. You weren't there yet.

VISITOR. Then we were trying to talk.

MAN. So what did you say to him?

VISITOR. I said, "The light is in my eyes."

MAN. You wanted the room darker. More intimate.

VISITOR. Then I said, "Your lips, they remind me . . ."

MAN. No, they didn't. They didn't remind you of anybody. You never said that. You probably said something like . . . you never saw . . .

VISITOR. That's right. I told him, "I never saw such perfectly shaped lips."

MAN. And he laughed, didn't he? He laughed . . .

VISITOR. . . . because he was nervous. Because my talk was silly. Because he knew I was going to part those lips with my tongue.

MAN. And you did.

VISITOR. Some saliva dripped from our mouths.

MAN. I remember.

VISITOR. He wanted to say something.

MAN. But you said, "Not now."

VISITOR. That's right. I said, "Not now. Later. Much later. We'll talk later."

MAN. There will be time to talk.

VISITOR. Later. When we're finished. After we know each other.

MAN. You wanted to know him first.

VISITOR. The kiss . . .

MAN. Yes?

VISITOR. Reminded me . . .

MAN. Of nothing.

VISITOR. Right. Of nothing I ever knew. It was like a first-time kiss.

MAN. Or a movie kiss.

VISITOR. Yes. Like one after a long separation. His tongue was full like his lips.

MAN. It was a long night, wasn't it? It was a long, staying-awake night.

VISITOR. He began to pull off his T-shirt, but I said . . .

MAN. You said, "Let me."

VISITOR. Yes.

MAN. I can remember.

VISITOR. I wanted to do the unveiling.

MAN. And you did.

VISITOR. From the T-shirt to his socks. He enjoyed the attention.

MAN. He was vain.

VISITOR. He was assured.

MAN. I remember.

VISITOR. His skin was tight — almost hairless. He smelled of youth, of possibilities. His small nipples looked as if they never had been touched.

MAN. But you touched them.

VISITOR. I did. And not all that gently. With my thumb and first finger, I squeezed them as I pulled his body near mine.

MAN. But you were still dressed.

VISITOR. Yes. Fully. I pulled his body on top of mine. He began devouring me.

MAN. It had been a long time for him.

VISITOR. It had been a long time for us both.

MAN. But your clothes? They were still on?

VISITOR. For a while, we wanted it that way. His nude body pounding at mine. His excitement slashing at my jeans.

MAN. Is that what you call it now? But then . . .

VISITOR. That's right. I wanted flesh to flesh. So we ripped my clothes off.

MAN. You both were still on the couch?

VISITOR. Stretched out on the couch. Me on the bottom. Him on the top.

MAN. That's the way you like it.

VISITOR. That's the way I like it. We really ripped the clothes off me. The button on my pants popped off. We tore my shirt. Did I tell you . . .

MAN. What?

VISITOR. . . . what it was like? His was not long, but fat. Fleshy.

MAN. Like a baby's arm.

VISITOR. How well you know. He smelled a bit of baby powder.

MAN. He used it to absorb his sweat.

VISITOR. Like a kid, he kept rubbing it against my belly. I brought my hand down there.

MAN. You had to touch it.

VISITOR. Put my hand around it.

MAN. And it felt like . . .

VISITOR. Home. Like a place of comfort.

MAN. What were you thinking?

VISITOR. When?

MAN. When you had your hand around his flesh.

VISITOR. So many things. One secret thought after another.

MAN. Tell me.

VISITOR. They're my secrets.

MAN. Please.

VISITOR. They were resurrection thoughts. My hand explored the head. It was surprisingly big — resurrecting the what-are-we-going-to-do-with-this thoughts. Giddy thoughts. Feelings were resurrected, smashing against so many memories. But my hand began squeezing it hard. Gripping, not wanting to let go.

MAN. Did he like that? Did he want you to hurt him a little?

VISITOR. His tongue was licking my face. Lapping at it. But then I caught that tongue, sucked at it, and trapped it in my mouth. (*The woman turns on the floor lamp. All lights brighten*)

NURSE. I brought you some Tylenol to bring down the fever.

MAN. Would you get out of here?

VISITOR. Relax.

MAN. She won't leave us alone.

NURSE. This is a hospital. I have a job to do.

MAN. To what? Torture me?

NURSE. (*To the visitor*) Is he having an anxiety attack? Does he need a sedative?

MAN. I need to be alone with my friend. You're not wanted here.

NURSE. This is a hospital room. On my floor.

MAN. Disappear!

NURSE. This is my floor. You're under my care. You can't treat me like this. There are things I can do if a patient is abusive.

MAN. What? Drain more blood?

NURSE. I'm going to report this to my superior.

MAN. What are you going to report?

NURSE. Your insubordination.

MAN. I had no idea I was in the army.

NURSE. What have I done wrong? Tell me! I always treat you with respect. When I'm on duty, I make sure your room is neat. I know that while you're here this is your home. I see to it that this home is as clean as mine. And that's not my job really. Some nurses are not that conscientious. I try to accomplish every procedure quickly. My mood is generally pleasant. I chat with you. I help you pass the time.

MAN. Go!

NURSE. When my superior gets back from her break, she's going to have to hear about this. She's going to tell me that I'm too sensitive, that I take things too seriously. She'll probably blame me. I don't care. She's going to hear about this anyway. (*Pause. The woman goes back to her stool*)

VISITOR. Was that a good idea?

MAN. What?

VISITOR. Treating her like that.

MAN. I hate her. I hate them all. Now ... you were squeezing it ... no ... no. What were you doing? His mouth. That's where you were.

VISITOR. I'm not in the mood anymore. Maybe tomorrow.

MAN. Tomorrow? I might not want to hear this tomorrow. I might not be able to. I might not be interested. Now is when I can listen to it. Now is when I have to remember. Now!

VISITOR. I wish the door had a lock.

MAN. But it doesn't.

VISITOR. It's a wish.

MAN. I remember those. The lights, please. (*The man playing the visitor walks over to the floor lamp and switches it off. All lights dim*) His mouth.

VISITOR. I wanted his mouth, his tongue to be the beginning. I wanted it to be the start. I wanted, by way of that full tongue, to suck into my mouth his whole body. His face would follow the tongue. Then the neck, the chest, the stomach, the groin, the legs, the feet, the toes.

MAN. Did he shake?

VISITOR. Like you did. Saliva was falling from our mouths. I caught some with my hand. Then I rubbed it . . .

MAN. On the head.

VISITOR. And the shaft. I was rubbing it . . .

MAN. Gently.

VISITOR. Roughly. I was too happy I was with him. He was too perfect. I was envious of his perfection. I wanted to disturb it. Hurt it. I had to create a distance between us. If I didn't, I would have been swallowed up by him. I would have disappeared. So I rubbed it roughly.

MAN. Did he say anything?

VISITOR. Oh no. There were no words. He was mine.

MAN. Totally?

VISITOR. Totally. My other hand was sliding down his back. Sliding down slowly. Down the center of the back. That blessèd valley. All the way down.

MAN. You didn't?

VISITOR. Of course I did. My hand went down the center of the back. All the way until it was exploring . . .

MAN. You did.

VISITOR. . . . until my hand was exploring the crack, until my finger was pressing into . . .

MAN. I know.

VISITOR. His hands were clutching at my chest. His fingers digging into me. He wanted to fight my possession. If only he knew . . .

MAN. What?

VISITOR. The truth. How completely in his power I was. But I pretended. I pretended to be in control. When his nails dug into me . . .

MAN. Show me.

VISITOR. I slapped his ass hard.

MAN. Show me.

VISITOR. The slap?

MAN. No. Where his nails dug into you.

VISITOR. Here?

MAN. Yes, here. Help me remember. (*The two men get off their stools and remove them from the center area. The man playing the patient puts on a hospital gown and connects himself to an I.V. He then sits in a chair. The man playing the visitor removes his shirt*)

MAN. Where were his fingers?

VISITOR. Digging into here. (*The visitor strokes his chest*)

MAN. Can I put my hand there? I want my hands where his were. (*The visitor places the other man's hand on his chest*)

MAN. (*After a moment*) I remember.

VISITOR. The slap surprised him. Stung him.

MAN. What did he do?

VISITOR. Whimpered. Like a child. And then he began caressing me as gently as you are. My finger pushed . . . pushed in. He tensed up for a moment. And then he covered my face with kisses. Veiled my face with his kisses.

MAN. He was grateful.

VISITOR. I pushed in deeper. He moaned. If you could have heard it. I wanted you to hear it.

MAN. Did he touch you . . . here? (*He puts his hand on the visitor's crotch. He strokes it tentatively*)

VISITOR. He was afraid to.

MAN. But I'm not.

VISITOR. You never were. Can I . . .

MAN. What?

VISITOR. Can I touch you?

MAN. Not there. Not tonight. Maybe never again.

VISITOR. Oh come on, we're kids. Come on, show me yours. Let me show you mine.

MAN. I'm afraid to remember.

VISITOR. Mine wants out. It feels like it's tightly slammed against a wall. It's in a vise. It's beginning to hurt.

MAN. Then ... then you have to let it out. But when you do, please, take your time, slip it out slowly.

VISITOR. Take your hand away. Now watch. Do you see? Can you see the beginning of it? (*The visitor stands in front of the other man, his back to the audience, and slowly pulls down his pants*) Touch it. Come on, stroke it. But be gentle. That's where your hands belong. That's where you should be. (*The woman switches on the floor lamp. All lights brighten. She gets off her stool and faces the men*)

NURSE. Stop it! (*The visitor pulls up his pants*)

MAN. Get out!

NURSE. What the hell do you think you're doing?

MAN. Out! Get out!

NURSE. How dare you?

MAN. Would you just leave and close the door!

NURSE. You shouldn't be doing that. You can't do that. You can't do that anymore.

MAN. Why?

NURSE. Because ... because this is a hospital.

MAN. It's my room.

NURSE. No. This room belongs to hundreds, thousands. This room is under my care. I want your friend to leave. I want you to go to sleep. That's what you should be doing here. Sleeping. Resting. I'm going to have to file a report. You have forced me to file a report. You're not supposed to be doing what you were doing.

VISITOR. Why?

NURSE. That's not what he's here for.

MAN. What am I here for?

NURSE. To recuperate.

MAN. That's what he's helping me do.

NURSE. I'm no fool. I'm a nurse. I have a degree. I know things. Every day it's a clean uniform. I have duties. I take them seriously. I'm going to have to file a report. It's best for everyone if I do. The hospital. Your friend. You. They may ask me to make it out in duplicate. Your friend has to go. You'll sleep. I'll take your temperature. I'm a nurse, God damn it. I try to do this job. The Almighty knows I try. And I try to do it well. Because I care.

MAN. Then help me. Help me get something back. Leave.

NURSE. No. I have to be more professional. That's my failing. Everybody says so. I want to get close. Sometimes too close. I want to make a difference. I want to nurse. Give attention.

MAN. Help me get something back.

VISITOR. Leave us.

NURSE. I should be welcomed here. This is where I should be performing my duty. This is my chapel. This is where I'm in service.

MAN. Then walk through the door and close it.

NURSE. I'm not professional enough. That's been my failing. That's what people tell me. I don't keep that distance. The distance that's required by all professionals. That distance that makes you enjoy your paycheck. That distance that, after a day when death drenches you, enables you to leave it all behind. That distance ... that distance is a drug. It makes you forget. It distances you from tears.

MAN. Turn your back on us and go.

NURSE. What should I say in my report?

MAN. That all is fine in this room. The patient is resting ...

VISITOR. And his friend is dozing, in an awkward position, in a chair. You saw nothing here. You don't want your supervisor to think you're a hysteric.

NURSE. She already does. But slowly, I'm dissuading her.

VISITOR. Then make no report.

NURSE. I get too close. They don't like that here. They eye you suspiciously if they expect you do. I cry. Do you believe it? I still cry. But I don't let them see me. I cry only in private. And the cries are getting quieter. I'm swallowing them. You see, I'm improving. Getting more professional every day. I don't remember their names anymore. I practice forgetting them. That's a promise I made to myself. Forget their names. I'll forget yours. In a week. In two. I'll practice. I'm learning how to forget.

VISITOR. You have to.

NURSE. So I can do my job. Relief is all I ever wanted to bring to them. A fraction of a second of relief.

MAN. Look in my eyes. Tell me what you see.

NURSE. No. If I look into them, I won't forget your name.

MAN. Please, look. Tell me what you see. Say it.

NURSE. (*After a moment*) Yes, it's there.

MAN. Relief.

NURSE. And I brought it, didn't I? You'll forget me — what I look like, those deep lines around my mouth, my name. But you'll remember the comfort. And maybe tonight, while I'm traveling home, I'll smile, because I did my job. These lights. The lights in this room are far too bright especially for such a warm night. (*The woman turns her back on the men. She walks over to her stool, sits down, and turns off the floor lamp. All lights dim. The visitor faces the man, moves in close, and buries the man's head in his arms*) Tea. That's what's needed. My superior will be coming back from her break. Then I can go on mine. I'll look at the newspaper. I'll think of other things. If they need anything, they'll call. They'll ring for me. I have to keep thinking of other things. (*Everyone is still for a moment. The nurse begins to speak again. As she is talking, the visitor dresses himself, stares at the man for a second, and then leaves the stage. The man removes the I.V. and hospital robe and returns to his stool*) So . . . so your friend is not here tonight. As a matter of fact, I haven't seen him for a few days. Maybe a week. It's the weather. It's too hot to move out there. He probably came home, intending to come here, having the best intentions, wanting to keep you company. A nap, he thought. I'll take a nap. He's probably there now. Lying on his couch. Sleeping. The television is on. And he's sleeping. Maybe he'll call later. But I wouldn't wait. I wouldn't hold my breath. In this weather you can't expect much from people. In this kind of weather people break promises. They forget to be kind.

MAN. He had to go away.

NURSE. I'm sorry. It always happens. Family problems. The friend is in the hospital for an extended stay, and for some reason, in some other city, there are family problems.

MAN. He'll be back. In thirty-nine more hours his plane will land. Then he'll come directly here.

NURSE. Don't watch the clock. Hide it. Don't make the wait an eternity.

MAN. My mind is drifting tonight. I can't seem to concentrate.

NURSE. I wish I had the opportunity to let my mind just float. I wonder where it would go.

MAN. I'm afraid.

NURSE. Don't say that. I have nothing for that.

MAN. I'm not tired, but my mind, it has nothing to hold on to.

NURSE. A massage. I'll give you a massage. Get the blood going. That might help.

MAN. I'm scared.

NURSE. I won't hurt you. I promise. My husband, he's on his vacation. Took my kid. They're visiting his mother. In Minnesota. I couldn't go. Had to work these two weeks. My home is so quiet.

MAN. Silence. It's all the time now. I'm so scared.

NURSE. My husband says he doesn't understand me anymore. He says that's why he won't touch me. But I know, it's because I'm not professional enough. I don't leave my work at work. That's what you're supposed to do. Leave your work at work. I'm trying to learn how to do that. But in the meantime, he won't touch me. I don't say anything about my work at home. Not anymore. I swear. He says I cry in my sleep. I think he lies. He just doesn't want to touch me.

MAN. I'm cold.

NURSE. It's warm in here. That air-conditioner of yours is not good. Close your eyes and remember warmth. Come on honey, close your eyes.

MAN. I'm afraid to.

NURSE. Feel my hands, honey. They're warm. You feel them. They're warming you up, aren't they? They're covering your body with summer.

MAN. Thank you.

NURSE. No. I'm a nurse. I have a uniform. I wear white. Feel my hands.

MAN. I'm so alone.

NURSE. I'm here.

MAN. I'm always lonely now.

NURSE. I know lonely. In bed with him, it's been three years now, he doesn't touch me.

MAN. Your hand ... where's it going?

NURSE. We know lonely, don't we? I work. Take care of my boy. He's fifteen. We only have one. I saw the silence coming. Felt it years ago. Didn't want to bring any more children into the quiet. I wonder how long I'll stay pretending. Perhaps, forever. I wonder what I am going to do. Forgive me. You must be envious. I can still "do." Do things. Do you hate me? Do you hate us all?

MAN. Your hand ... please ... no ... not there.

NURSE. But tonight, let's just remember.

MAN. Take it away. I want your hand away.

NURSE. Don't lie. You like it there, don't you?

MAN. Yes ... no. I can't ... not anymore.

NURSE. Sure you can. I remember a summer night. Years and years ago. Young years. It was the only time I lifted my skirt in the open air. Outside. It was in a field. I was visiting my cousin. She lived in the country. I dreaded the visit. Dreaded the boredom of country nights. Dreaded a summer's evening with no streets to parade up and down. My cousin arranged a date for me. We double-dated. We went to a drive-in. What a novelty that was for me. But halfway through the first feature, we had to leave. Had to bring my cousin and her date back home. Her date got a headache. Said we parked too close to the screen.

MAN. Your hand ...

NURSE. Yes ...

MAN. Lower.

NURSE. After we dropped them off, my date said we were heading back to the drive-in.

MAN. Right there. Yes. That's it.

NURSE. We never made it back to the drive-in. I knew we wouldn't. I knew what we were going to do. What I wanted from him. Oh, those young years. We parked the car. Walked hundreds of feet into the field. He laid me down. I'll tell you about him.

MAN. Should you?

NURSE. Of course. Broad features. Handsome. Big thick hands

that were not clumsy. His clothes were not stylish. New, but not fancy. Shopping-mall clothes. His full, tight body looked like it was about to explode out of those clothes. He laid me down. Stood over me. He undressed first. The smell of his skin filled the air. I remember that smell. I still search for it.

MAN. Yes, I know.

NURSE. I felt wet and wanted to kiss him. The only part of his body near me was his feet. I kissed them. He fell on top of me and with those massive, kind hands freed my body from the cloth that covered it. His smell, I can remember.

MAN. Yes. Remember. (*The woman gets off her stool, stands behind the man, and places her arms around him*)

NURSE. I wanted him to take his time. I wanted him to break all time. I wanted no time. I wanted forever.

MAN. And . . .

NURSE. My body . . . his lips wove a blanket over my body. (*The woman places her hand on the man's crotch and begins stroking it*)

MAN. Gently . . . slower.

NURSE. My body . . .

MAN. Yes?

NURSE. Every cell. I began feeling every cell.

MAN. I remember.

NURSE. And they were alive. (*Blackout*)

intimacies/
more intimacies

■

BY

MICHAEL KEARNS

▼

intimacies/more intimacies

In the bowels of New York City's subway system, I saw a man: fortyish, his head swathed in bloodied bandages, wearing fuzzy bedroom slippers and a hospital identification bracelet. Clearly gay and in the throes of dementia, he was part stand-up comic, part drag queen, and part social activist. Like many "crazy" people, his diatribe resonated with the truth. I thought to myself, "What would it be like to *be* him?"

This turned out to be the inspiration for *intimacies*. After writing Denny's monologue, I continued to create characters you wouldn't find on the pages of *People* magazine: the disenfranchised faces of AIDS, not the usual media darlings. As an actor-writer, I put myself in their shoes (sometimes high heels), finding parts of me — parts of all of us — in them. I avoided the "innocent" teenage hemophiliac story in favor of a junkie, a whore, the homeless and unloved. When six characters began to breathe, I premiered *intimacies*.

more intimacies is a continuation of my original desire to bring to life those PWAs who had virtually been ignored, to give voices to the unheard: a middle-aged hemophiliac, a lesbian, a bisexual Latino, a deaf young man.

When I was a nine-year-old child in St. Louis, Missouri, I was taught the Stanislavski method of acting by Marian Epstein. A very controversial approach in the fifties — especially for young children. Miss Epstein taught us, above all, to always search for ourselves in the characters we portrayed. It remains my greatest gift as a writer and actor: the ability to empathize. I thank Miss Epstein and dedicate these works to her and all the valuable teachers since.

Michael Kearns

Written and performed by Michael Kearns, *intimacies* premiered in May 1989 at Highways in Santa Monica, California; produced by Ron Myers; directed by Kelly Hill; with original music written and performed by Darien Martus.

Written and performed by Michael Kearns, *more intimacies* premiered in November 1990 at the Los Angeles Theatre Center in Los Angeles, California; produced by LATC; directed by Kelly Hill; with original music written and performed by Darien Martus.

CHARACTERS

intimacies

DENNY .... fortyish, suffering from dementia

BIG RED .... a female black street hooker, late 30s

PATRICK .... a gay beauty clone, thirtyish

RUSTY .... a teenage street hustler on drugs

MARY .... a Southern religious fanatic in her 60s

PHOENIX .... a homeless ex-con, black or Hispanic, 50s

more intimacies

FERNANDO .... a Hispanic flamenco dancer, fiftyish

JESSE .... a middle-aged black lesbian druggie

FATHER ANTHONY .... a Roman Catholic priest, 35–45

MIKE .... a redneck hemophiliac, fortyish

DEEDE .... a pregnant yuppie, thirtysomething

PAUL .... a hearing-impaired young man, mid 30s

The plays may be performed with one or more actors in one or more roles.

THE MONOLOGUES

DENNY. Don't talk to me about gay brotherhood, girlfriend. They wish I was dead. I'm the type that gives gay liberation a bad name. My name, by the way, is Denny, but you can call me Creme Dementia. These fuckin' hospital slippers won't click, click, click. There's no place like homeless; there's no place like homeless; there's no place like homeless. Benefits for homeless and AIDS and alkies — oh, my! I'm a walking telethon, girlfriend. But I ain't seen a leftover quiche from any of Cleopatra's parties. So I'm producin' my own. (*Sings*) "Please don't talk about love tonight . . ." This is my farewell tour, honey. (*Sings*) "Please don't talk about sweeeet love . . ." Don't tell George Bush: I use American flags for diapers. Then I burn 'em. If you think I'm demented now, honey, you should have seen me then. I was sooo demented . . . I was sooo demented, I shot up crystal and went to brunch with the family on Mother's Day. (*Sings*) "I'll always love my Mama 'cause she's my favorite girl . . ." I don't have twenty-five cents for the fuckin' pay phone and these fuckin' fags have phones in their jeeps. I asked one of 'em to call my agent. My travel agent. Book me a spiritual plane. To the big death valley. Spare me the faith healers and prayer meetings. The idea of a new miracle drug is about as exciting to me as . . . Calvin Klein underwear. I'm ready for my close-up, Mr. Undertaker. If my T-cells get any lower, I'm gonna name the motherfuckers. They tell me I'm suffering from OBS — Obnoxiously Bad Sex. Calvin Klein underwear. I was sooo demented . . . I was sooo demented, I wore a butt plug to my tenth year high school reunion. I've been writing my will. I have only three requests: bury me with my tambourine; no Stephen Sondheim songs; send all donations to Save the Baths.

I love this new expression: Self Delivery. I went to the Post
Office and asked how much. "How much would you charge
to self deliver me?" You shoulda seen that bitch's face. "I'll
have to ask my supervisor." She had on one of those big "Just
Say No" buttons. I thought she would "just say no" but,
nooo, she asks her supervisor. Now this big black stud is
standin' there — more chains around his neck than Sammy
Davis Jr. on an opening night. "You want to what?" "I want
to suck on your big black hard piece of meat, honey." Then I
ran out onto the street. And this big buck is chasin' me. I start
screamin' "Rape! Rape!" at the top of my damaged lungs.
Well, it worked. Of course people believed this mean black
dude was chasin' this glamorous white woman. So he stopped,
realizin' he'd be tarred and feathered before I would. Besides,
he probably figured I'd like to be tarred and feathered. And
he's right! As long as the feathers match this hospital gown.
I'm thinking about getting into the phone sex business: 976-
DEAD. Maybe I'll answer, maybe I won't. You all heard of
the Names Project. That's me, tryin' to remember my old
boyfriends. Calvin Klein underwear. In case you're wonderin',
I'm open to another marriage but the only man who'd marry
me is hooked up to an oxygen machine and can't possibly say
"I do." I don't regret one of my marriages and I lost track
somewhere in the seventies. There isn't one inch of my slightly
deteriorated body that hasn't been pinched or punched or
poked or prodded. How many of you can say that? When
they came in me, they stayed in me. They left souvenirs:
damaged childhoods, fucked-up adolescence, disapproving
parents, and outraged wives. I don't believe their bodily fluids
gave me AIDS. We been poisoned by something but not
bodily fluids. We been poisoned by hate, hate from moms and
dads and uncles and aunts and priests and nuns and school
systems and mayors and the Moral Fucking Majority and
Miss Jesse Helms and Calvin Klein underwear and the Reagan
Fucking Administration. Bodily fluids gave me life, honey.
Hatred is what's killin' me. Oh, yeah, I read those lists: No,
Don't, Stop. I would have died without bodily fluids. I refused
to abstain. The only thing harder to put on than false eyelashes is

a fuckin' rubber. I needed to feel their semen settlin' in my soul, their spit activatin' my heart. Making me alive. I even indulged in an occasional piss cocktail now and then. That's a sure cure for any of yous sufferin' from fear of intimacy. You probably won't read about me in *People* magazine or see me on *Nightline*. Besides, I don't have a thing to wear. I traded in my LaCoste shirts for a hospital gown. Tried to get into Studio One the other night but they didn't like my hospital slippers. Get real, girleen. So I stood outside. Some big burley number with a sissy voice told me to split. "Listen here, you overripe piece of fruit, I'm a safe sex advertisement; havin' to look at me is better than any of those keep-your-tongue-outa-buttholes lists. You'll have to carry me away, Mr. Big Stuff." (*Sings*) "Mr. Big Stuff, who do you think you are?" Listen, honeys, windin' up like this was not my life's ambition. When I was young and pretty — younger and prettier — I went to the parties with the gay elite, the gay effete. I took the same drugs and sat on the same cocks. Some are just luckier than others. (*Sings*) "I love the nightlife, I love to boogie . . . "

BIG RED. Between hand jobs, I concentrate on forgiveness. That's all I got time for these days. It's jus a matter of time. I been lucky. I got a few lesions on my head and this tiny one on my face. I'm special! Most womens don't get lesions: that's what they tole me at the clinic. Little bitch who tole me was makin' a point, knowin' my profession. Lesions is God's way of punishin' a whore like me, she was sayin'. I don't believe that shit. How'd I git it? How long have I had it? Now what the fuck difference does it make? Probably from a drug addict. Or maybe up the ole poop shoot. You'd be surprised how many guys hire a whore so they can act like they're a faggot. "Suck my dick; let me fuck you in the ass." I made my tricks wear rubbers back when Ayds was somethin' I took to keep the weight off. But, sure, there were times when the fuckin' things broke. You hear me? Uh-huh. And there mighta been a few druggies shootin' up — you never know about that. And, yeah, I forgot. I forget a lot these days. It might be the disease. Uh-huh. Walter. Now he swears he ain't got it but he ain't been tested neither. We got back together a few years ago. He's the only man I ever loved so I'd like to think I got it from love and not from some druggie stranger who popped open a rubber. You hear me? Uh-huh. Walter could be the one. He's been shootin' drugs mosta his life. And fuckin' with transsexuals. And transvestites. I don't know which is which. Sometimes I think that's why he comes back to me: I can suck dick and I dress like a drag queen. Uh-huh. First time I got paid to suck dick I was eleven or twelve years old. This nasty uncle — my mother's brother — paid me to keep my mouth shut. I mean, to keep my mouth wide open, then shut up tight. I was a quick learner. Probly because I like it. I liked the feel of warmth shootin' inside me. And I liked the cash. I liked bein' good at somethin'. Eventually, I started givin' blowjobs to teenage punks in a downtown movie theatre. I'd be lucky to get a box of jujubees. But I liked it. That's where I met Walter. I was fourteen. He was a few years older. A real tough guy. Juvenile delinquent. He liked to watch me go down on his buddies as much as he liked gettin' it hisself. Some guys — now, baby, this might surprise you — some guys, they need a finger up their butt to keep it hard. Walter was one of them guys. He even liked a finger up there when he fucked me. Which he did — not at the movie theatre, in his car, where one of his nasty friends would watch. I married him. Four or five months pregnant at the time. Got a ten-year-old daughter to prove it. Farrah. My one and only babychild. Walter went to jail when she was a baby and my mama had to raise her. I hit the streets and I been here ever since. Uh-huh. You must wonder why I can't get off these streets. Listen, I ain't doin' nothin' dangerous. You hear me? Jus hand jobs these days. Most I can make is twenty, thirty bucks. How many hand jobs will it take to send Farrah to college? Tell 'ya this: beats the fuck outa bein' a waitress. I tried that — jus another form of hustlin'. I was lyin' to ya when I tole you I only got one daughter. I got a baby, Annie is her name, and she's only eight months old. One of them popped-open rubbers. Or Walter. Walter could be her daddy. Jus couldn't handle it. I can take care of myself, thankyou-

243
▼

verymuch, but Annie's in bad shape. She and I got somethin' in common. You know. Wears a colostomy bag, that tiny baby. Weighs less than a pair of my high heels. That disease is in her. It's jus a matter of time. Oh, she's okay right now. Livin' in a big, beautiful house with a big, strong lady who wouldn't have no babies of her own. Right after Annie was born, I started gettin' chemotherapy. My hair started fallin' out by the handful. I bet you already figured this is not my real hair. A bald whore is worse than a diseased whore. You don't always see the disease. God has been good to me. Gave me a beautiful head of red hair. My best feature. Some guys would pay me just to tickle their balls with my long, red hair. My hair has been my callin' card. That's my nickname: Big Red, named after my hair. God took that hair back and gave me some beauty marks on my head. That's what I call 'em: beauty marks. And one tiny beauty mark on my face. God knew I could buy a wig. God knows I need to keep workin' so I can send money to Farrah's grandma who takes care of her. They don't know I'm sick. Farrah don't know she's got a dyin' mother and a dyin' baby sister. Secrets. I keep secrets. My mother, Farrah's grandma, she knew her brother was payin' me to have sex. I keep so many secrets. If I was gonna start blamin' people for my life, I guess I'd start there. But what's the point? Huh? Big Red is gonna keep on truckin'. God ain't punishin' me. How could he punish a baby like Annie and not punish my mama for encouragin' her own daughter to become a slut? That don't make much sense now, does it? I just try to forgive my mama. She promises me she's not pimpin' Farrah and I gotta believe her. And I forgive that nasty uncle. And Walter. Or the asshole who broke open the rubber. Whoever gave me these beauty marks and a baby born to die. It's jus a matter of time. You hear me? Time for forgiveness. Who knows? Maybe someday I'll forgive. . . . Forget that. I ain't got that much time left.

PATRICK. Shortly after I had my chin implant, I told this guy my name was Patrick and he said, "Did you say 'Perfect?'" I'm close to perfect. I paid for it; I wasn't born this way. Teeth, nose, cheekbones: all done. Best haircutter in the city. And I go to the gym — three hours a day, seven days a week. Easy to imagine someone thought my name is Perfect. Being perfect ain't easy. I work at it. I also have the perfect car, condo, and closetful of clothes. Barry, my lover, also perfect: rich, gorgeous, powerful. We're in the entertainment industry. He's an agent at William Morris; I'm an accountant at Disney. Perfect. People are always saying I look like I'm an actor but that's just because I'm gay. Not that I'm completely out of the closet. Neither is Barry. I mean, we're out. Except to our parents. And at work. We even take dates to office functions. We have to; it's just part of the Hollywood game. We don't need to march in gay pride parades or any of that bullshit. We make a yearly donation — $50 each — to AIDS Project. Anonymously. Our lifestyle is really our own business. When I asked about these (*Indicating swollen glands*) I really resented my plastic surgeon suggesting I have the test. Look at me; do I look sick? Barry and I have been together for seven years. "Has it been a monogamous relationship?" the doctor wanted to know. "It's been perfect," I told him. It's really none of the doctor's fucking business. I know Barry has been faithful to me and I've only cheated a coupla times. Not really cheating. Fooling around. The gym. "Do you and your partner have safe sex?" the doctor had the nerve to ask. Of course not. Why would we? We've been together seven years. We're perfectly monogamous — Barry thinks. I can't destroy that. Besides, he might leave me and I can't stand to be alone, for Chrissakes. Barry doesn't like to fuck. I do the fucking in the family so when this really hot guy came on to me at the gym, I let him fuck me. You don't usually carry a condom into the steam room at the Sports Connection, now, do you? It happened at least once a week for several months. It was perfect. He is an actor. To die for. Clean cut. Look at me. Do I look sick? "Fuck it," I said, "I'll take the test." There's no way. No way. Get AIDS in the steam room at the gym, looking the way I do? It's so clean in there. No way. Get serious. When my doctor told me I was positive, I thought he must be kidding. Not me. Look at me. Do I look sick? Then I thought about the actor. He didn't look sick. He couldn't have given it to me; he's a TV star! There was this kid a couple of years ago — maybe it was him. I let him fuck me in the john on the lot at Disney. That was before we knew anything about AIDS. He worked in the mailroom. Dick of death. He was black. Even though he was clean, Barry would die. Who? Who gave it to me? I can't be positive. "Are you sure about your lover?" the doctor asked, like he's in some third-rate movie of the week. "No," I lied, "It probably is his fault." But I know Barry. He's not a good liar like I am. I'd know. The doctor lectured me about protecting Barry. Immediately. But I can't. I can't tell anyone. And I sure as hell can't tell Barry. Tell him I've given him AIDS for Christmas? C'mon, get serious. The only answer is to kill myself. I never wanted to get old anyway. What's that line? "Live fast, die young, and have a beautiful corpse." I'm just gonna disappear. They'll be no revelations. No screaming parents. No raging lover. No obituary in *Variety* or the *Hollywood Reporter*. No crow's-feet. No fortieth birthday party. No twentieth high school reunion. No tenth year anniversary with Barry. No more lies. No more bullshit. No more plastic surgery. No more hating myself. No more hangovers. No more sex in bushes and johns. No more poppers. No more cocaine. No more steroids. No more. No more. No more. No more hope. Like Norman Maine in *A Star Is Born*, I'm just gonna walk into the Pacific Ocean. At sunset. Judy will be singing in the kitchen. A perfect Hollywood ending. Perfect.

RUSTY. My name is Rusty. Somebody once tole me only hookers, strippers, and lesbians are named Rusty. I am not a lesbian. I'm not really a stripper — not 'til tonight. I got this gig by accident. This fuckin' movie producer picked me up off the street. Fancy fuckin' car. Figured I'd have a place to spend the night. I'd do almost anything for a warm fuckin' bed and twenty bucks. Since Richard left, I been sleepin' in fuckin' cars, in the fuckin' park, under the fuckin' freeway — you name it. Turns out this prissy producer just wants me to dance to some fuckin' disco music from the seventies. I was

born in 1970, for Chrissakes. Donna Summer does not get me
off. Anyway, I dance. Like I actually like all that love-to-love-
you-baby shit. He jerks hisself off — from clear across the
room — without even touchin' me. He thought it was so cool
I didn't take my shirt off. "That's hot," he kept repeatin'.
"That's so hot. Leave your shirt on. Hot. Show me your butt.
Show me your dick. Show me your tits. But leave your shirt
on. Hot." I guess he thought he was directin' some fuckin'
movie. He shot his load all over his fuckin' fat belly and then
asked me if I'd be interested in makin' a hundred bucks.
That's five times what I'm used to. All I had to do was strip at
this party for a bunch of his phoney faggot friends. So here I
am. "Keep your shirt on. It's hot," he orders me in that
whiny, bitch voice of his. Reminds me of my mother, that
voice. "Of course I'll keep my shirt on, you fuckin' asshole.
Your fuckin' alcoholic, martini-mouthed prissheads wouldn't
want to see track marks on my arms, now, would they?" A
hundred bucks would buy me a day's supplya crystal. I usually
have to turn five or six tricks a day to survive, keep high.
And let me tell you — most of 'em want more than a fuckin'
dance routine to some seventies disco beat. One fuckin' maniac
actually tried to stick a loaded gun up my butt. Said he
wanted to see if I trusted him. Another dude — you mighta
read about him in the papers: Doctor Max. He liked to take
polaroid pictures of body parts. Legs, thighs, shoulders, neck.
Sounds like I'm orderin' fried chicken, huh? I even let him
take a picture of my arms. Track marks and all. Five bucks a
shot. He wasn't as squeamish as these Hollywood fags. A few
nights later, Doctor Max took a chainsaw to Leroy, one of
my buddies. Sawed him up and buried the pieces up and
down the California coast. I just barely escaped that looneytune.
Couldn't dance very well without my legs, now, could I?
Only other time I made a hundred bucks was paintin' a house
one weekend. I actually tried to get my shit together. Went to
this rehab program for street kids. Stopped doin' crystal for
about ten days. Had a place to stay. Got this job paintin'
houses with this really cool dyke in A.A. I even went to a
fuckin' counselor who asked me a million fuckin' questions

about my family. You see, my scum-of-the-earth parents kicked me outa the house when they found out I was smokin' dope. They are these fuckin' heavy-duty winos but they go to church every Sunday — after beatin' each other up every Saturday night — so it's okay. If they knew I was fuckin' with guys, they'd shit. If they knew I had the Big A, they'd have a fuckin' heart attack. Which is the one — and only — reason I might tell 'em. What if these holier-than-thou fags found out I got it? One thing is for sure. No fuckin' refunds! That hundred bucks will be dancin' in my veins before the night is over. I've only been on the streets for about a year. Got tested when I was in that rehab place. That did it. Figured I might as well get back on the streets and party. Nobody — *nobody* — could stop me. Yeah, they taught us all about safe sex. I dare anyone who's shot up crystal to put on a fuckin' rubber. It ain't my responsibility. One of them assholes gave it to me. Right? They ain't all assholes. There is a few cool ones. This one dude, he drives a white Toyota. He took me to see *Rain Man* with that fox Tom Cruise. Now lookin' at him makes me think I'm gay. I fuck girls, too. I'm not sure what I am. The guy who took me to the movies — his name is Richard — all he wanted to do was kiss my eyelids. Jesus. Pretty weird, huh? He bought me this yellow-and-black checkered shirt — longsleeve — at the Army/Navy Surplus. He taught me to eat with chopsticks. He kissed me on the eyelids — that's all, I swear. He died about four weeks ago. That's when I started gettin' sick. Sometimes the speed makes me sick but this is different. This is it. Richard killed hisself when he found out he got it. I don't got the guts. Whenever I see a white Toyota, I think it's him, gonna save me. His neighbor tole me. I went over there one night — he used to let me sleep on his couch — and his neighbor tole me that Richard hung hisself 'cause he caught AIDS. He handcuffed hisself so he couldn't chicken out and change his mind at the last minute. I went there to have my eyelids kissed. No charge. No shit. Those motherfucking handcuffs. I need to get high. How much longer do I have? To do this fuckin' striptease? What the fuck time is it?

MARY. Holy Mary, mother of God, pray for us sinners now and at the hour of our death. Amen. The hour of our death. Amen. Death. Amen. No matter how far apart, you beat in my heart. Pray for us sinners now and at the hour of our death. You beat in my heart. Amen. It was my turn to receive the valentine this year. We began sending it back and forth in 1974 — imagine! — fifteen years ago. David sent it to me in January of '74, the occasion of my first heart attack. It started out as a get-well card; it wasn't really designed as a valentine — or a get-well card, for that matter. No matter how far apart, you beat in my heart. Seemed like the perfect valentine. So I just found an envelope and returned the card to him on Valentine's Day that year. Then, a year later, on February 14, 1975, he airmailed it back to me. We've cherished it as a yearly valentine ever since — except for the Big One — my 1984 heart attack (five years ago, that's when I was transfused) when it resurfaced as a get-well card. No matter how far apart, you beat in my heart. There is ample proof to indicate I will not be alive next Valentine's Day. David does not know this but I must, I must, tell him. And I must return that dilapidated card for the last time. No matter how far apart, you beat in my heart. AIDS is God's punishment. Pray for us sinners now and at the hour of our death. Amen. My sin was in loving my son too much. David was six or seven when I divorced his father. An ugly traumatic parting. His father never paid any attention to him and then he tried to prove I was an unfit mother. Unfit? If anything, I overloved him. I overloaded him with love. Whatever Davey wanted, I gave him. Whatever I could. After his father left, leaving us with next to nothing, David became my friend. My best friend. He understood when I had a little too much to drink. He understood my need to find a replacement for his father. Such a good boy. By the time he was nine or ten, he'd stay by himself without a babysitter. He'd iron my clothes; I taught him how to hem my skirts. Some Saturday nights, he'd do up my hair. Of course, there were accusations from family members: "Mary, you're turning him into a mama's boy." I didn't pay much attention. I wanted to find a man to help me raise David. Of course, I wanted to find someone to love but nobody loved me as much as that child. Nobody. By the time I did find an excuse for a second husband, David had followed in my footsteps: drinking too much and looking for men. I tried to accept his being homosexual but I knew in my heart it was wrong. I knew it was a sin. A mortal, unforgivable sin. I couldn't accept it — any more than I could accept him marrying a woman. My Davey. Nothing could destroy our bond. God knows I don't love my second husband the way I love David. And I can't accept the idea of his so-called male lovers. The word makes me queasy. Lover. Accept my son's male lover? And, believe you me, he's had his share. When I first heard about this disease which is killing me — even before they called it AIDS — I just knew he'd get it. This has got to be God's punishment. And David flaunts his homosexuality. Openly queer. Why does he have to be open — especially now? I prayed, night after night, week after week, month after month, that God would forgive David and spare him. I could not live without his phone calls, his letters, his postcards, our valentine. My prayers have been answered. David does not show any signs of AIDS and I'm going to die from it. I ask myself, Mary, what did you do to deserve this? Am I being punished for my son's behavior? "You're turning him into a mama's boy." There were those nights, after I'd been out too late, drinking too much, when I'd come home and find David asleep in my bed. I'd try to wake him, I'd try to move him. I knew it was wrong for a ten-year-old boy to sleep in the same bed with his mama. But his body made the bed warm. I was afraid to be alone and so was he. Sometimes I'd hold his hand — so little compared to his father's. Or the big, crusty hands of the men I'd meet at Blueskies, the neighborhood bar. David's hand was so soft in my hand. With my other hand, I'd stroke his babyfine blond hair which smelled of my favorite shampoo. One night I woke up to the sound of my own crying, startled, knowing his skin was pressed up against mine, holding me. Tight. Loving me. Part of me. This is my sin. Not his. AIDS is my punishment. I am ashamed. I deserve to die. God has given it to me and spared

David. He has answered my prayers: there is a God! Holy
Mary, mother of God. How will I tell David his mother
deserves to die? Pray for us sinners. My heart hurts, missing
my boy. My hands are empty, missing my boy. No matter
how far apart, you beat in my heart. Now and at the hour of
our death. Amen.

PHOENIX. Yo, bro. My name is Phoenix — named after the city,
not the bird. I've snorted MDA, swallowed LSD, shaken
from the DTs and flown without the help of TWA. I tested
positive for HIV and gone blind from CMV. That's right: I
can't S-E-E. Now for the good news: I'm sixty-three days
clean and sober. No shit, man. No fuckin' shit coursin' through
my veins, bro. I been shootin' dope since I was a teenager.
Learned how to in the joint. Learned how to do a lot of things
in the joint. I been in and out of the pen for the past thirty
years — mostly in. First time was for petty theft. Nothin' big
time but I learned they treat ya better in there than they do
out here on the street. Think about it: three meals a day, roof
over your head, family. Got out this most recent time in '85.
That was for armed robbery. I been livin' on the streets ever
since. Got me a comfortable little abode right under the
Hollywood Freeway. Bein' locked up doesn't exactly prepare
you for a job. Can you imagine me at the B of fuckin' A? I
pretty much been keepin' outa trouble. Beggin' for money
insteada stealin' it. Easier to beg now that I'm blind. Got a
quarter, bro? Was shootin' dope even though I knew it was
killin' me. About six months ago, I got a killer case of the
shits. Which is pretty unfuckinusual for a junkie since weeks
go by when I can't even take a shit. The diarrhea kept up —
even though I was hardly eatin' a thing. Then I started losin'
my vision. First one eye, then the other. I knew. I didn't need
no doctor to tell me. I read the paper. I read the paper. Now
I'm fuckin' blind with the fuckin' shits all the fuckin' time.
That's the one nice thing about bein' homeless: when you
gotta crap, you don't gotta run to the bathroom. A coupla
months ago — sixty-five days to be exact — some young kid
with a soft voice came to my abode and offered me a handful

of syringes and some bleach. I'm real sensitive to voices since I can't fuckin' see. And smells. This kid smelled like a laundromat — clean. He musta been twenty or twenty-one years old. Sounded real educated. And a little superior. But gentle. Like I said: soft. Couldn't believe it when he tole me he was a drug addict. "I'm recovering," the kid said. "I'm a recovering drug addict with AIDS and while I'm alive, I want to stop spreading the disease." I tole him he was knockin' on my door a little bit late in the fuckin' day but thanks, anyway. Max came back the next day. I mean Luis. That's his name: Luis. I was all fucked up. Nasty. Shit in my pants. Foul. He said he wanted to take me to a meeting for drug addicts with AIDS. He smelled sweet. After he cleaned me up — that's when he tole me he was gay, somethin' I already kinda figured. Didn't make no difference to me. I was too sick and too tired to say no. He smelled like flowers. I don't remember much about that first meetin' 'cept they was all men. And their voices — some of them real masculine, others more soft, like Luis's — were filled with laughter. Alcoholics and drug addicts with AIDS — laughin' their butts off. Luis later tole me I was lucky I was blind 'cause I didn't have to see the expressions on their faces when he pranced me through the door. But, after a few days, they accepted me. Most of 'em. Tole me I was "chemically dependent"; I always thought I was a junkie. I call everybody "Bro." They like that. "Hey, bro, what's happenin'?" Luis gave me this cat, Max. We had a big fuckin' fight because I won't move from under the freeway. I went to the fuckin' clinic, wasn't that enough? No, he says, it's important for me to share a home. To touch somethin', someone. So he gave me Max, a cat without balls. Lives with me. Sometimes I call the cat Luis and I call Luis Max. Might be the disease. Sometimes I pet Max and it's Luis's long, silky hair against my hands. Might be the disease. I been tryin' to kill myself for the past thirty years and it's finally gonna work. Godammit. The past sixty-three days have been a fuckin' miracle, man. I been loved, finally, by a queer boy and his cat. And I don't want to die. I want to love. I mean, live. Might be . . . but you know what? I'm ready, ready for

... whatever. He smells like morning. He smells like rain. He smells like life.

FERNANDO. "A man needs to be fucked." Those were his exact words. This white boy with yellow hair, the color of corn. From Ohio. Or Iowa. I do not know the difference. "A man needs to be fucked." Jim. I call him Jim-Boy because he looks like he could have been on *The Waltons*. That's my children's favorite show; they watch all the reruns. Jim showed up at the club where I have been dancing for the past twenty-three years — since before he was born. He'd seen my picture in a newspaper advertisement. "I like manly men," he said to me. "Macho men, dark men, older men. Men with sturdy legs and strong stares." "I guess I fit the bill," I said to this boy with much guts, "but I am not gay." He did not blink. Those clear blue eyes stared right through me, penetrating me. "A man needs to be fucked," he whispered. Everyone assumes male dancers are queer. Not true! I grew up with kids taunting me. "Here comes the dancer," they'd say. As if dancer meant fairy, pansy, fruit. "Here comes the dancer." I learned to outrun them. Most of those guys are dead by now. Gang fights. I outran them and I outlived them. Dancing was not what my father had in mind for his only son. "Dancing is for sissies," he'd hiss. In order to go to dancing school, I had to prove I was no sissy. I became a ladies' man at a very early age. My father was impressed — if not with my dancing ability, with my ability to attract beautiful girls. I got married to please my Dad. I was seventeen. Marrying Gabriella made it easier for my father to accept the idea of me becoming a dancer. There was never any question about what kind of dancer I'd be; from the time I was a little boy and saw a picture of a flamenco dancer, I knew. While other boys wanted to be Superman, I longed for the power and the passion I saw in that dancer's strong stare. His impenetrability. I tore that picture out of the book and carried it in my pocket. For inspiration. Thank God I was good enough to get a steady job, flamenco dancing, about the same time Gabriella got pregnant. After I moved away from home, I remember only

253
▼

two serious discussions with my father and both of them were about ass-fucking. One of these "man-to-man talks," as he called them, was when Gabriella ballooned up from the pregnancy. "You must not commit adultery," he said, being a strict Catholic. "Yet, being a man, you'll have urges and your wife will be too sick or too fat or too something," he said, looking me in the eye. "Find a boy, a puto, to fuck in the ass," he said, as if this was the Eleventh Commandment. "Find a puto to fuck in the ass. Feels great," he said. "You won't know the difference." Like Ohio and Iowa, I thought. So I did. And it did. Our second man-to-man talk came when Gabriella was pregnant with our third child, less than three years later. "You obviously haven't figured out how to practice birth control," he said. I knew he wasn't talking about rubbers, forbidden by the Church. "You must learn to fuck her like you fuck those pretty boy putos. Then no more babies." Suddenly I knew why I was an only child. Gabriella wouldn't go for it — "hurt too bad," she said — so we had two more kids in as many years. Five hungry kids to feed on the salary of a flamenco dancer was not easy. Many women at the club had offered me gifts. And I accepted. I knew they wanted to feel what was between the flamenco dancer's sturdy legs. When a lady presented me with a hundred dollar bill, I knew she wanted more than a feel. I blamed Gabriella. If she'd let me do what my father suggested, I wouldn't need to fuck this old bag for a hundred bucks. But I did; the kids needed to eat. It became a weekly ritual with this rich old broad. Then I started servicing her girlfriends. I was exhausted but I was making an extra thousand dollars a month. That was fifteen years ago. I still — even at my age — get offers. As long as they don't see my feet, I can make a few extra bucks. As long as it doesn't spread up my legs. Onto my face. Into my mouth. There's one conversation my father and I did not have about butt-fucking. A conversation that might have saved my life. "A man needs to be fucked," Jim-Boy said. He's rubbing my feet. We're in his hotel room, which he's rented for the weekend. The picture of me in the newspaper advertisement is on the dresser. "You have so much attitude when you're onstage," he says. I don't understand "attitude." "Charisma," he says. "Oh! *Garbo* is what you're meaning." "Garbo? Like in Greta Garbo?" he asks. We laugh. He begins licking my feet, putting each toe in his mouth, like they are cherry popsicles. Sucking my toes. I am feeling things I have never felt before. He tickles my feet with his silky yellow hair; I feel his finger slide into my ass as he works his way up from my feet, kissing my ankles, my calves, my knees, my thighs, my balls. I am completely wet. His tongue is inside me. I will never be the same. He fucks me with his tongue and then he's on top of me, kissing my face, whispering in my ear. "Tell me how much you need it," he says. "Tell me how much you need it." "I need to be fucked," I hear myself say, under the spell of this boy from Iowa. Or Ohio. It does not hurt but I feel tears on my face. Or could it be the juices from his mouth? I am coming. I am gay! I am not gay! I am a husband and a father. A good Catholic. I am a Spanish flamenco dancer. I am not Mexican. I am a ladies' man. Those are not lesions on my feet. They are badges of passion, purple tattoos oozing from places on my skin where his lips touched, feet first, then moving up my legs, inside my ass, up my chest, inside my mouth, until I am covered with his lovely kisses, his deadly marks. A violet shroud of love and death. I will not die. He gave me his youth. Injected me with immortality. Into my brain. I do not have AIDS. I am not gay. I am not a grandfather: I am impenetrable. Superman. Immortal. Spanish, not Mexican. A ladies' man. A man needs to be fucked. I am a ladies' man who needs to be fucked. Now I know the difference. Before Jim-Boy I did not know the difference. Between straight and gay, life and death, Ohio and Iowa. Now I know. The truth.

JESSIE. This here dyke don't hate men. I hate dick. I got them three words tattooed on my left arm: "I hate dick." You ain't never seen a black broad with a tattoo? This one's got two. The one on my right arm says "Mom." Readin' those tattoos is like readin' chapters of my life. The track marks is the table of contents. But nobody's gonna read me today. Curtain is closed. Longsleeve shirt is hidin' all clues leadin' to Jesse's true story. A mournful story of love and hate, the kind sung by a drugged-up diva. I grew up listenin' to them bluesy mamas singin' from their bleedin', gin-soaked guts. Every time my mama'd get shit on by a man, she'd listen to Bessie or Billie and cry her eyes out. In bed. She was always in bed — either gettin' fucked or gettin' over gettin' fucked. The only time she got dressed up was to go find another man and that didn't take long 'cause she was a beauty — even at the end. These men were all alike. She'd force me to call 'em "Daddy" whether they was there for an hour or a month. My real daddy was as foreign to me as the king of fuckin' Siam. These men were a bunch of dicks, always leavin' her. She'd lie on that bed, sheets smellin' of sex and cigarette smoke and scotch. She'd turn her records up full volume and wail along like she was a tortured star. Which she was. I became the man of the house by necessity. I took care of her day and night. Sometimes these motherfuckers would give us money; sometimes I'd pick their pockets after they passed out. I'd do odd jobs to make money — passed myself off as a boy to mow lawns. Then I got a steady job workin' for a white lady who ran a laundry. Part of the deal was I got to wash mama's sheets for free. But I had to hide from the customers 'cause they wouldn't want to think their lily white linens had been folded by colored hands. That's what we was then: "colored." One day — when I was twelve or thirteen — I came home from the laundry and found mama dead. Fresh blood all over one of them snow white sheets I'd scrubbed and folded myself. With my colored hands. Billie was singin' on the victrola. Mama'd slashed her wrists. Over a dick. That's when I vowed never to let a dick ruin my life. That's also about the time when I got my "Mom" tattoo — "Mom" written on the inside of a bleedin' heart. I went and lived with my grandma who forced me to wear a dress to school. I hated her for it. I knew what I wanted to be, what I wanted to wear. I discovered my first lez bar before I was old enough to drink — a bar where half the women wore dresses and the other half of us dressed like men. Fuck Grandma! This was the fifties; walkin'

up to that bar, we was passin'. On account of the fuckin'
police. This bar I'm tellin' you about was my salvation. It was
a jazz club with an all-female jazz band. One night I got up to
sing — "God Bless The Child" — and the place went wild. I
was jus' imitatin' those records I heard all my life. But I
learned how to sing. I also learned how to shoot up. One
night when we was high, I got me my second tattoo. "I hate
dick." Even though I walked like a man, talked like a man,
dressed like a man, and sang like a man — there was always
some dick who thought he could change you. I'd show 'em
my arm, track marks and tattoo, which I never bothered
coverin' up in those days. Now that I manage this apartment
building, I have to play the game. Hide my habits. I been
managin' this building for about fifteen years. Although I'm
not supposed to discriminate, I do: Womens only. With one
exception: this sorry ass deaf and dumb dude I rented to a
coupla years ago. I figured he'd be nice and quiet and wouldn't
be complainin' about the broads' noise — bitch fights and
butch fights and cat fights and bull fights. This kid — I think
he's a fairy, but I ain't seen nobody visitin' him — keeps to
hisself. Me too, since my marriage died. Literally. Miss Jill.
What's known as a lipstick lesbian. Femme fatale — all dolled
up like one of them Charlie's Angels. A drunk. Now I'm one
of those tough motherfuckers who can handle drugs and shit.
Some people liven up their weekend with hot dogs. Or Häagen
Dazs. I prefer heroin. But I know when to stop. Miss Jill had
a problem with booze 'n shit. Didn't know when to stop. I
stopped givin' her money but she kept comin' home pissed to
the tits. Nice tits, by the way. We was husband and wife for
two years. I wore the pants in the family. During the last
year, she spent mosta her time in bed. Sick as a bitch. At
night, she's sweat like a motherfucker. I'd change the sheets
every morning. Thank God this building's got a laundry
room. She was always a skinny chick — weighed about halfa
what I do — but she started lookin' like a skeleton. I couldn't
stand seein' her shrivel up and die. I started shootin' up — but
only days endin' in "y." Miss Jill never shot up; she was your
garden variety alkie. She said she was afraid of catchin' AIDS

by shooting' drugs. I tole her I shared needles with people I wouldn't drink outta the same glass with and I ain't caught no fuckin' disease. Dick is what carries AIDS, baby: that's what I tole her. Turns out I was right. Jill died of AIDS. Finally admitted she was gettin butt-fucked to pay for her booze. She thought only queers could get AIDS up the ass, she said on her deathbed. Everybody in the building — includin' that faggot deaf mute — heard me screamin' the night she tole me. I hate dick. Some dick is killin' my gal. It was an ugly death. This time I had to burn the sheets. I started losin' weight about a month later. Thought it was because of the death. Diarrhea all the time. Thought it was the drugs. Sweatin' all night long like my mama did — I mean, like Jill did. I looked in the mirror one day and I realized I was wastin' away to nothin'. Then I figured it out: that dick had infected me through Jill. Dicks have been tryin' to destroy me my entire fuckin' life. This dick did the trick. I needed to talk to someone. I needed to tell someone I was dyin'. But I didn't want no fuckin' lectures. I just wanted someone to listen; someone who wouldn't talk back. I knocked on his door — hard as I could. I musta pounded on that door for halfa hour. I knew he was in there. Finally, I used my master key and let myself in. I musta scared the shit outta him. He looked pissed off at first. I didn't say a word. We was like two animals, just sensin' each other. He could probably smell death all over me. All of a sudden, this weird, sweet smile came over his face and he opened his arms. Nobody in my life has ever understood my pain. Next thing I knew, I was bein' held by a deaf-and-dumb dick. A dick. And I was cryin'. Then singin'. And he was rockin' me, cradlin' me in his arms while I sang.

FATHER ANTHONY. We were not identical twins — not identical in any way. Even as kids, my mama says, we were as different as day and night, black and white. For one thing, Vinnie has — *had* — this bright red hair, from the time he was a baby. A red-headed Italian. My hair's always been black — like the rest of the family. Vinnie was this rambunctious kid, always overactive. I remember he broke something three summers in a row. His arm. His collar bone. His wrist. He wasn't athletic as much as he was physical: climbing trees, bike-riding in the pouring rain, showing off on the monkey bars. He drove our folks crazy with hospital bills. I was the opposite of Vinnie. Even our names, Vincent and Anthony. How's that for two Italian Catholic boys from New York? Nobody ever called me Tony. Ever. To this day. But he was always Vinnie; nobody ever called him Vincent. I was always the good boy — serious, studious, determined to make our parents proud. When I went into the seminary, Vinnie enrolled in cosmetology school. I swear he did it just to infuriate our parents, especially our father. A hairdresser! I stayed close to home while Vinnie traveled all over the world: London, Paris, Los Angeles. We lost touch with him. Then, one Sunday evening a couple of years ago, I was visiting my parents — I have dinner with my folks every Sunday night — and this news segment came on TV. Something about Gay Pride Day in San Francisco. And there was Vinnie: red hair and all, bigger than life, in a parade. Twirling a baton! My parents became hysterical. Lots of tears from my mom and shouting from my father. They decided to disown him. There were lots of AIDS victims in the parade and I remember my father saying it was God's will. The following Sunday in church, my sermon upheld the teachings of the Catholic church: homosexuality is not condoned; there is no such thing as safe sex; abstinence is the answer. At least my parents had one son to be proud of. I was shocked to hear from Vinnie about a year later. We had hardly spoken during our entire adult life. He had two tickets to go to Paris, he said, and he wanted to take his twin brother. I don't know why, but — without telling my parents — I went. The first night there, we went to this elegant restaurant: Dodin Bouffant. Vinnie chose it — partly because of the name, a hair reference. "Bouffant, as in girl singers from the fifties," he said. He could be very funny. There was a beautiful woman at the table across from us who mesmerized me. I guess you could say she was a free spirit. She was flirting with an older bald man — kissing him on his shiny, smooth head, running her long red fingernails along his neck. Very sexy.

Seductive. When she stood up to leave, I got a look at her long black skirt, slit all the way up, revealing these incredible legs. She was so uninhibited, so comfortable with herself. So passionate. She reminded me of Vinnie. The next day we went to the Louvre and saw the David show. There was a woman, being yanked away from the exhibit by her crude husband. "You've seen enough," he said. Determined to please him, she left, looking longingly over her shoulder at those dramatic, sensual masterpieces. She was wearing a blouse, buttoned to her neck, strangling her. She looked constipated. Squelched. I saw myself in her. Those two women were as different as Vinnie and me. The Paris trip didn't make sense to me until I got word, about six months later, that my brother was in the hospital and would probably not leave. Again, unbeknownst to my parents, I went to his side. I'll say this: he never lost his sense of humor. He was shaving one day — he insisted on shaving himself even though he was terribly weak — and he dropped the hand mirror. It shattered. There was a pause. "In my case, that's seven *days* bad luck," he said. He died eight days later. He'd lost all his beautiful red hair. I've been a priest for almost ten years and being with my brother when he died is the only spiritual experience I've ever known: I kissed his bald head and caressed his neck with my fingertips. After he died, I told him a secret: "We are identical," I said. "I have AIDS, too." I did not get infected from handling my brother's shit; I did not get infected from wiping my brother's tears; I did not get infected from touching my brother's vomit; I did not get infected from tasting my brother's saliva. I loved his puke. I loved his diarrhea. I loved his sweat and I loved his spit and I loved his tears. I got infected from having sex with boys in my parish, hustlers off the street, husbands of wives who come to me for marriage counseling. Being a good Catholic, I didn't use a condom. Neither did they. Even a disposable condom was too much evidence for Father Anthony. Not only have I — in the name of Holy Mother, the church — killed my own twin brother, I've murdered all my brothers. How many Hail Marys should I say for penance? Perhaps I should splatter, not red paint, but my own blood on the steps of the Vatican. Perhaps I should pin a pink triangle on my long black skirt. Perhaps I should learn how to love my fellow man. If it weren't for my parents. They're in their seventies. It would kill them. I'm all they have. Father Anthony is all they have. If there is a merciful God — which I doubt — surely he will take them before me.

MIKE. My mama always tole me that boys with hemophilia had three things in common: we was bright; we was good lookin'; we was all daredevils. My name is Mike. I'm an alcoholic. And a daredevil. My brain cells and my looks are ancient history, but I'm still a fuckin' daredevil. Or I wouldn't be here. I been called a lot of other things — from "Mama's boy" to "motherfucker." When I was a kid, I was called a "sissy" because I couldn't do sports. On account of the danger. I had to be real careful: bleedin'. In gym class I was graded on how I'd put the equipment away and take the roll call. My fuckin' mother wouldn't let me out of her sight. She was always guilt-trippin' herself about me. "It's all my fault," she'd piss and moan. "It's all my fault." Drove my old man fuckin' nuts. She never paid no attention to the poor bastard so he eventually split. That's when she really started drinkin'. That's when I started drinkin'. If I did have an accident — even a bump against a piece of furniture could cause internal bleedin' — it'd be real painful. She began medicatin' me with a few sips from her drink. Tasted good. Then she started pourin' me a drink whenever she poured herself one. Which was pretty fuckin' often. By the time I was in high school, I had learned to outdrink her. After she'd pass out, I'd go out and get into some trouble. Drunk on my butt. Lots of times I'd hurt myself and wind up in the emergency room for a blood transfusion. She'd come rescue me, hysterical. "You're all I've got," she'd say. "It's my fault." I started hatin' her. I started stayin' out all night. When I'd come home the next mornin', she'd be in a panic. Drinkin', wringin' her hands. When I got me a girl, Jeaneanne, she became insanely jealous. Insane. She was either beggin' me to stay home or threatenin' to kick me outa the house. I got Jeaneanne pregnant! Proved I was no sissy! I decided to marry her. For one thing, it would get me out of the house, get me away from that hysterical, drunken, smothering bitch. Jeaneanne had a boy. A healthy boy! He was normal; he would have a normal childhood — somethin' I never knew. Jeaneanne started givin' him a bunch of attention. "I got two little boys to take care of," she always liked to say. It's true, she did take care of me. I didn't work, couldn't hold down a job. I was drinkin' pretty heavy and startin' in with motorcycles. Motorcycles got me outa the house, away from Jeaneanne and Little Mike. I was only happy when I was on a bike, stoned outa my mind, on my way somewhere. Nowhere. I had a bunch of accidents and wound up in the emergency room. By this time, we bleeders had this blood concentrate shit which made life easier. But I had already begun gettin' arthritis from bleedin' in my joints and was in chronic pain. Motorcycle wrecks didn't help none. Had to have a shoulder replacement. And a knee replacement. Jeaneanne raised Little Mike pretty much by herself. He was a tough little bastard. By the time he was a teenager, he really fuckin' hated me. One night I had this gigantic blowout with Jeaneanne. I was drunk outa my mind and I guess I hit her pretty bad. Well, Little Mike freaked out and almost killed me. Seriously. Missed my face and punched me in the neck. Started bleedin' internally, in my throat, and couldn't breathe. Can't say I blame him; I asked for it. That's when he forced her to choose. Between him and me. She said she couldn't make the decision so he made it for her. He split. More than ten years ago. That's when we hemophiliacs started hearin' about AIDS — a disease for faggots and drug addicts, spread by butt-fuckin' and needle-sharin'. They warned us that concentrate may have been polluted by these fuckin' degenerates so a bunch of hemophiliacs started gettin' the AIDS test. Not me! No fuckin' way was I gonna volunteer to go to a fuckin' doctor's office. I spent my life goin' to the doctor. I survived this far; no fag disease was gonna kill me. Only bad people got AIDS. I thought if a hemophiliac got it, he must be a secret cocksucker or fuckin' axe murderer. Jeaneanne tried to get me to wear a fuckin' rubber — like some scared sissy. "I'm not the pussy — you are," I'd tell her. "And if you don't let me fuck you without a faggot rubber, I'll find some broad who will." And I did — plenty of 'em. Jeaneanne had enough of my shit and started goin' to meetings for wives of alcholics or some such bullshit. "Shouldn't I be the one goin' to meetings?" I asked her. She seemed to be gettin' happier while I was gettin' sicker. The booze wouldn't even kill the pain. I was exhausted, constantly sick and tired. I couldn't ride my bike — fuck, I couldn't walk across the room. She'd be at her meetings while I'd be at home, burnin' up with fever and shittin' in my pants. One night I had to call my ole lady to come over and clean me up. "My baby," she kept sayin' over and over again, like she was thrilled shitless I was covered in crap. "It's all my fault." Jeaneanne took care of me less and less but she agreed to take me to get the AIDS test. The doctor took one look at me and knew. I jus' couldn't believe it. What was I bein' punished for? Jeaneanne started laughin' when I said that. Laughin' in my face. I remember — barely, 'cause I was drunk at the time — grabbin' a knife and goin' for her throat. To stop the laughter. People been laughin' at me my entire fuckin' life. She knew it was time to kick my ass out for real. After more than twenty years. I had nowhere to go but home to my pathetic ole lady. That was the worst moment of my entire, miserable, fucked-up life. Rock bottom. I began to pray: "Let me die quick." Started thinkin' about slashin' my wrists. Losin' blood didn't scare me. Bleedin' to death is what I been doin' all my fuckin' life. Found out that Little Mike came home to see Jeaneanne. I wanted to see him before I fuckin' did myself in. "He won't see you if you're drunk," Jeaneanne said when I called her. "Then I'll get sober," I said. Simple as that. "I dare you," she said. I tole you I'm still a daredevil. Jeaneanne gave me a number to call and I been sober for twenty-five days. Livin' in a halfway house, away from my poor old lady. Got together a coupla weeks ago with Little Mike, who is bigger than I am. He's queer. That's what he tole me. Gay! "Jesusfuckingchrist, is it my fault?" He says it ain't; he was born that way, he says, like I was born hemophiliac. It's natural to him; he likes bein' different. I asked him if he caught AIDS yet. He says he don't have sex. "Then how you know you're gay?" I ask. He just laughed. But not at me. I laughed, too. For the first time in years and fuckin' years. I guess I gotta lot to learn.

DEEDE. His final three words to me were "I love you." I'm lying. His final three words were sprayed on the mirror of the guest bedroom with that stuff that makes snow on Christmas windows. It was big, flowing, white snowy letters: "I HAVE AIDS." Those were his final three words. "I have AIDS." Not "I have AIDS, I'm gay." Just "I have AIDS." Why didn't he tell me? I've been around gay guys all my life; there's never a time when they weren't around. My mother loves gay men. When I was a little girl, I called them my uncles. Some of them would call themselves my aunts. As a kid, I never thought about what they did in bed. It was presented to me as natural so it came as a big shock to me to learn that homosexuals were not considered normal by every family on the block. I wound up going to art school where, again, gays were pretty much the norm. I got into interior design — a friend of my mom's, naturally. I started doing massage back in '83. I was twenty-four. A virgin. Can you believe it? I was. And I had boyfriends — straight ones — but I just never felt like going all the way. Don was a client. He was in the midst of a heavy-duty divorce. Stressed to the max. He had these knots in his neck and shoulders, like rocks. After a few sessions, he started to relax. He asked me out. We fell in love. But I wouldn't have sex with him until after his divorce was final. I'd waited that long! It's funny when I think about it. My girlfriends were always joking that I, at least, would never come down with AIDS. A lot of my mother's friends were getting sick around this time. I massaged some of them. It was scary at first but I knew there was no chance of catching it. Don never objected to me working on these guys with AIDS. That really endeared him to me. When I think back, there were probably clues. But I'd never had a fulfilled sexual relationship with anyone. Even after his divorce, we didn't have sex. He didn't want to; he said he was recovering. We made out — lots. When we finally did do it, it wasn't what I'd anticipated. What I'm trying to say is that he didn't like to have intercourse as much as he liked me to go down on him. According to most of my girlfriends, that's not so unusual. A coupla years ago, we stared watching porno videos during sex. I used to pick them up at the video store next to the grocery store. It was just like selecting another flavor of soup. But one day I picked up a tape — without paying much attention, I guess — with two guys in it. Two guys and a woman. *Bi and Beyond*. I'll never forget watching that tape, lying there in bed with Don, and these two guys start going at it. I apologized and said I'd made a mistake. "It's all right, honey," he said. Well, we had great sex. I honestly think that's the night I conceived. We must have done it — I mean it — four or five times. At the time, I didn't think much about it. We went back to straight movies and he never mentioned it again. I found out I was pregnant a coupla months later. Due around Christmas. This made Don ecstatic. He had this lousy childhood — never knew what it was like to celebrate the holidays. So having a baby on Christmas was making him hysterically happy. *It's A Wonderful Life* is his favorite film. I'm not kidding. As I got more pregnant, *It's A Wonderful Life* replaced the porn movies. He watched it until he knew every word by heart; he could recite the entire movie. It's been a rough pregnancy. I was sick a lot. Then Don started getting sick. Someone suggested it was sympathetic illness. He had the flu. Started around Thanksgiving. I remember when we got the Christmas tree, he could barely carry it to and from the car. I was gaining weight and he was losing. He refused to go to a doctor. A month-long flu where we live is not unusual. He stopped working and turned our guest bedroom into a Christmas fantasy. There was an electric train, dozens of beautifully wrapped presents for me and the baby, and a video of *It's A Wonderful Life* playing around the clock. We live on the thirty-seventh floor. Sometimes the wind was so fierce, it would cause the Christmas tree to sway back and forth. Beautiful. He loved that. He looked out the window and talked about the power of the wind. He seemed feverish at times. He'd wake me in the night, sweating. He knew I needed my sleep so he began sleeping in the Christmas room where I imagine he was very happy. By the time Christmas arrived, he couldn't get out of bed. No baby yet. I'm two weeks overdue now. We celebrated. Tried to. He was very groggy. The morning after Christmas, I went in to check on him. He seemed a little better. I brought him some orange juice and he drank a coupla sips. "I love you," he said. And he patted my stomach. He asked me to turn up the volume on *It's A Wonderful Life*. I went back to sleep in the other room. The next thing I heard was pounding at the front door. It was two policemen. "Do you know a Don Swerling?" one of them asked. I didn't even answer — I ran into the Christmas room. The window was wide open. The only comfort I've had is in watching that porn video. *Bi and Beyond*. Two guys and a woman. When I think back, that's probably the most honest he ever was with me. I watch those two guys — one blond and one brunette — and I fantasize he's one or the other of them. He's the blond one getting screwed from behind. He's the dark one getting sucked. He's being kissed, licked — his neck, his nipples, his face, his feet. He's being loved. And I'm watching. Not judging him. Just accepting him. As he is. Was. I watch that movie, over and over and over. Two men having sex. It's okay. If only he'd told me.

PAUL. (*On tape in "normal" voice*) I remember screaming. What it was like to scream. To cry. To express myself. I remember the sound. The sound of my voice. Screaming. Crying. I remember the sound of his voice, screaming. And the sound of her voice, crying. I do not remember the sound of laughter. Or "coochy-coochy-coo." I do not remember hearing "I love you." I do not remember hearing my name. Paul is my name. I have been deaf all my life, almost. Since I was five years old. "High fever," is what they told me. Two words: high fever. Like high school, high tide, high noon, high hopes. That was the explanation: high fever. I do not remember laughing. Or hoping. No hope. No high hopes. No sound.

No voice. No more screams, no more cries. I knew I did something wrong; I knew I was bad. It was all my fault. Even though I couldn't hear, I knew he was screaming at me. And she was crying because of me. It was all my fault. I could not hear. I could not speak. I was bad. I was a freak. They sent me to a normal school with hearing kids. I was not really deaf, they insisted, I would get over it. I was forbidden to learn sign language. I attempted to read lips. I only knew one other deaf person my age, a boy I was forbidden to see. I met him accidentally in a park; he was there with his parents who were also deaf. They were a happy family, speaking sign language. "They look like animals in the zoo," my father said. Scott was his name and he'd come to my house when my parents were not home. He taught me how to sign. He taught me how to jack off. We were ten or eleven. He taught me to speak with my hands and fingers: "Feels great," he'd say, putting my hands on his cock and balls. Then he'd put his hands on mine and I'd sign, "Feels great." He taught me to speak without words, with my tongue and my mouth. He stuck his tongue inside my ear and for a moment I thought I heard the words "I love you." He spoke with his tongue and his fingertips. "Feels great," I'd sign, a good student. My father caught us, in bed, naked. We'd fallen asleep in each other's arms with our worn-out fingers entwined. My father beat the shit out of me and told Scott's parents — wrote them, actually — about their "deaf and dumb faggot of a son." I went to sleep that night smelling Scott on my sheets and tasting blood in my mouth. The message was clear: The only thing worse than being deaf was being a fag. (*Live in deaf accent*) I learned to speak to please my Dad. I got married to please my Dad. To a hearing girl, naturally. It was a disaster. I could not fuck any better than I could speak. Once in awhile, remembering Scott's soft, wet tongue in my ear, I could perform. But mostly I'd fail. She thought it was because I was deaf; I guess she thought all deaf guys are impotent. Don't laugh. Most people think we can't drive a car. I began — secretly, of course — pursuing men. In the park. In public johns. Anonymous encounters where I didn't have to speak. I gave new meaning to playing hard to get. Guys would ask me my name, I wouldn't respond. Guys would ask me what I liked to do, I wouldn't respond. Guys would ask me for my phone number, I wouldn't respond. Remember, this was the seventies. They didn't think I was deaf, they thought I was hot. I became a star of the anonymous sex circuit. A silent star but a compulsive one who never once even said "thank you." I divorced my wife, much to the dismay of my parents. I divorced my parents. I isolated, collecting SSI and trying to fit in by reading books about hearing people and watching movies about straight people. Sex was my only human contact. On bodies of nameless strangers, I composed love songs with my tongue, wrote sonnets with my fingertips. And I could do it all — fuck, get fucked, suck, get sucked, you name it — *standing up.* Just don't ask me to talk dirty. I didn't consider myself gay, any more than I considered myself deaf. I thought you had to go to bed — to a man's bedroom — to be gay, to get AIDS. I began getting mysterious ailments in 1986 or '87. I went to the free clinic. They tested me. Two weeks later — after daily unsafe and unsound encounters against cold white porcelain and under dying dry brown branches — I got the results. Positive. "There is an available counselor who knows how to sign," the doctor wrote, under the word "Positive." He also handed me a pamphlet: *AIDS and the Deaf.* I ripped up the pamphlet and stormed out of the clinic, realizing for the first time in my life: I am gay, I am deaf, and I'm going to die. Alone. No friends, no family, no one to tell. No way to tell. Nothing. Suicide. I could blow my brains out without hearing a thing. Instead, I went back to the clinic to find that pamphlet. *AIDS and the Deaf.* I went to this meeting. There was a room, filled with gay, deaf men, using sign language, communicating passionately. They were all infected with HIV. We sat in a circle and everyone told his story — in sign. Even though I didn't fully understand, I got enough. What I didn't get, this really cute guy wrote down for me. When my turn came, thank God I remembered those words Scott had taught me to sign: "Feels great." Gradually, I began to get honest with myself. (*Live in deaf accent, accompanied by signing*) I finally learned to sign. I finally admitted what I've known all along: my deafness was not caused by a high fever. My father had beaten me into silence. "It doesn't matter how," this guy in the group says. "Deafness is a gift." He also believes being gay is a gift. And having HIV is a gift. His name is Billy. He describes himself as part Helen Keller and part Mary Poppins. He's the opposite of me. But I love him. Except for Scott, Billy is the only person I've ever had sex with in a horizontal position. The only person I've ever made love with — that's a gift. For sure. (*Sign only*) Feels great!

Annunciation

■

BY

CARL MORSE

▼

Annunciation

To pay the rent, I work for a major publisher of school textbooks — the kind with Teacher's Editions that say, "Explain that smelling is something people do with their noses," and "Introduce distinguished people and people in authority first."

This is also the major publisher where I noticed in *¿Habla español?* that Cuba was missing from the endpaper map of Spanish-speaking countries. Like, not there. And it's the company where a close-up photo of the pistils of a tulip blossom got deleted from high school science for being "too suggestive."

Voicing my misgivings about these and similar matters only got me tagged as a troublemaker by my superiors. This got worse when I tried to achieve gender balance in social studies by making an art request for "1 male, 1 female, 1 androgyne." And things really came to a head when I took a count of the pregnant women on our floor — and there were ten — and I sent them a memo about my count and how according to Kinsey one of them was *certainly* going to have a fairy — and how I just wanted to be one of the first to share their joy.

But not one of them answered me in a rejoicing way.

So I wrote this play — in case somebody besides me wants to rejoice.

Carl Morse

Annunciation was first presented by P.I.A. Productions in *Homosexual Acts*, an evening of short gay plays, at the Theater at 224 Waverly in New York on April 5, 1991. It was directed by Rich Rubin. The scenic design was by Jamie Leo; lighting design by Glenn J. Powell; costume design by Gregory Melendrez; sound design by Chuck Brown; and property design by Ross Fusca. The cast was as follows:

MELISSA .... Kristina Keefe

MICHAEL .... Ted Senecal

CHARACTERS

MELISSA — a determinedly independent, bristly, and very pregnant woman

MICHAEL — a nervous and excitable gay angel

PLACE

A business office.

THE PLAY

A very pregnant woman is working at a computer terminal. She turns a manuscript page. It falls to the floor. She rises, carefully attempts to stoop and retrieve it without losing her balance, but decides to give it up and sits down again. The baby kicks, and she goes "Ah!" and holds both hands on her belly.

MELISSA. Easy now, easy. Be nice and help mommy finish her typing. You'll be out soon, Julian. Lovely Julian. Dear Julian. Just be patient. (*Pats her tummy*) There, there. That's a good boy. Mommy wishes she were home, too. But she can't be. I just hate this damn machine — and it's not good for you either. (*Looks at her watch; sighs*) Okay, just hang in there for two more hours, and we'll be home and have a nice bowl of soup and some nice rye bread. Whaddya think, rye or whole wheat? And a great big bowl of vanilla ice cream with butterscotch sauce and marshmallow sauce and sprinkles and nuts while we watch *Jeopardy*, okay? But right now . . . (*She turns the pages of a manuscript*) right now, did you know that . . . (*She reads aloud as she types words from the manuscript into the computer*) Definition. Boldface. All caps. Community. Colon. Community . . . is people living . . . near each other . . . and working together. Period. Cap P. People . . . in a community . . . take good care . . . of each other. Period. (*As Melissa speaks, Michael, a gay angel, nervously wanders down the hall looking in doorways, until he comes to hers. He stops, starts to retreat, but gathers his resolve and listens to her speak and type until she finishes*)
MICHAEL. (*First crossing himself*) Hello.
MELISSA. (*Finishes typing her sentence without looking up*) Hello.
MICHAEL. You're Melissa, aren't you? I'm Michael.

275

MELISSA. (*Looks up*) Hello, Michael. Can I help you?

MICHAEL. Oh, yes. I work upstairs — in Personnel. You don't know me.

MELISSA. No. Can I help you with something?

MICHAEL. I've got a message.

MELISSA. Not again. Look, I can't work late tonight.

MICHAEL. No, that's not it. It's a different kind of message. You're pregnant, aren't you?

MELISSA. (*Swiveling her chair belly-out*) Oh, no.

MICHAEL. That machine's not good for the baby.

MELISSA. (*Snappish*) I just happen to like to eat — and have a roof over my head.

MICHAEL. Of course. I'm sorry. (*Turns as if to leave*) I'd better go.

MELISSA. (*Starts to do a breathing exercise*) Hey, wait up. Don't be so jumpy. I'm a loudmouth. What's the message?

MICHAEL. It's really quite good news.

MELISSA. Great. I could use some.

MICHAEL. I wouldn't want you to get upset.

MELISSA. Why should I get upset? Out with it.

MICHAEL. Well, you may have noticed that there are a number of women in our company who are going to have babies — an extraordinary number, in fact. Like almost contagious maybe.

MELISSA. (*Laughs*) I'll say.

MICHAEL. Like Miss Fullner in Editorial and Mrs. Lombardo in Publicity and . . .

MELISSA. Actually, we've been kidding about it for months. It's almost getting to be a joke. I mean, even Ellen Rasterman, and she's forty-three and never had one, and her husband's over sixty. Maybe there's a germ going around.

MICHAEL. There are nine others in all, actually. You're the tenth. And that's why I'm here.

MELISSA. Oh, do I get a prize or something?

MICHAEL. Sort of. You see, uh . . . maybe you already know, uh . . . well, there's only one way to say it and that's just to say it. One out of every ten children born in America is gay — and I just wanted to tell you that you're the tenth — right around here in this company anyway. So . . .

MELISSA. (*Stops exercising*) Hey, are you trying to tell me my baby's gonna be gay?! Now just a goddam minute!

MICHAEL. I was sort of hoping you'd be glad.

MELISSA. I think maybe you'd better leave. I have a lot of work to do.

MICHAEL. I just wanted you to know *I'm* very glad. And I was hoping you would be, too.

MELISSA. Sure I am. I'm insane with joy.

MICHAEL. You see — with so many fairies dying now, we need new ones — you know — to paint pictures and go on demonstrations and things.

MELISSA. I am *not* having a fairy. Please leave.

MICHAEL. They can be really good painters. You like the Sistine Chapel, don't you?

MELISSA. (*Picking up the phone to call Security*) That's it. I've had enough. Are you sure you work here?

MICHAEL. Oh, yes. Personnel. Extension 3333. It was very hard to get that number. (*Looks as if he might cry*) Please don't report me. I'm only trying to do my best.

MELISSA. (*Putting down phone*) Oh, for heaven's sakes. Don't snivel.

MICHAEL. I didn't mean to upset you.

MELISSA. You haven't. But, c'mon — you can't just walk into people's offices and tell them their baby's gonna be a goddam queer. (*Michael flinches as if he has been struck*) Sorry.

MICHAEL. It's all right. I *am* queer. Very. Actually, having a fairy is a wonderful thing — like quite patriotic these days — and maybe it's just you don't really know any — except me, and I'm not necessarily representative.

MELISSA. You've made that clear.

MICHAEL. But you still don't like the idea.

MELISSA. Well, I suppose it's not absolutely the worst thing that could happen.

MICHAEL. Oh, no, it isn't. I mean, it could be abnormal or something — but it's not going to be, is it?

MELISSA. Not if kicking means anything. (*Draws back*) Hey, you're not sick or anything?

MICHAEL. No — although I'm generally very positive. Are you sure you don't know any gay people besides me? There's nobody you can think of gay in your family?

MELISSA. Certainly not. (*Beat*) Well actually, I did have a cousin that never got married.

MICHAEL. Oh, wonderful!

MELISSA. And my mother used to talk about her Aunt Ida.

MICHAEL. Oh, excellent!

MELISSA. I didn't say she was gay.

MICHAEL. No, you didn't. Not at all. I agree. But having one or two possibly friendly relatives helps. If they *are* friendly. There's no guarantee.

MELISSA. I don't have any relatives anyway — alive — they're all dead — or in jail where they belong.

MICHAEL. Say, you wouldn't mind *making* a relative, would you? It's just like making friends, only it takes a little longer sometimes — though usually you can tell right away — like I knew right away when I first saw you months ago when you'd just started walking funny. Your fifth month, I think it was.

MELISSA. My god, you've been spying on me!

MICHAEL. No, no. Just keeping an eye out in case you wanted help with anything. But you didn't. You're very independent.

MELISSA. Yes. Yes, I am. Any objections?

MICHAEL. Oh, no. It's much better than the other way. But pretty lonesome sometimes maybe. It's nice to have company available if you ever decide to need it.

MELISSA. I am *not* lonely. Alone, yes — but not lonely, okay?

MICHAEL. Okay. It's quite a decision deciding to bring up a baby by yourself.

MELISSA. Well, there just comes a point if things haven't happened to you in your life like you thought, or wanted — you know, the right guy and stuff — then you just have to decide, make up your mind. Nobody else is going to. So I did. Lots of people do these days.

MICHAEL. But you're unusual.

MELISSA. Don't get back on that fairy thing!

MICHAEL. You *would* love it anyway, wouldn't you?

MELISSA. I don't know. (*Beat. Almost in tears*) Oh, for Christ's sakes, of course I would. (*Frightened*) What's going on here anyway?

278
▼

MICHAEL. Oh, I'm so relieved. I just know it will be all right — even if you do have certain reservations. You're working right up to the last minute, huh?

MELISSA. Yes. I could have it right here if I had to. I've been trained.

MICHAEL. Lamaze? Leboyer? Leboyer is good.

MELISSA. Sort of Leboyer.

MICHAEL. Leboyer is wonderful.

MELISSA. Well, mine is more like . . .

MICHAEL. (*Excited*) Straight into a warm basin of water — right away. And very dim light, so nobody gets startled or frightened — and lay right on top of mommy first thing before anything — right on mommy's tummy and smell her good and feel her heart beating, that's the best. And mommy doesn't mind if you're purple and all bloody and wrinkled — and it's almost like still being inside mommy if it's done right.

MELISSA. You know a lot about this.

MICHAEL. Oh, I studied some. Not formally — but I pay attention to different things that interest me — and it does make sense not to hit them on the back right away and shine those bright lights in their eyes. What was your cousin like — the one that didn't get married? Say, you're not married either.

MELISSA. No. He was a sissy. He wouldn't fight. The other kids beat up on him.

MICHAEL. Oh, dear.

MELISSA. Even me, I remember making fun of him and calling him a sissy.

MICHAEL. (*Indicating the computer screen*) Is that sociology you're working on?

MELISSA. Yes, third grade.

MICHAEL. How discouraging. When I was a kid if you wanted sociology you just stepped out the door and caught a snowball behind the ear. I guess your cousin got plenty of sociology.

MELISSA. (*Laughs*) More than enough, I'd say. It was sad, but nobody could do anything.

MICHAEL. Wouldn't fight at all, huh?

MELISSA. The only time I ever saw him fight was when this kid down the street was pulling all the bark off of this tree — and

279
▼

my cousin went crazy. Scary crazy. I thought he'd kill him. We didn't make fun of him after that — but nobody really talked to him.

MICHAEL. Did he like music, and big words, and insects? Did he try to tell people things they didn't understand?

MELISSA. I don't know. He sang in the choir. I remember one day I was going by the chicken coop, and I heard this voice — and it was him talking to the chickens. He had names for every one of them. Over a hundred. I told him I was gonna tell on him, and he started crying.

MICHAEL. Did you?

MELISSA. No. And then after high school he went away and never came back, and never wrote to anybody or anything. I think maybe he died. Somebody said he might have.

MICHAEL. Yes, he did. It was too bad. He was a very nice person.

MELISSA. How do you know that? Excuse me, but I'm scared.

MICHAEL. Don't be scared. I'll be going now. I just came to let you know that there's a whole lot of us out here rejoicing on account of you and your baby — and how glad we all are, and ready to welcome little Julian into the world.

MELISSA. (*Backing away*) Jesus, you know his name. How the hell do you know his name? Nobody knows his name but me.

MICHAEL. Your cousin's name was John, right?

MELISSA. (*In awe*) Oh my god in heaven . . .

MICHAEL. Oh, no. Nothing like that. However . . . (*Michael slowly raises his arms, which turn out to be absolutely magnificent wings — which he points straight up. A light glows all around him. Melissa shields her eyes from the light. Michael lowers his arms and looks ordinary again, and the lights go back to normal*) Please don't be frightened.

MELISSA. I'm not frightened.

MICHAEL. I don't do that very often.

MELISSA. No.

MICHAEL. Before I go, could I ask just one favor?

MELISSA. Yes, anything.

MICHAEL. Could I listen? Just for a minute? (*Melissa nods yes. Michael kneels and lays his head against her belly and listens, as the lights fade down and out*)

About the Authors

■

BETTE BOURNE

Bette Bourne, cofounder and director of Bloolips, was trained by Edith Evans and Mae West. Bloolips won an OBIE for their New York production of *Lust in Space*. Bourne directed and starred in *Get It While You Can*, by Larry Mitchell, as well as *The Plate, Colonial Boy*, and *Gland Motel*, all by Ray Dobbins. Recently, he appeared in *Sarrasine*, by Neil Bartlett and Nicholas Bloomfield, in productions throughout the U.S. and U.K.

VICTOR BUMBALO

Victor Bumbalo was the 1987 winner of an Ingram Merrill Award for playwriting. His award–winning play *Niagara Falls* followed its off Broadway run with subsequent openings in over fifty cities throughout the United States, England, and Australia. *Niagara Falls and Other Plays*, a collection of comedies, is published by Calamus Books. His play *Adam and the Experts* opened to critical success off Broadway in the fall of 1989, and is published by Broadway Play Publishing Inc. Bumbalo has also been the recipient of two MacDowell Fellowships and residencies at Yaddo and the Helene Wurlitzer Foundation. His other works include *628 Blandina Street, Show, And Then*, and *What Are Tuesdays Like?*

JANE CHAMBERS

Jane Chambers (1937–1983) began her career in the late 1950s as an actor and playwright, working off Broadway and in coffee-house theatre. Her plays have been produced off Broadway, in regional theatres, in community theatres both in this country and abroad, and on television. She has been the recipient of the Connecticut Educational Television Award (1971, *Christ in a Treehouse*), a Eugene O'Neill fellowship (1972, *Tales of the Revolution and Other American Fables*), a National Writers Guild Award (1973, *Search for Tomorrow*, CBS), the New York Drama-logue Critic's Circle Award, the Villager Theatre Award, the Alliance for Lesbian and Gay Artists Media Award, the Robby Award, the Oscar Wilde Award, the Los Angeles Drama Critic's Circle Award, a Proclamation from Los Angeles for Outstanding Theatre (1980–83, *Last Summer at Bluefish Cove*), two Betty Awards (1987, *Kudzu*; 1985, *The Quintessential Image*) and the Fund for Human Dignity Award (1982), among others.

Published novels include *Burning*, originally published by Jove Press in 1978 and then rereleased by JH Press in 1983, and *Chasin Jason*, published by JH Press in 1987. Her articles have appeared in such publications as *The New York Times* and *Harper's*.

She was a founding member of the New Jersey Women's Political Caucus and of the Interart Theatre in New York City, and a member of the planning committee of the Women's Program of the American Theatre Association. She was also a member of the Writers Guild East, the Dramatists Guild, the Authors' League, Actors' Equity, and East End Gay Organization for Human Rights.

On February 15, 1983, she died of a brain tumor at her Greenport, Long Island home; she is survived by her mother, Clarice, her two step-brothers, Ben and Henry, and by her life's companion, Beth Allen.

Women in Theatre (originally the American Theatre Association–Women's Program) in 1983 created the Jane Chambers Playwrighting Award to encourage the writing of new plays that address women's experiences and have a majority of principal roles for women.

Ms. Chambers is taught in women's studies programs, writing

programs, and acting programs in colleges and universities throughout the United States.

VITA DENNIS

Vita Dennis, a Chicago-based actor and playwright, founded
Footsteps Theatre Company in 1987 to create more opportunities
for women in Chicago theatre. Not surprisingly, the company's
first production was *Last Summer at Bluefish Cove* with Vita as
Dr. Kitty Cochrane. As artistic director she has guided Footsteps
through five seasons of critically acclaimed "theatre from a
woman's point of view," including ground-breaking productions
of Shakespeare's *The Two Gentlemen of Verona* and *Hamlet*, each
with an all female cast. In 1991 Vita played Josie in Chambers's
My Blue Heaven — a production that Beth Allen went to Chicago
to see and that initiated the discussion that would lead to Vita's
being asked to revise *Eye of the Gull* for a world premiere at
Footsteps. Vita's other credits include writing and performing
comedy with the group Cowboy Chow; a one-act play, *Twins*;
and *My Soul to Keep*, a full-length play about an adult survivor
of incest.

TERRY HELBING

Terry Helbing began his gay theatre career in 1973, appearing in
the Boston and New England touring company of Jonathan Ned
Katz's *Coming Out!* He also acted in the original TOSOS production
and The Glines revival (at the Spike Bar) of Doric Wilson's *The
West Street Gang*. He produced and starred in Terry Miller's *Pines
'79* for The Glines, and served as general manager for their Sixth
Anniversary Rep. He was cofounder and codirector of Meridian
Gay Theatre from 1983–1987. For Meridian he appeared in Doric
Wilson's *Street Theater* at the Mineshaft, starred in *The Demolition
of Harry Fay*, and appeared in *Franny the Queen of Provincetown*. In
1991, he acted in *Cocktails at the Red Rooster*, which was a benefit
for Joseph's Surgical, an AIDS organization.

He publishes gay/lesbian plays by Jane Chambers, Robert Chesley, et al. under the JH Press imprint, which also published his 1980 work, *Gay Theatre Alliance Directory of Gay Plays*, which he compiled, edited and introduced.

His weekly theatre column, "The Fourth Wall," runs in *New York Native*, of which he is theatre editor; it includes reviews of shows, theatre compact discs, insider news, and information about upcoming shows of all types.

Since 1977 his articles on theatre, books, video, and music have appeared in *Christopher Street, The Advocate, Soho News, 7 Days, Genre, Theaterweek*, and many other publications.

MICHAEL KEARNS

Michael Kearns is a writer–performer–director who has been concentrating on AIDS art since 1984, establishing himself as one of the country's most consistent and respected theatre artists.

His two theatrepieces, *intimacies* and *more intimacies*, in which he portrays a dozen culturally diverse PWAs, have been produced in Los Angeles, San Francisco, Chicago, Portland, Eugene, Tucson, Phoenix, Washington, D.C., New York City, Hartford, New Haven, Northhampton, and Sydney (Australia).

Other writing for the theatre includes his autobiographical *The Truth Is Bad Enough* and *Rock*. He also wrote the lyrics for *Homeless, A Street Opera*.

Kearns directed and coproduced the Artists Confronting AIDS' landmark productions of *AIDS/US* in 1986 and *AIDS/US II* in 1990.

He also directed the Los Angeles premieres of Robert Chesley's *Night Sweat* and *Jerker*, Rebecca Ranson's *Warren*, and Doug Holsclaw's *Life of The Party*, all plays depicting AIDS.

As an actor, he appeared in *Jerker* (Los Angeles, San Diego, Des Moines) and continues to tour, nationally and abroad, in James Carroll Pickett's *Dream Man* (which has played New York City, L.A., Washington, D.C., Atlanta, Edinburgh, Dusseldorf, and London). His television credits include *Cheers, Murder She Wrote, The Waltons, Knots Landing, General Hospital, Days of Our*

Lives and *The Fall Guy*. On film he appeared in *Kentucky Fried Movie* and Brian DePalma's *Body Double*.

Kearns has received numerous acting awards, including the 1989 Bay Area Theatre Critics Award, Best Solo Performance, for *intimacies*. As a humanitarian, he has been honored by the *L.A. Weekly*, PFLAG (Parents and Friends of Lesbians and Gays), and the Gay and Lesbian Rights Chapter of the ACLU. He has received grants from L.A.'s Cultural Affairs Department and the Brody Foundation. He is a member of the Dramatists Guild and PEN Center USA West.

He lives in Los Angeles where he teaches acting and contributes regularly to *Edge Magazine*.

CARL MORSE

Carl Morse made his first New York stage appearance at the Caffe Cino in 1959. Playwright, poet, and political activist, he is the author of *The Curse of the Future Fairy* (poems), of the revenge oratorio *Impolite to My Butchers*, and of *Breeder Slime Never Die: 3 Comedies of Fertility and Free Will* (including *Minimum Wage, Shootout! Or He Died for Beauty*, and *Dover Beach*). His most recent full-length plays are *Flesh & Blood in Cincinnati* and *The Sunshine State*.

For a number of years as writer with Medicine Show Theater Ensemble, Morse provided lyrics and speeches for productions performed throughout the United States and Europe, including at the Berlin, Bordeaux, and Lincoln Center Summer festivals and at the Whitney Museum of American Art. *Impolite to My Butchers, Dover Beach*, and *Flesh & Blood in Cincinnati* have been presented in readings at La MaMa La Galleria, New York, and at the Oval House, London. *Minimum Wage* was performed in La MaMa E.T.C.'s short play festival in 1990. *Annunciation* and *Fairy Fuck-In* were produced as part of *Homosexual Acts*, an evening of short gay plays at the Theater at 224 Waverly, New York, in 1991.

A selection of Morse's poems appears in *Three New York Poets* (GMP, London, 1987). Morse is also the translator of a major biography of Verlaine and of the essays of André Maurois.

Morse was for several years Director of Publications at The Museum of Modern Art, and he was a 1989 Fellow in Playwrighting of the New York Foundation for the Arts. He is writing a new play.

PAUL SHAW

Paul Shaw is a long-standing member of the Bloolips gay theatre group. He spent a season as assistant director at the Glasgow Citizens Theatre and designed sets for Larry Mitchell's *Get It While You Can* and Ray Dobbin's *Colonial Boy*. During the last year he has toured with *Belle Reprieve* and has been involved with adapting Lilly Walden's *Maria Stuart* (originally in German) for the English stage. He has also redesigned the set for Split Britches' *Dress Suits to Hire* and is learning to play the ukulele.

PEGGY SHAW

Peggy Shaw began her acting career in 1974 with the gay theatrical company Hot Peaches. From 1978 to 1981 she worked with Spiderwoman Theatre, touring Europe and the United States. She has been an actor and collaborator with the Split Britches Company since its beginning in 1980 and is a cofounder of Women's One World Cafe (WOW), a women's performing space in New York City. In the spring of 1988, Shaw won a Village Voice OBIE Award for her performance as Deeluxe in *Dress Suits to Hire* by Holly Hughes. She was a 1988–89 winner of the New York Foundation for the Arts Fellowship in performance art. She collaborated with Lois Weaver on *Anniversary Waltz*, a piece about their ten-year relationship, which was presented at the Club at La MaMa in 1990. She is currently collaborating with Weaver and Deb Margolin on a piece called *Lesbians Who Kill*.

PENNELL SOMSEN

Pennell Somsen, a professional actor, began writing for the stage a year ago. Besides *One Tit, A Dyke, & Gin!* Pennell has completed a selection of monologues entitled *Within & Beyond*, which played at The Vortex in September 1992. She is presently working on a full-length play, *Beer & Chocolate*, which will open at The Vortex in 1993. As an actor, Pennell has worked exclusively with new scripts since she moved to New York City. Her regional acting credits include Miss Ramsden in *Man and Superman* with E.G. Marshall at Center Stage in Baltimore, Ouiser in *Steel Magnolias* at Horse Cave Theatre in Kentucky, and Kate in *Brighton Beach Memoirs* at Petrucci's Dinner Theatre in Maryland. She studies playwriting with Stuart Spencer at Ensemble Studio Theatre and is an associate member of the Dramatists Guild. She lives in Chelsea with her computer, Schmendrick, and is the mother of two grown children, Sara and Brendan.

ROBIN SWADOS

Robin Swados lives in Manhattan, where he divides his time between his writing and a career as an editor at Alfred A. Knopf, Inc. *A Quiet End*, his first play, has received wide critical acclaim at theatres including Theatre Off Park, New York; the American Repertory Theatre, Amsterdam; the Offstage Theatre, London; the International City Theatre, Long Beach, California; and the Repertory Theatre of St. Louis.

LOIS WEAVER

Lois Weaver is an actor and collaborator with and the director of the Split Britches Company, which tours four shows in repertory: *Split Britches, Beauty and the Beast, Upwardly Mobile Home* and *Little Women: The Tragedy*. She created and directed the role of Michigan in *Dress Suits to Hire* by Holly Hughes, and made her film debut in Sheila McLaughlin's *She Must Be Seeing Things*. Weaver is a founding member of Spiderwoman Theatre and co-founder of the Women's One World Cafe in New York City where she directs and teaches acting. She has also conducted workshops in Italy, Denmark, Great Britain and throughout the U.S. She was a 1988−89 winner of the New York Foundation for the Arts Fellowship in performance art. Weaver and Peggy Shaw collaborated on *Anniversary Waltz*, a piece about their ten-year relationship, presented at the Club La MaMa in 1990. She is currently collaborating with Shaw and Deb Margolin on a piece called *Lesbians Who Kill*, and has been appointed co−artistic director of Gay Sweatshop in London.